GREAT BRITISH CYCLING

www.transworldbooks.co.uk

GREAT BRITISH CYCLING

The History of British Bike Racing
1868–2014

Ellis Bacon

BANTAM PRESS

LONDON • TORONTO • SYDNEY • AUCKLAND • JOHANNESBURG

TRANSWORLD PUBLISHERS
61–63 Uxbridge Road, London W5 5SA
A Random House Group Company
www.transworldbooks.co.uk

First published in Great Britain
in 2014 by Bantam Press
an imprint of Transworld Publishers

A CIP catalogue record for this book
is available from the British Library.

ISBN 9780593073100

Addresses for Random House Group Ltd companies outside the UK
can be found at: www.randomhouse.co.uk
The Random House Group Ltd Reg. No. 954009

The Random House Group Limited supports the Forest Stewardship Council® (FSC®),
the leading international forest-certification organisation. Our books carrying the
FSC label are printed on FSC®-certified paper. FSC is the only forest-certification scheme
supported by the leading environmental organisations, including Greenpeace. Our paper
procurement policy can be found at www.randomhouse.co.uk/environment

Typeset in 12/15.25pt Ehrhardt by
Falcon Oast Graphic Art Ltd.
Printed and bound in Great Britain by
CPI Group (UK) Ltd, Croydon, CR0 4YY

2 4 6 8 10 9 7 5 3 1

For my dad, and time-trial pusher-offers everywhere:

'Left a bit . . . Right a bit . . .'

'Three . . . Two . . . One . . .'

'Thank yooooouuuu . . .'

CONTENTS

FOREWORD

To say that I'm proud to have been president of British Cycling between 1997 and 2013, and to have overseen bike racing's unprecedented success and subsequent growth in Great Britain, would be a bit of an understatement.

At the end of 1996, after decades of underachievement in our sport, albeit illuminated by occasional sparks of brilliance, my colleagues and I were elected to bring about a major change in the way things were done. We set about comprehensively restructuring the sport, adopting a bold new strategy and setting new standards of governance and management. In doing so, we were able to invest the influx of money so gratefully received from the National Lottery wisely. But the results – both in terms of the sport and in the growth of cycling in general – surprised even us and resulted in an astonishing uplift in the sport's profile.

Our strategy had three simple elements: to make cycling Britain's most popular and successful sport; to boost membership of the federation to 100,000; and to put Great Britain at the top of the UCI's rankings. It is perhaps worth remembering that it was received with disbelief and derision in some quarters! Yet who would argue with that now?

On the sporting side, first Peter Keen, and then Dave Brailsford, with the help of Shane Sutton, Steve Peters and their numerous expert colleagues, brought the best out of what would prove to be an immensely talented crop of young British riders, many of whom had come through our newly established development programmes, and it was at the 2008 Olympic Games in Beijing that that talent overflowed, impossible to ignore any longer by the British press and public.

Looking back to when I first joined a cycling club in 1965, we had already had a number of top riders flying the flag for Britain – world champions such as Beryl Burton and Tom Simpson, Tour stage winners like Brian Robinson and Barry Hoban – and I can remember following their exploits in magazines like *Cycling* and *Sporting Cyclist*. Meanwhile home-based riders like Les West and Hugh Porter put up world-class performances whenever the opportunity arose.

Then, later, we had riders like Robert Millar, Mandy Jones and Sean Yates, and successful pursuiters and team-pursuiters, too. All of these ploughed something of a lonely furrow in their racing careers, certainly without anywhere close to the kind of support that they deserved and that today's top British riders enjoy. A different era, a different approach, though of course we should not forget that many people worked hard behind the scenes with the resources available at the time.

Now, as well as the elite-level successes, there are two other things of which I am proud. Firstly, the grass-roots activities that show people of all ages and ability the joys of our sport and pastime. And secondly, those development and coaching programmes that are ensuring an ongoing stream of talented young men and women, and providing a sustainable level of success – over half the GB Olympic cycling team at London 2012 came directly from those programmes.

So, from right back in 1868, when British cyclist James Moore first put his country on the bike-racing map, British cycling has enjoyed more than its fair share of ups and downs, and I'm immensely proud to have played a role in one of those ups and to have been part of the amazing journey so wonderfully told in these pages.

In the modern era, Dave Brailsford, as Performance Director, became the media face of British bike racing's success, but I'm sure he won't mind me saying that none of it would have been possible without the help of so many others, whose efforts truly were invaluable.

Alongside me at British Cycling, I always enjoyed the support of an excellent board and expert commissions, and a highly professional management team, led first of all by chief executive Peter King, and then his successor, Ian Drake, both of whom played vital roles in steering the ship firstly into a safe harbour and then onwards to exciting voyages of discovery.

And that's without having mentioned people such as Chris Boardman, Doug Dailey, John Mills, Jonny Clay and Rod Ellingworth, and the hundreds of others who worked so hard to develop the sport and to push British riders to the top of the medal tables. In fact, there are so many people behind the scenes who deserve huge recognition – but who humbly and uncomplainingly worked, and continue to work, so hard for the good of cycling in Great Britain – that I'd run out of pages were I to name them all.

Despite leaving my post with British Cycling to become president of the International Cycling Union (UCI) in 2013, and although my office is now at the UCI headquarters in Switzerland, I'm proud to maintain an active interest in both British cycling and British Cycling – that is, the sport's growth in the UK, and the federation that continues to nurture burgeoning cycling talent.

And where next for British bike racing? I'm thrilled to now be in a position in which I can witness – and hopefully help – other burgeoning cycling nations as they play catch-up to a federation that is truly at the top of its game. But I'm entirely confident that British Cycling, under its new president Bob Howden, will continue to thrive, be it continuing to introduce more youngsters to the sport, helping newcomers to take part in races and sportives, encouraging more people to ride their bikes to work, or bringing through talent capable of winning even more Olympic medals, world championships and Tour de France titles.

The future's brighter than it's ever been for cycling in Britain, and I was honoured to be in Yorkshire when the Tour de France came to town for its 2014 *Grand Départ*, while all the towns along the route – from Leeds to Harrogate, from York to Sheffield and then from Cambridge to London – gave the race such an overwhelming reception that Tour director Christian Prudhomme was left in no doubt that he was witnessing the confirmation of Britain as a bona fide cycling nation.

Onwards and upwards.

Brian Cookson
President of the International Cycling Union (UCI)
Aigle, Switzerland
July 2014

INTRODUCTION

It may feel as though British cycling has come on in leaps and bounds in recent years. And although that's hard to argue with – Olympic golds by the bucketful, three BBC Sports Personality Awards for cyclists in the past six years, multiple honours bestowed for sporting excellence – British cycling talent has in fact always been there; athletes had simply been sidelined by limited opportunities to compete on the world stage and a lack of media coverage.

Chris Hoy, Bradley Wiggins and former British Cycling performance director Dave Brailsford, who is now concentrating on running Team Sky, fully deserve their knighthoods, as does Sarah Storey her title of Dame, but these are the rewards of standing front and centre of the cycling revolution: of being in the right place at the right time, if you like.

That's to take nothing away from those athletes' hard work, dedication and resulting victories, and Brailsford's achievement of really having put British cycling on the sporting map. But all of this is the culmination of what came before, and so this book will chart that rise to world domination, identifying how the tide changed, and unearthing the source of Britain's cycling success.

Many may well be surprised at just how successful Britain was at the dawn of bicycle racing in the late 1860s. But while mainland Europe – and the hotbeds of France, Spain, Belgium and Italy, in particular – embraced cycling for its charm and simplicity, arousing passion and competitiveness in those brave enough to race, and encouraging similar passion and adulation in those watching roadside or at the velodrome, British riders battled against laws brought in to prohibit competitive, massed-start events on the nation's roads. While the Continent has embraced road racing, with organizers working regularly and easily with local police forces to close roads in order that events can take place, in Britain it's always been an uphill battle. Today's struggles with the authorities to close the roads for road racing are nothing new.

As far back as 1890, British cyclists turned to time trialling: timed, individual racing against the clock, with no need for road closures. The only requirement was that other road-users see you and take the necessary precautions to avoid mowing you down. Easier said than done, it turns out. On today's better road surfaces with the resultant higher speeds, the inherent danger of riding a bicycle per se is increased by the very real threat of getting ploughed into by an inattentive HGV driver, or getting side-swiped by a caravan-pulling car's wing mirror.

Nevertheless, Britons excelled at this individualistic form of racing, and it remains the case today with by far the majority of Britain's top professionals more than a little handy when it comes to racing against the clock.

Bike racing has always at least appeared an eccentric pursuit: it embraces funny clothing, shaved legs, pointy hats and people riding along dual carriageways not long after the sun's come up. Yet for many that was always part of the appeal. While on the one hand wishing for more recognition and better media coverage, many cyclists now feel mildly put out that 'their' sport has become mainstream, creeping, unbelievably, ever closer to the all-powerful football.

But try telling that to the likes of Bradley Wiggins and Lizzie Armitstead. The home-grown heroes and heroines who only a few years ago were anonymous, unrecognized, Lycra-clad freaks – the public oblivious to their talent when failing to wait for them at that notorious T-junction – are now reaping the benefits of the sport's growth. Young riders coming through now as potential world-beaters have never had it so good.

Tom Simpson had, of course, won the BBC Sports Personality Award for the cycling community in 1965 on the back of his road race world championships title that year – part of what was a golden era for British cycling, coming just ten years after Brian Robinson and Tony Hoar had become the first Britons to complete the Tour de France. Robinson would also become the first British winner of a Tour stage, too, in 1958. At the same time, Beryl Burton began tearing up British roads: her sporting reign would last a quarter of a century, and would include her winning the road-race world championships in Germany and the Netherlands in 1960 and 1967, respectively.

But 1967 also saw the tragic death of Tom Simpson during that year's Tour de France, and when doping was found to have contributed to his death, it dampened the building enthusiasm for the sport at a time when doping was a hidden, yet accepted, practice.

The sport plodded on after that, with flashes of brilliance from the likes of Barry Hoban, Sean Yates and Robert Millar, the latter winning the King of the Mountains title and finishing fourth over-all at the 1984 Tour. However, it wasn't until 1998 – the year when Chris Boardman, arguably the 'pioneer' of the next big push for cycling's popularity after his gold medal on the track at the 1992 Olympics, took the yellow jersey after winning the Tour de France prologue in Dublin – that doping was seriously acknowledged and the cogs were set in motion to try to eradicate it from the sport.

Compared to Europe's more Mediterranean cultures, Britain has stayed relatively clear of doping scandals. But in 2004, Boardman's successor, David Millar, who was at one point even being touted as a future Tour winner, admitted to having turned to performance-enhancing drugs in the wake of a police investigation in France, and there was heartache yet again for British cycling fans. The nation would have to wait a little longer yet for that Tour winner.

And when he came, in the shape of Bradley Wiggins, it was as a prelude to Lance Armstrong's downfall, and on the back of phenomenal British cycling success, which arguably peaked at the 2008 Beijing Olympics and remained 'peaked' from then on as Mark Cavendish sped into the national consciousness, ably backed up by Victoria Pendleton, Nicole Cooke, Chris Froome, Hoy, Wiggins, and a resurgent, and repentant, Millar.

Despite the long wait for consistent success, there is now much to celebrate. The Herne Hill Velodrome – used for the 1948 Olympics, but in danger of closing down as recently as 2011 – is enjoying a new lease of life in south-east London, while the Manchester and Newport velodromes go from strength to strength, and new velodromes spring up around the land – in east London for the Olympic Games, in Glasgow for the Commonwealth Games in 2014, and, soon, in Derby, too. Britain is supplying world-class venues at which young cyclists can learn their craft safely away from the nation's trafficated roads, and safe in the knowledge that the likes of the aforementioned Hoy, Storey and Wiggins learned how to race on the track, while the new generation of riders such as Laura Trott, Jason Kenny and Becky James prove that, for the gifted few, it's a legitimate way to earn a living in this age of manufactured pop bands and televised talent-contest winners.

But to label the British public a fickle bunch who respond only to success is only half the story. While athletes have struggled to showcase their talent and make their voices heard, so, too, behind the scenes, have hundreds and thousands of volunteers and cycling-club members worked tirelessly and all but invisibly over the years to keep the marginalized sport alive.

And it is to those people – too numerous to mention, such is their number – that this book is dedicated.

As big as football? Not yet, but it is the efforts of the few for so long that have borne fruit in the shape of the many who now enjoy the benefits of world-class cycling coaching and training facilities, and, more broadly – from commuters to 'weekend warriors' – the enjoyment of riding a bike.

1

A BRITISH WINNER

I don't believe in ghosts. But I was surely in the right place to see one.

I'd paid my admission fee, and the staff of Ely Museum, fifteen miles north of Cambridge, had let me into their charming building in the centre of town. It was a damp October afternoon – a humble start to autumn after a blisteringly hot British summer – and, once inside, there was not another soul around. Or so I hoped.

The museum is housed in the city's old gaol (so old that it's spelled like that), and who knows what unspeakable horrors its walls must have seen?

I followed the one-way arrows through the exhibitions of British life past, pausing occasionally out of respect for the museum's function rather than from any overwhelming personal interest in the other displays. I was here for one exhibit only, and there it was, suddenly – unexpectedly, somehow: the bicycle ridden to victory in the world's first-ever bike race.

It seemed surreal when I thought about it too hard. Really, I decided, it should have been encased in glass – pickled, perhaps, like a Damien Hirst mammal or big fish. But here it was, imprisoned now in the quietude of Ely's old gaol: the wooden velocipede ridden to victory on 31 May 1868 in Paris's Parc de Saint-Cloud by Englishman James Moore.

I didn't dare touch it. Something stopped me. It seems irresistible now, something so old, so important, and I wish I had, but something definitely stopped me.

'It's actually mainly wrought iron,' says Moore, 'and the wheels and spokes are wooden, with a metal rim.'

I could imagine him correcting me and proudly talking through the details of his winning machine, but this is John Moore – James's grandson – proudly telling me more about the bike from his home in Hertfordshire a few weeks later.

'My grandfather was born in Bury St Edmunds, in Suffolk, in 1849,' Moore tells me, 'but moved with the family to Paris in 1853 for his father's work.'

James Moore's birth certificate says that his father was a black-smith, but his new job was as a farrier, taking care of horses' hooves, working at the prestigious Maisons-Laffitte horse-training centre to the north-west of Paris. The Moore family lived closer to the centre of Paris, and a young James Moore grew up on the corner of the Cité Godot de Mauroy – today the rue de Boccador – and Avenue Montaigne, just off the Champs-Elysées, opposite the Michaux family.

Pierre Michaux was a coach builder – coaches of the horse-drawn variety – but would go on to mass-produce the first pedal-driven velocipedes in 1868, having supposedly pioneered the first true bicycle a few years earlier, with cranks and pedals that directly drove the front wheel, versus the feet-on-the-ground-driven 'hobby horses', or 'dandy horses', or *draisiennes*, that had come before, invented by German Karl Drais.

There's some contention over whether it was actually Pierre Michaux or his son, Ernest, who was the true inventor of the pedal-powered velocipede, but Moore got to know the family, and was taught to ride by Ernest.

These bicycles became known as boneshakers for good reason, thanks to the iron frames and metal-rimmed wheels, and the one displayed at Ely Museum is a prime example; it perfectly matches the old photographs and illustrations depicting wealthy Parisians aboard their Michaux machines. A closer look reveals a length of string – one end twisted around the handlebars, the other attached to a small metal 'arm' on a pivot just in front of the rear wheel – that serves as a rudimentary braking system.

'It's just a very thin string on my grandfather's bike there in the museum now,' Moore points out, 'but it actually used to be more of a thick cord, like you might get on bay windows.'

Up front, the pedals are weighted underneath, so as always to be 'right-side-up' and ready to ride, and are attached to cranks that are slotted so that the pedals can be adjusted to different riders' leg lengths. Almost 150 years later, optimal crank lengths are still being discussed and argued over.

The Parc de Saint-Cloud gravel flicked up at the cyclists chasing behind, tink-tinkling the metal frame on its way. The boneshaker's front wheel did all the work; the smaller rear wheel, around two-thirds the size, dutifully, if with a little less purpose, trundled along behind.

James Moore's hands were – where else? – on his handlebars, but poised to stop, if need be, by way of a twist of the handlebars; this would gather up the piece of cord running below him to the back wheel, pivoting the brake, which would grind against the metal rim. But Moore didn't want to slow down. He was in a position to win the world's first bike race, and crossed the finish line victorious. Only then did he twist his handlebars.

But had he won the world's first bike race? For so long, history – and Moore himself – said so.

'My father used to say that it was the first bicycle race,' says Moore's grandson, John. 'But what we're saying now is that it was the first formal bicycle race, with wheels of one-metre diameter.' He hopes this new information can soon be added to the display in Ely.

Some further fishing by Japanese bicycle historian Keizo Kobayashi made Moore's race only the second race of that day in 1868. It was a discovery put to Moore's grandson by Nick Clayton – the editor of British organization the Veteran-Cycle Club's tri-annual magazine, named, appropriately enough, *The Boneshaker*. Moore recalls the correspondence, and remembers writing back to Clayton to ask why, if his grandfather's race hadn't been the first race that day, no one had ever challenged the claim.

'That was some years ago, when I used to be quite active about it, but recently I haven't done so much,' says Moore. He suggested to Clayton that there might have been something different about the first race – that it was perhaps open to riders of the old-style 'hobby horse' machines – and indeed the programme of races uncovered by Kobayashi suggests that it was only in the second race, in which James Moore took part, that the velocipedes had to have a front-wheel diameter of one metre, which could mean that they had to be Michaux boneshakers – supposedly the first pedals-and-cranks-driven machines.

Moore's medal from the race, on display with the bike in Ely, is engraved: '*1er Prix James Moore*', and, around the edge, '*1ères courses de vélocipèdes*'. Confirmation of the multiple events that day is evidenced by the plurals – 'the first velocipede races' – while the official nature of the medal is in no doubt, stamped as it is with the head of Napoleon III on the reverse.

Yet, when he was later interviewed by H. O. Duncan for his 1926 book *The World on Wheels*, Moore told him: 'It was the first bicycle race with cranks and pedals.'

'I don't know why my grandfather didn't mention anything

about the one-metre-diameter wheels,' says John, who owns a copy of the book. 'That's the thing that Kobayashi really picked up on; that, apparently, is the important thing.'

On 31 May 1938, soon after James Moore's death, a plaque, specifically naming him as the winner of the first bicycle race, was erected in the Parc de Saint-Cloud, commemorating the 70th anniversary of the race.

'I went to see it once,' his grandson says, 'but it was no longer there.'

What certainly isn't in question is that James Moore also won the first-ever massed-start road race, proving his domination in the fledgling sport.

The Paris–Rouen one-day race, held on 7 November 1869 – a year and a half after the first bike races in the Parc de Saint-Cloud – was sponsored by sports newspaper *Le Vélocipède Illustré*, beginning a long, and still continuing, connection between the cycling media and the sport. Just as the Tour de France was started in 1903 by the sports paper *L'Auto*, the intention of *Le Vélocipède Illustré* was to boost sales figures through the running of the 123-kilometre event.

On the start line at the Arc de Triomphe with Moore and 118 others was 'Miss America': an Englishwoman, despite the fantastical moniker. She was one of only 34 finishers, and the only female. It seems more than a little extraordinary that a woman took place in that first road race – especially when the question of whether it was right and proper for women to ride bicycles at all was still to come in the decades that followed, and when, even today, women's racing struggles to find its voice versus the more established men's racing.

Moore's winning time of 10 hours and 40 minutes gave him an average speed of 11.53 kph, but the bike he won on is not to be found in any museum. It's quite likely to be rusting at the bottom of a Rouen canal, in time-honoured fashion, having been stolen while it was left unattended at a later celebratory banquet. It's quite heartbreaking to imagine that some thieving Frenchman nicked it, and more heartbreaking again trying to imagine where such an important piece of history has ended up today.

'That kind of thing obviously didn't happen as much then as it does now, but clearly someone must have thought it was worth having,' says Moore's grandson, John.

As an aside, John tells me about the infuriating number of occasions when writers and historians have confused the dates and details of the various races his grandfather won. He gives the television quiz show *Mastermind* as an example.

'I happened to be watching it a year or so ago, and, to my horror, one of the questions was about the first cycling road race, which they said was Paris–Brest–Paris. I pointed the error out to them, and they apologized, but when I asked whether they would point out the mistake in their next edition, they said they couldn't because the shows are all pre-recorded.'

Less than a year after his victory at Paris–Rouen, cycling had to take a back seat as James Moore and his father were called up to serve in Paris's 1st Arrondissement Ambulance Corps during the Franco-Prussian War, which started on 15 July 1870. During the Siege of Paris that winter, a year after standing proudly at the Arc de Triomphe for the start of cycling's first road race, Moore and his father were forced to eat rats to survive.

But with the war over in 1871, Moore decided to move to England, where he studied veterinary medicine in London and befriended fellow veterinary student John Boyd Dunlop. In either a strange quirk of fate or (who knows?) perhaps influenced by Moore's tales of bike racing, Dunlop, while working at a veterinary practice in Belfast in 1887, would develop the pneumatic bicycle tyre.

*

Despite his aspirations to qualify as a veterinarian, Moore's bike-racing career was far from over, and his Michaux boneshaker isn't alone in that Ely Museum display.

Tucked behind it, a little criminally, is a penny-farthing, or Ordinary, or high-wheeler. No matter; its huge front wheel towers above the Michaux. Far from penny-farthings having been the earliest type of bicycle, as is widely imagined, the front wheel outgrew the one-metre diameter of the Michaux as a direct result of riders requiring a bigger gear. Like the boneshaker before it, the penny-farthing's pedals remained attached to the front-wheel hub, which meant that the same 1:1 gear became 'higher' due to the increased diameter. But while the front wheel grew, the rear wheel dropped in size compared to the boneshakers; surplus to requirement, almost, save for its role in stability. It also helped offset the extra weight from the larger front wheel.

It may not have quite the same cachet as the Michaux, nor the missing bike from Paris–Rouen, but the penny-farthing on display in Ely nevertheless served Moore just as well, carrying him to further race victories and international titles between 1873 and 1877.

'My grandfather said that he'd built it himself, mainly out of a gun barrel,' explains John Moore. 'His father was a blacksmith, or a farrier, remember, so he knew what he was doing.'

In 1874, at the Molineux Pleasure Grounds in Wolverhampton – which later, in 1889, became, and remains, the home of Wolverhampton Wanderers football club – Moore rode the bike to victory at the one-mile world championships, contested over three meetings on the purpose-built cycling track there.

A 1933 edition of *Cycling* magazine, which was founded in 1891 and is still in existence today as *Cycling Weekly*, has the times recorded by Moore as three minutes and two and a quarter seconds on 7 April 1874, three minutes and two and a half seconds on 2 May, and then a record-breaking three minutes and one second for the mile on 26 May. Moore was awarded a cup for his achievements at that 'Championship of the World' in Wolverhampton, and only in 1877, aged twenty-eight, did he finally decide to hang up his wheels, having won his final race: the International Championship, back in France, in Toulouse.

Having qualified as a veterinarian, Moore remained in Paris and started a stud farm, where he owned and successfully bred racehorses – his other great passion besides bike racing. 'He was quite successful as a trainer, and became quite well known as a horse breeder because of his veterinary experience; he was able to use that,' Moore's grandson explains. 'As he was always very competitive, he successfully transferred that to his horse racing.'

In 1921, having retired from horse breeding, Moore returned with his family to his native Britain, settling in Hampstead, in north-west London, and enjoying cycling and golf in his retirement. He died on 17 July 1935, aged eighty-six.

Many of the medals, plus the cup won in Wolverhampton, that Moore collected throughout his nine-year racing career are on display at Ely Museum, but his last medal, won in 1877, is missing.

'In 2001, I lent some of the medals to the New York Hall of Science (NYSCI) for a special exhibition, partly against my better judgement,' his grandson admits.

The NYSCI – located in Flushing Meadows–Corona Park, which is also home to the US Open tennis tournament – welcomes thousands of schoolchildren through its doors each year.

'We weren't told about that,' Moore's grandson continues, 'although we did go over everything – all the security aspects of it – and convinced ourselves that they'd be safe. But, unfortunately, despite the security cameras, that medal somehow got stolen. This wasn't discovered until February 2002, but we think that the police were still a little preoccupied with the aftermath of 9/11.'

Luckily, photographs and measurements had been made, and

compensation was paid out, so John Moore now intends to have a replica made.

'It can sometimes be that things do turn up again after many years,' Moore says, perhaps a little philosophically. It would be fantastic if his grandfather's 1869 Paris–Rouen bicycle somehow turned up again, too.

As to how it was that Ely Museum ended up with what is a magnificent collection of James Moore's bicycles and medals, it was because Moore's son, also James – John Moore's father – and his family moved to nearby Witchford in 1958.

'My father had these bicycles in the garage, and so after he died my brother and I decided to loan them to Ely Museum,' explains John, who later also came across a draft of a letter his grandfather had written to a friend. 'In it, he'd said that he thought that the bicycle would one day become as commonplace as an umbrella. And he was right!'

John doesn't remember his grandfather, but he has a feeling that he was told they met.

'I was born in 1934; he died in 1935. We overlapped by one year, so he would have known me,' he says. 'All my knowledge of him is from my father, and he could only go on what his father had told him, and by hearsay. My father died thinking that his father had won the first bicycle race, but in a way I'm grateful for Keizo Kobayashi's research; it's nice to know the truth, and in some ways it enhances the significance of my grandfather's achievements.'

In 2018, John points out, it will be the 150th anniversary of the races that took place in the Parc de Saint-Cloud.

'I don't know if I'll still be alive by then, but I could easily be!' he laughs.

Thanks to James Moore and his successes in the early days of bike racing, British bike racing's victory tally was up and running. But it was to be a long journey to the Olympic and Tour de France successes that would be enjoyed later.

2

GREAT EXPECTATIONS

While British bike racing's successful beginnings owe everything to the Paris-based James Moore, it wasn't long before the French craze for all things bicycling also appeared on the northern side of the Channel.

Indeed, the very day after the first-recorded bicycle races in the Parc de Saint-Cloud, where Moore won his race, Britain's first official bike race was staged, close to the Welsh Harp (or Brent) Reservoir in north London. It was won by Arthur Markham, whose son, A. G. Markham, later set the Road Records Association's (RRA) unpaced tricycle record for 100 miles.

That same year – 1868 – Rowley Turner, the Paris-based agent for the Coventry Sewing Machine Company, had witnessed at first hand France's passion for the velocipede and took a Michaux boneshaker back to Coventry to show to his uncle, Josiah Turner, who was a manager at the sewing-machine company. Sales of sewing machines had not been going too well, and so the company subtly changed its name – to the Coventry Machinists' Company – and its focus to building boneshakers, which soon flew out of the door.

Not that everyone was initially convinced about the newfangled machines. John Mayall Junior, a friend of Rowley Turner's, set off from Clapham in south London in January 1869 on such a machine with the intention of riding to Brighton, but had to give up, exhausted, at Redhill after only 17 miles, and catch the train home again.

In the Suffolk Sporting Series' 1898 book, *Cycling*, George Lacy Hillier – whose idea it was to build the Herne Hill Velodrome – describes Mayall's second, slightly more successful attempt at his London-to-Brighton ride in those early days. This time, he made it, in 16 hours, but 'as some three weeks later the brothers Chinnery *walked* to Brighton' – Hillier's italics – 'in eleven hours and twenty-five minutes, the advantages of the new steed . . . were considerably discounted'.

The Coventry Machinists' Company soon switched to making the new penny-farthings, although, like the boneshaker, that form of the velocipede was also relatively short-lived, and had all but been superseded come the 1880s by the 'safety bicycle' – so named simply for the fact that the rider was no longer perched dangerously high off the ground; instead their weight was evenly distributed between two evenly sized wheels.

Like Josiah Turner, James Starley was a manager at the Coventry Machinists' Company, but it was his nephew, John Kemp Starley, who popularized the safety bicycle in 1885 with his mass-produced Rover model, which morphed later into the Rover car manufacturer. The safety bicycle was also rear-wheel-driven by way of a chain, which made steering a lot lighter, easier and far less dangerous. And very little has changed in terms of bicycle design between then and now; indeed, modern bicycles are safety bicycles in all but name.

Coventry became the bicycle-producing capital of the world, and, from being home to seven bike companies in the 1870s, by the 1890s it boasted more than fifty.

*

By the late nineteenth century, bicycling in Britain was in full swing, as was bike racing, on all kinds of machines, and the establishment of the Road Records Association in 1888 ensured that the popular distance, time and 'place-to-place' record attempts being made all over the country were officially logged and verified.

Ten years earlier, in February 1878, the Bicycle Union had been founded to oversee bicycle racing in all its forms, established by members of both London's Pickwick Bicycle Club and the Cambridge University Bicycle Club. The Pickwick Bicycle Club was one of Britain's first cycling clubs, formed in June 1870, when their first meeting, of six founding members, took place at Hackney Downs.

At first, they didn't have a club name, but at their second meeting in July, and in honour of the writer Charles Dickens, who had died that year, on 9 June, it was decided to name the club after the Pickwick Club in Dickens's first novel, *The Pickwick Papers*. It was also decided that each member of the cycling club should adopt the name of one of the many characters from the book, and so today the 200-member club still operates a rather macabre waiting list for prospective new members. There's less actual cycling going on at the club these days; it's more about meeting up to eat, drink and be merry, which they do twice a year at a luncheon at the Connaught Rooms near Covent Garden. Members – all male – wear the club uniform, which includes a straw boater, and, at least until recently, a clay pipe was placed at the table setting of each member, in a box on which was printed the friendly command: 'Gentlemen – you must smoke.'

The Cambridge University Cycling Club, as it's called today, was founded as the Cambridge University Bicycle Club in February 1874, and was soon – quite rightly – locked in battle with its Oxford rivals the Dark Blue Bicycle Club in an inter-varsity

80-mile race held that June between the two cities. And it was Cambridge who came out on top through Trinity College pair Edward St John Mildmay and John Plunkett, who took first and second place.

The first official British national cycling championships were hosted by the Bicycle Union three months after its formation, on 11 May 1878, at the new Stamford Bridge arena in London, which later, in 1905, became home to Chelsea Football Club.

Cambridge University's own Ion Keith-Falconer – another Trinity man – became Britain's first national champion by winning the two-mile event in a time of six minutes and 29 seconds, before A. A. Weir won the longer 25-mile event in a very respectable one hour, 27 minutes and 44 seconds.

In 1883, the Bicycle Union was renamed the National Cyclists' Union (NCU), having merged with the Tricycle Association.

Tricycles were as ubiquitous as two-wheeled velocipedes as the world whizzed its way towards the twentieth century; the three-wheeled machines were popular with women, in particular, as their skirts and dresses didn't get tangled in either of the two rear wheels set either side of the rider, as opposed to underneath the rider on a conventional safety bicycle. Riders who found it tough to balance on just two wheels could be comforted by the stability-giving security of a third wheel, although the tricycle also had – and still has – a legitimate racing class of its own; cornering at speed requires a deft technique to ensure that rider and at least two wheels retain contact with the ground.

Tandems – the 'bicycle made for two', immortalized in the song 'Daisy Bell' of 1892, sung by Harry Dacre ('Daisy, Daisy, give me your answer, do . . .') were indeed aimed at couples. But as it was most polite to allow the lady to go first – i.e. at the front of the machine – many of the early tandems had rods leading from the woman's handlebars at the front to the man's handlebars behind her in order to put him in control. A married couple sitting one behind the other with their handlebars connected, however, sounds as though in 'real life' it could be a recipe for disaster, or at least for falling off.

In his autobiography *It's Too Late Now*, the creator of the Winnie-the-Pooh children's stories, A. A. Milne, recalls riding a 'rear-steer' tandem-tricycle (a tricycle made for two!) as a young boy with his brother, in around 1890: 'Ken sat behind, and had the steering, the bell and the brake under his control; I sat in front, and had the accident.'

Worry about falling off a bicycle, tandem or, less so, a tricycle was very real, right from the word go when Parisians first took to the velocipede and James Moore showed the world how to race them. 'Riding schools', which operated in a very similar manner to horse-riding schools, with wide, usually indoor, arenas in which cyclists could learn, and then show off, their skills, sprang up in cities across Europe to help people join in with the new craze.

It was still a little early in the day to say that riding a bike was as easy as riding a bike, but certainly some people took to it like a duck to water.

By 1901, some riders had become so comfortable aboard their bikes that they had started to experiment with balancing and doing tricks, and the publication that year of the book *Fancy Cycling: trick riding for amateurs*, by Isabel Marks, makes fascinating reading and viewing. Manoeuvres such as 'Backward Stationary Balance – Removing Jacket' and 'Stationary Balance – Foot on Saddle and Pedal' are just as impressive-looking as they sound, while poses such as 'Coasting – Knees on Handle-Bar, Feet on Saddle' are just asking for trouble.

Viewed with today's world-weary eyes, the book's innocent 'moves' look somehow almost unreal; it's as if they've been set up simply to illustrate a modern 'comedy' greetings card, lacking only a pithy, deadpan sentence along the lines of: 'Julie hadn't realized that you were supposed to look where you were going when commuting to work by bike.' Even more impressive is the fact that this was still in the relatively early days of the bicycle, and the irony is that much of the trick riding caught in the black-and-white photographs at various London riding schools puts many modern-day freestyle BMXers' tricks to shame.

Those BMXers could be said to be the natural progression, but the truth is that trickery to the extent illustrated in *Fancy Cycling* simply never caught on in the UK, although it clearly had more of an audience elsewhere in Europe. While Britain has embraced track and road racing, as illustrated by our more recent achievements in those disciplines, in Germany what's called artistic cycling is immensely popular: a competitive discipline in which riders – in singles or pairs – perform gymnastic-style moves to music on bicycles. Also in the same category of 'indoor cycling' is cycle-ball, which is more or less the opposite of artistic cycling; players use their wheels to flick the ball towards their opponent's goal in a game not too dissimilar to polo – a cycling discipline again dominated by the Germans, and the Swiss.

In the late nineteenth and early twentieth centuries, cycling was still a fun gimmick for many, but increasingly a viable means of transport for others, while the hardcore racing men revelled in the ever-increasing number of competitive events. In 1890, however, the NCU banned all racing on public highways in Britain, having deemed it too dangerous, and it would remain that way until the Second World War. The RRA was still permitted to stage its official place-to-place attempts, but racing was otherwise confined to closed circuits and velodromes, which had sprung up all over the UK, with some two dozen in London alone, built mainly in the 1880s and '90s.

One of those tracks, which has arguably become the best-known and most-loved velodrome in the world, was Herne Hill, which opened its gates on Burbage Road in south London in 1891. The banked track was the baby of George Lacy Hillier, who was unhappy that the track at Crystal Palace, which was built in 1880, didn't feature any banking (although it later did), and it was on the new wooden Herne Hill track in 1893 that Frederick Thomas 'F. T.' Bidlake set his 24-hour tricycle record of 410 miles.

Bidlake, who became president of the RRA in the 1920s, was always dead set against both mass-start road racing and women's racing, and was happy to state such opinions in his regular contributions to the pages of *Cycling* magazine, although he had nothing against a lady riding a bicycle at a more genteel pace. He also founded the Road Racing Council in 1922 to oversee clubs that organized time trials. Their races differed from RRA events in that multiple riders took part, but they started at minute or two-minute intervals, and therefore raced alone against the clock.

F. T. Bidlake's 24-hour tricycle track record was never broken in his lifetime – he died in 1933 – and his sporting and administrative achievements are remembered through the F. T. Bidlake Memorial Trust, which, since his death, has awarded the Bidlake Memorial Plaque to the person the committee considers to have achieved the most outstanding performance in, or contribution to, the sport each year. What he would have thought of top women racers such as Eileen Sheridan, Beryl Burton, Mandy Jones, Yvonne McGregor, Nicole Cooke and Julia Shaw later winning 'his' prize is anyone's guess; perhaps he would have mellowed by then.

But Bidlake's opposition to women racing was far from uncommon, and women riding bicycles at all was frowned upon until well into the twentieth century. Female *vélocipédistes* may have joined James Moore during the first massed-start road race, Paris–Rouen in 1869, but they were to suffer years of disdain, even from within their own ranks.

For the 1898 book, *Cycling*, George Lacy Hillier was joined by two co-authors in the form of H. Graves – 'councillor of the CTC [Cyclists' Touring Club] and NCU, and former captain of the

Oxford University Bicycle Club' – and Susan, Countess of Malmesbury. 'Susan' was Susan Harris, née Hamilton, who'd acquired her title through marriage to James Howard Harris, 3rd Earl of Malmesbury, later remarrying after the earl's death and becoming Susan Ardagh.

Anyone who's seen BBC comedy *Harry Enfield and Chums*' sketches in which spoof public-information films warn women that they should 'know your limits' and only talk about things they truly understand, such as fluffy kittens, rather than join in with their husbands' complex conversations, will be only too familiar with the tone as the countess, in the book's final section, 'Bicycling for women', at least appears to warn women not to go too far.

'The tricycle was used by a few [women] who felt they needed more vigorous exercise than could be obtained by walking or playing a quiet game of croquet, and were unable to provide themselves with the more expensive luxury of a saddle-horse,' she writes. 'Cycling in traffic is a vexed question; many consider it better for the weaker sex to abstain from doing so, but the matter really depends on the skill, nerve and judgment of the rider,' she continues. 'A woman who cycles in the streets of the metropolis or any other large city must learn the police regulations which prevail, and conform to them. She must not suppose her sex excuses her from doing exactly the same as others. Any act of courtesy on the part of cabmen and other drivers of vehicles should be acknowledged.'

Her words do, however, smack rather of a perhaps-disapproving male editorial hand, especially when contrasted with an earlier article by the countess for the *Badminton Magazine of Sports and Pastimes*, in 1896, in which she writes a somewhat sarcastic appeal to the drivers of hansom cabs – London's horse-drawn taxis – to be considerably more careful: 'I cannot help feeling that cycling in the streets would be nicer . . . if he did not try to kill me.'

Hillier, meanwhile, is the book's racing expert, described as 'amateur champion at all distances in 1881'. His writing style is measured and sensible, and he writes in praise of racing as a means of furthering cycling's popularity more generally.

'Cycling has many claims on the community outside the race path, and it is quite conceivable that it might in course of time have attained its present position without the aid of racing, but its rapid advance is indubitably due in a very great degree to cycle racing and racing men,' writes Hillier. 'The roadster of today is simply the racer of yesterday,' he adds, which is an opinion that could easily apply to today's cycling boom, too: that manufacturers meet bike racers' demands by making better bicycles and equipment, the technology from which then trickles down to lower-priced bikes.

The book's principal author, H. Graves, begins by explaining how to ride, and look after, your bike in what is a viciously condescending tone, although one that was popular at the time: 'Too many beginners are under the impression that when once they have mastered the difficulties of steering, mounting, and dismounting, their cycling education is complete,' he writes. 'How general this fallacy is can be seen by looking at three out of every four cyclists one meets, who, while sufficiently expert at controlling their machines, are entirely lacking in that finish which stamps a good rider.'

It's tantamount to writing, 'You're all rubbish, and I'm brilliant,' although, to be fair to Graves, he does go on to explain, in some detail – if still quite condescendingly – just how the reader can become as brilliant as him, which, really, would be the purpose of buying such a book. His tips include how 'nursing the machine' can prevent a fall, and he ensures the reader understands that 'nervousness is absolutely fatal' when dealing with 'greasy roads'. It sounds as though he'd be a hoot to ride with.

Graves's own associations – the NCU and the CTC – are,

naturally, fantastic, although he admits that there is 'much need-
less duplication of work and jealous competition between the two
bodies; we look forward to seeing all matters affecting the public
rights of cyclists dealt with by a joint board of both Associations'.

Understanding his demeanour, it's no wonder, then, that the
NCU were very much against the dangerous practice of road
racing on open roads. If you have to do it, the message appears to
be, at least minimize that danger by doing it on closed-road
circuits.

Graves also initially praises the RRA for their past good work of
'certifying the authenticity of claims for records on the road over
the classic routes and distances'. But then he turns nasty, and gives
it to them with both barrels: 'We are however strongly of the opinion that, as road records are now rarely attacked by amateurs, this
institution, which exists for little more than the purpose of hall-
marking trade advertisements, is marring a glorious past by a
sordid present, to say nothing of the odium raised against cycling
in general by the widespread publication of these advertisements.'

Why advertising is so terrible is unclear, but the sporting-
amateur idealism of the day can't be very far away as a reason.

Graves's parting shot reveals what he thinks the solution is: 'If
the Association were gracefully to dissolve itself, the inherent
corruption in modern road record-breaking, freed from its one
antiseptic influence, would speedily [sic] work out its own
destruction.'

George Pilkington Mills would never have agreed with H. Graves's
assessment of the RRA. Mills was a prolific record-breaker, and it
was achievements like his penny-farthing record from Land's End
to John o'Groats of five days, one hour and 45 minutes – which
still stands for a penny-farthing – that garnered him invites to
other events, such as the first running of the Bordeaux–Paris in
1891. The French race's 600-kilometre distance was no great

challenge to Mills compared to what he was used to; he polished off the lot in just over 26 and a half hours, beating fellow Briton Montague Holbein by an hour and a quarter. Holbein later re-invented himself as a cross-Channel swimmer, but failed at his first attempt in 1901. The following year, he tried twice more, but never made the full distance.

Five years later, at the 1896 edition of Bordeaux–Paris, a British rider again put his mark on the race, although this time it was as joint winner. Arthur Linton went off course when he looked certain to win in Paris and, after a brief consultation by the judges, was deemed to share first prize with the man who was first across the line, Frenchman Gaston Rivière. Little did anyone know that this would be the last time a British rider would win a 'Classic' – the term used to describe the most prestigious one-day races – for sixty-five years, until Tom Simpson won the Tour of Flanders in 1961. Simpson also won Bordeaux–Paris himself, in 1963.

But the late nineteenth century was a period in bike-racing history when new events came thick and fast. In 1888, the German federation had suggested an official world championships to its fellow cycling federations, but it wasn't until 1893 that the first of these were held, in Chicago.

There were no British riders present for those first Worlds, but there was British representation at the second world champion-ships in 1894, held in Antwerp in Belgium. Jack Green was the runner-up in both the 10km and 100km paced event, but the following year, in Cologne, Germany, Welshman Jimmy Michael, a professional with the Dunlop team, went one better. At eighteen years old and just five feet tall, Michael took the top honours in the paced 100 kilometres, and Britain had its first official world champion.

But what connects the Bordeaux–Paris – the Classic in which British riders had such early success – and the world championships is a man named James Edward 'Choppy' Warburton. A former professional runner himself, two of Warburton's charges in his role as a rider-manager were 1896 Bordeaux–Paris winner Arthur Linton and Britain's 1895 world champion Jimmy Michael.

Less than two months after winning Bordeaux–Paris, Linton's health declined dramatically, and, suffering from typhoid, he died, aged just twenty-seven. Michael's death in November 1904 – also, like Linton, at the age of twenty-seven – came on the back of a period of drinking and gambling. Having spent all of his money, Michael had signed a lucrative contract to race in the USA, but died on the ship on his way there, the cause of death consistent with the symptoms of alcohol withdrawal. Linton's brother, Tom, was one of Warburton's boys, too, and, like his older brother, also died of typhoid, again young, at thirty-nine, in 1915.

Just what was it that their manager, Choppy Warburton, would habitually give them from his 'little black bottle' before a race? Although it was no great secret that bike racers took stimulants in those days to help them stay alert (and awake), it's certainly unlikely that the little black bottle contained anything particularly good. Even if its 'magic' – Warburton's own explanation for what was in it – was something completely harmless and just had a placebo effect, the early deaths of the Linton brothers and Jimmy Michael nevertheless don't sit well.

Warburton died himself of heart failure in December 1897, at the age of fifty-two. There was never any concrete proof that he had doped his protégés – it's one of those stories that has almost become truth, and we're unlikely to ever know – but, either way, in Jimmy Michael, Warburton will also be remembered for having given Britain its first world champion.

James Moore's old veterinary pal, John Boyd Dunlop, invented the pneumatic bicycle tyre in Belfast in 1887, which was used in anger for the first time in 1889 when Dunlop handed the captain of the Belfast Cruisers Cycling Club, Willie Hume, a pair of his new tyres to try at a race meeting held at the city's Queen's College (later Queen's University). They were an instant success: Hume won all four of the races, and eagerly headed to Liverpool with his Dunlop-equipped safety bicycle for another series of races later that year, at which he was victorious in all but one event.

It was a significant leap forward in the bicycle's development, immediately improving its comfort and speed, if compromising a little on its reliability over the old solid, puncture-proof metal 'tyres'.

By 1896, all the riders at the first modern Olympic Games in Athens were kitted out with pneumatic tyres. Britain's love affair with the Olympics started at the very beginning, and Britain's cyclists enjoyed a modicum of success, too. Edward Battel, who worked at the British Embassy in Athens, took part in the first cycling event: an 87-kilometre road race, out and back between Athens and Marathon, in which he finished third, despite crashing.

Battel's embassy colleague, Frank Keeping, then went one better in the 12-hour race – held at the velodrome! – taking the silver medal after having been beaten by a single lap by Austria's Adolf Schmal. Keeping's son, Michael, would later follow a different sporting path, playing professional football for Southampton and Fulham, before becoming manager of Real Madrid between 1948 and 1950.

When the Olympics were held for the first time in London in 1908, it was a veritable gold rush for British cycling, with the team taking five golds from seven events. Benjamin Jones was the star of the cycling events, winning both the 5,000 metres and the team pursuit, and taking silver in the 20-kilometre event, which was won by Jones's teammate, Clarence Kingsbury. Victor Johnson won the 660-yard event: a one-lap sprint of the track at the stadium in White City – the area that would later become home to the BBC. And Charles Bartlett was the winner of the

100-kilometre race, out-sprinting compatriot Charles Denny, while Jones and Kingsbury linked up with Leon Meredith and Ernest Payne to also take gold in the team pursuit, beating Germany in the final.

For the first and last time, track cycling events weren't held at the 1912 Olympics in Stockholm. The British team – which stood to do rather well, going by the London Games four years earlier – had protested, but, as Sweden's sole velodrome had been razed to make way for the new Olympic stadium, there was nothing to be done.

There was no road race, either – just a huge 196-mile individual time trial on the terrible rutted roads around Lake Mälaren, just outside Stockholm. The race doubled as a 'team time trial' with the four best finishers from each nation counting towards the team prize. The race was won by South Africa's Rudolph Lewis by more than nine minutes from GB's Fred Grubb, while there was another silver for Grubb, and teammates Leon Meredith, Bill Hammond and Charles Moss, who were beaten by hosts Sweden in the team competition.

After the First World War, at the 1920 Games in Antwerp, Tommy Lance and Harry Ryan won Britain's sole gold medal of those Olympics in the always spectacular 2,000-metre tandem race. Their win marked the last time that Britain would win a gold medal in cycling for seventy-two years, all the way up until the '92 Barcelona Games, where Chris Boardman thrilled the nation by winning the individual pursuit, and which eventually – by the turn of the century – helped open the floodgates to a raft of cycling golds.

The post-war years of the 1920s saw Britons taking to the roads on bikes in their thousands, and one of their best sources for where to go, what equipment to use and where to stay was 'Kuklos', or cycling journalist Fitzwater Wray.

Kuklos – the Greek word for wheel, which Wray used as his

byline – wrote regular columns for the London *Daily News* (founded, and initially edited, by Charles Dickens) around the turn of the twentieth century, while *The Kuklos Annual* was published in 1923 (and reissued in 2013 as *The Modern Cyclist, 1923*, using the author's original copy illustrated with pictures of the day from *Cycling* magazine).

Longer weekend rides became popular with riders of all abilities, who would stay overnight at a relatively inexpensive guesthouse or hostel (it was often called 'hostelling' by club riders, who saw the practice as a good way to extend their training, and it was still popular in the 1970s), and Kuklos's book lists scores of what must now be mostly long-gone places to stay across Britain, Ireland and France.

The rest of the book is packed with solid advice and the voice of experience to help Kuklos's fellow cyclists enjoy a day or two out on their bikes. The anonymously written foreword, written in the third person but quite possibly penned by Wray himself, explains that Kuklos is quite happy to correspond with readers who require any further information on, charmingly, 'matters of the wheel', the only stipulation being that 'a stamped addressed envelope for reply must be enclosed'. Who needs email or Twitter?

While earlier literature teaching people how to ride and behave on a bicycle appears to have had quite a curt, condescending tone, Kuklos's popularity may well have been thanks to his more encouraging voice. 'Any cyclist, man or woman, who is good enough in physique and health to ride 50 or 60 miles on a Saturday or Sunday holiday, can double it in the course of a long summer day without undue fatigue and without special preparation,' he writes, 'supposing that he is decently mounted and does not encounter a strong head wind all the way.'

Riders wishing to circumnavigate London, meanwhile, are encouraged to follow Kuklos's directions on the quieter roads that these days trace nigh on exactly the route of the M25, although he does concede that 'there are cyclists who *want* to ride right through London, for various reasons, and have no strong objections to traffic riding. It is worth remembering, too, that on Sundays the complete transit of London is easy'.

There's sage advice, too, for riders brave enough to take a trip to the Continent. Getting through Customs can sometimes be costly, Kuklos warns; even visitors are likely to have to pay import duty when taking new bicycles into France. He's ready to help his fellow rider with a quick fix for that, though: 'If your bicycle is new, or looks new, rub it over with mud.'

He assures readers that they're unlikely to have any such problems at the Franco-Belgian border, however, where proof that you're only visiting will mean that no duty has to be paid: 'If the officials at some inland frontier station are disposed to be awkward, point to this sentence: "*Je suis ancien combattant, et je fais la visite des champs de bataille – séjour de quinze jours seulement*,"' Kuklos suggests. ('I'm a former soldier visiting the battlefields, and am only here for a fortnight.')

But while bicycling fans enjoyed the green and pleasant lands of Britain – or, even, the then less salubrious environs of Belgium's battle-ravaged countryside – on two wheels between the two world wars, the racing scene was hotting up as British riders ventured ever further afield in pursuit of new races and challenges.

The Tour de France had first been held in 1903, and, like many races of the day, was a marketing exercise – in the Tour's case, to sell more copies of the sports newspaper *L'Auto*. Initially it attracted mainly French racers, as well as a handful from Belgium, Switzerland and Germany, and in the years that followed the Tour grew rapidly to become the world's most famous bike race of them all – although it took until 1937 for it to welcome the first British riders to the start line.

Charles Holland had won an Olympic bronze medal in the team pursuit at the 1932 Los Angeles Games, and finished fourth in the road-race world championships in Leipzig in 1934. But the opportunity to ride the 1937 Tour de France only came about because, out of curiosity, Holland simply entered as an individual rider, which you could still just about do in those days. He was put together with fellow Brit Bill Burl, who crashed out of the race on stage two, while Canadian Pierre Gachon, who was the third member of their British Empire team, didn't even make it through the opening stage.

Holland pushed on alone, but was forced to retire from the race on stage 14c – split stages were rife at that time; 14c was the third stage in the same day – between Ax-les-Thermes and Luchon after losing too much time due to a puncture, although the not-overly-shiny silver lining appears to be that he was brought a beer by friendly roadside spectators to slake his thirst while working on the repairs.

Putting the Tour behind him, Holland, sponsored by Raleigh–Sturmey Archer, set about trying to break various RRA place-to-place records, successfully setting new times for Liverpool to Edinburgh and Land's End to London. The war spelled the end of his professional career, but he later made a successful return to veterans' bike racing.

Being one of the first two Britons to take part in the Tour de France should really have brought him a lot more recognition in his lifetime – Holland died, aged eighty-one, in 1989 – but Britain's current interest and success in the event has meant that the efforts of riders like Holland and Burl are finally being acknowledged.

Holland's also remembered as one of the early winners of the British Best All Rounder (BBAR) competition, which he won in 1936, the year before he rode the Tour. It was a competition dreamed up by *Cycling* magazine as a way of finding the season's best time triallist over a 50-mile, 100-mile and 12-hour time trial, ranking riders by their average speeds.

Today, the BBAR is run by Cycling Time Trials (CTT), which used to be called the Road Time Trials Council (RTTC), which started life before that as the Road Racing Council (RRC), which in turn had been started by that man F. T. Bidlake in 1922.

The NCU just about tolerated time trialling on the open road – individual riders racing against the clock wasn't too dissimilar to individual riders trying to beat RRA records – but participants were nevertheless careful to be as discreet as possible, lest they attract the attention of the police and risk not being able to race on the roads at all: they did this by dressing all in black, and 'not talking about Fight Club' to anyone they couldn't trust; early-morning starts and code numbers for each course ensured the secrecy of their little cult.

3

THE OPEN ROAD

Percy Stallard had represented the national team – and therefore the NCU – at the world-championship road race for three years in a row from 1933 to 1935, finishing 12th in Montlhéry, France, sixth in Leipzig, in Germany, and 12th again in Namur, in Belgium. Road racing in Britain was still then limited to closed-road circuits, so 'proper' road racing on the Continent was a thrill for British riders like Stallard.

In 1942, he went to the NCU with a proposal for a massed-start road race from Llangollen, in north-east Wales, to his home town of Wolverhampton: it didn't even require the roads to be closed, he told them, thanks to the lack of wartime traffic on the roads due to petrol rationing. He'd sought permission from the governing body for his race – which wasn't forthcoming – and so he did what all of history's great leaders have always done and went ahead with his plans anyway; to hell with 'the Union'.

The programme for the race, which took place on 7 June 1942, reads: 'The event is run with the kind permission of the Chief Constables of Denbighshire, Shropshire, Staffordshire and Wolverhampton.'

The NCU were furious that Stallard had managed to garner the support of the police forces in the counties that the race ran through, and, to really rub it in, Stallard ensured that all proceeds from the event went to charity, while the winner, E. A. Price of the Wolverhampton Road Racing Club, even added his £3 voucher prize to the charity pot. Stallard's race was a great success with those who rode it. Whether they knew they'd all be banned by the NCU for having taken part, as was Stallard, the race was nevertheless vital in setting in motion the eventual acceptance of massed-start racing on British roads.

Stallard started a new governing body for road racing – the British League of Racing Cyclists (BLRC) – later in the year, and set about recruiting riders who were keen to race en masse on the open road like their fellow cyclists in Europe. To join 'the League', however, meant being thrown out of 'the Union', and often your club, so riders simply set about starting new BLRC-affiliated clubs.

After imposing their ban on Stallard and his co-conspirators, the NCU asked the RTTC to ban them, too, which they did. But the RTTC were very much 'the other woman' – or, indeed, 'the other man', if you prefer – to the quarrelling NCU and BLRC. They may have appeared to have sided with the NCU, but they tended to remain quite aloof, quietly getting on with doing their own thing, which was enabling riders to race against the clock.

The BLRC were seen as promoting 'continental-style' racing, which it was, but its formation began a really quite nasty 17-year feud with the NCU.

In his foreword to Peter Whitfield's excellent *The Condor Years: A Panorama of British Cycling 1945–2000* – a book that covers a lot more than just the famous London bike shop and frame builder of the title – Alf Engers, the prolific winner of time-trial national championships throughout the 1960s and '70s, and the first to ride

35

under 50 minutes for 25 miles, writes that it made for a wild time: 'Training groups would pass each other, and a shout of "Up the League" would go up; in return a shout of "Fuck the League" was the reply.'

Against the backdrop of the NCU–BLRC feud on the road, track cycling in post-war Britain enjoyed huge popularity, and one rider in particular was the David Beckham of his generation: track sprinter Reg Harris regularly sold out track grandstands wherever he raced in the country.

In 1944, at the age of twenty-four, Harris became track national champion in the two sprint distances at that time – the quarter mile and the 1,000 yards – as well as possessing the stamina to win the five-mile event. He 'three-peated' again in 1945, before becoming amateur sprint world champion in Paris in 1947.

Having reached his mid-twenties, and having proved he was the best amateur sprinter, Harris was champing at the bit to turn professional and take on the very best track sprinters in the world, but retained his amateur status in order to compete in the 1948 London Olympics. However, that March, just a few months before the start of the Games, Harris fractured two vertebrae in a car accident. Having recovered enough to start riding again, he then crashed and sprained his wrist during a race at the Fallowfield track in Manchester, just a month out from the Games.

He was then temporarily excluded from the Olympic squad in the build-up after refusing to come to London to train on the Herne Hill track with his British teammates, preferring to convalesce closer to home in Manchester and train at Fallowfield. But Harris was not going to miss his 'home' Olympics; his fans would never have allowed it. These were the so-called 'Austerity Games'; post-Second World War, the global economy was not in great shape, and London – rather sportingly – had agreed to host the first Games since the infamous 1936 Berlin Olympics.

The track programme at Herne Hill had just four gold medals on offer, with Harris set to do battle in both the sprint and tandem events. He would also have been the first choice for the 1-kilometre time trial, but the tight schedule meant that the spot went to Tommy Godwin, who was usually more of an endurance rider than a sprinter. Harris made it into the final of the sprint, spurred on by a partisan crowd, but was beaten by his rival, Italy's Mario Ghella, in 'straight sets'; that is, twice in the best-of-three final.

Harris then partnered Alan Bannister in the tandem event, but the pair were beaten to the gold by the Italian duo, Teruzzi and Perona, and Harris had to settle for his second silver. Godwin took bronze in the 1-kilometre time trial, and there was bronze again for Godwin when he joined David Ricketts, Robert Geldard and Wilfred Waters for the team pursuit.

The 1948 Olympic road race, meanwhile, was held at Windsor Great Park, and was won by France's José Beyaert. Britain's best finisher was Bob Maitland in sixth place, which, with Gordon 'Tiny' Thomas in eighth and Ian Scott 16th, was good enough to give them the silver medal as the second-best team – the competition for which required three finishers.

Putting his disappointment with his two silver medals behind him, Harris turned professional with Raleigh following the London Games, and his star rose yet further. He won the world professional sprint title in Copenhagen in 1949, becoming the first British rider to do so, then won again in Liège, in Belgium, the next year and, for a third time in a row, in Milan in 1951.

He'd take the title once more – in 1954 in Cologne – before retiring from professional racing in 1957. But you can't keep a good man down, as they say, and Harris emerged from retirement in 1971 to take bronze in the British sprint national championship. By 1974, he had found his rhythm again, and took the British title at the ripe-old age of fifty-four.

Harris continued cycling into his seventies, and died in 1992, aged seventy-two. But as they race and train at the Manchester Velodrome, the latest generation of British track riders are watched over by a bronze statue of Reg Harris, no doubt helping to inspire young athletes who require a little added heritage beyond that provided by modern-day sprint heroes like Chris Hoy and Victoria Pendleton.

Back on the road, in August 1944 the BLRC organized Britain's first stage race, mimicking the format made popular by such great European races as the Tour de France. All three stages of the Southern Grand Prix started and finished in the small Kentish town of Farnborough, which has all but been swallowed up by Orpington these days.

Appropriately enough, it was Stallard himself who won the opening stage, outsprinting Les Plume. Plume would go on to win the race overall, beating Len Hook by just one second, with Ron Filsell almost four minutes back in third. Stallard finished eighth.

Stage racing in Britain was up and running – just as it was on the Continent – and 'the League' grew rapidly, leading to a BLRC-organized 'Tour of Britain' in 1945: a five-stage stage-race, which went from Brighton to Glasgow and was initially called the Victory Cycling Marathon, to celebrate the end of the war. The event changed name frequently after that, becoming simply 'Brighton–Glasgow', and then, in 1951, the first official Tour of Britain, sponsored by the *Daily Express* newspaper. The 1951 BLRC race ran from 19 August until 1 September – a 14-day stage race contested by British regional teams, sponsored teams of independents – 'semi-pros' – and national teams from Scotland, Ireland and France.

A small-format *Daily Express* publication, which sold for two shillings and told the story of that first official Tour of Britain, was littered with advertising pages almost as interesting as the account of the racing itself: for the bicycle brands used by the race's star riders, for saddles and tyres, and even for signature Reg Harris gloves.

Staring out, too, from the pages of the list of starters is the Yorkshire regional team's Oscar Savile – here nicknamed 'The Duke' – and better known, later, as Sir Jimmy Savile, of 'Jim'll Fix It' fame, and now infamous since his death in 2011. Having been accused of multiple sexual offences in the 1960s and '70s, he has become the catalyst for a wider, ongoing police investigation into the entertainment industry of the time, which saw the jailing of entertainer Rolf Harris in July 2014.

Savile appears not to have completed the first stage between London's Hyde Park and Brighton, which was won by France's Gabriel Audemard, just nine seconds ahead of his national team-mate Edmond Pierre. Ordinarily, this should have made Audemard the race leader, but the stage winner was docked 30 seconds by race officials that evening – the lead passing to Pierre – when it emerged that someone had carried Audemard's bike across a railway bridge for him after the level-crossing gates had gone down near Newhaven, just a few miles short of the finish on Madeira Drive in Brighton. The chasers were so close behind him that they, too, had to carry their bikes across the bridge, and a picture shows some startled-looking members of public caught on the stairs as the riders come up and over the bridge.

But the British public and the BLRC would have been hoping for a home winner at the inaugural Tour of Britain, and Ian Steel took the race by the scruff of the neck, and the French team to task, by winning the third stage into Plymouth. He'd win two more stages on his way to overall victory by the time the race had looped back to London over 12 stages – taking two rest days along the way – via Cardiff, Steel's home town of Glasgow, Newcastle and Norwich. Steel was also the winner of the 'Berlin–Warsaw–Prague' Peace Race in 1952 after the BLRC had sent their own 'national team' – albeit an unofficial one – to take part in the prestigious Eastern European stage race.

It was significant, too, in that the International Cycling Union, known best by its French acronym, the UCI (Union de Cyclisme Internationale), took note of the win by the unofficial British team, and threatened to expel the NCU from the world union if a solution to the continued BLRC–NCU battle was not found.

By the third edition of the Tour of Britain, in 1953 – when the race was won by the same Tiny Thomas who had taken a team silver medal in the 1948 Olympic road race – the *Daily Express* had had enough of the BLRC and the NCU continuing to be at each other's throats, and pulled the plug on their sponsorship. The *News of the World* had also sponsored the 'Brighton–Glasgow' in 1947, but similarly withdrew its sponsorship after just one edition once it became aware of what was happening.

With the BLRC losing the support of the *Daily Express*, and with the NCU trying to cope with the UCI breathing down their neck, something really needed to be done.

The warring of the parties had led to the creation of a 1954 government report on massed-start cycle racing by the Ministry of Transport and Civil Aviation Committee on Road Safety, which hoped to clear things up. When the Ministry of Transport received identical letters, dated 30 August 1953, from each of the BLRC, NCU and RTTC, all parties pledged to work together in the future: 'From a domestic point of view the Committee [joint committee] would point out that this year, after a long period of bitter struggle, full agreement was reached between the three bodies responsible for the control of cycle racing in all its forms in this country and there is no longer any dissension between them which could, as in the past, be reflected in the control of massed-start cycle racing.'

Interestingly, the report revealed how things had already begun to go in the right direction after an agreement was reached between the NCU, BLRC and RTTC as to who should pay for what at the 1953 world championships in Lugano, Switzerland:

(1) The costs of the professional road team shall be met, and the receipts from the professional road race shall be received, by the League.
(2) The costs of the amateur road team and the receipts from the amateur road race shall be shared equally between the Union and the League.
(3) The costs of all track teams shall be met, and the receipts from the track championships shall be received by the Union.

A thaw in relations between the NCU and the BLRC helped lead the (now defunct) Milk Marketing Board to take on sponsorship of the Tour of Britain, and in 1958 the Milk Race was first run – the name replacing the various iterations of the race that had run since the mid-1940s.

The Milk Race was initially open to both amateurs and 'independents', before becoming a strictly amateur-racers-only event from 1960. It was a race that would help raise home-grown talent, that would eventually be capable of taking on the more experienced European riders at their own game. Professionals were permitted to ride, too, from 1985 until its last edition in 1993.

In 1959, a year after the creation of the Milk Race, and to Percy Stallard's chagrin, the NCU and BLRC finally merged, creating the British Cycling Federation (BCF), although the RTTC remained a separate body, regulating only time trials, which it still does, now as the CTT.

The CTT still runs the British Best All-Rounder competition, and has separate national championships over each standard time-trial distance. The BCF – these days simply 'British Cycling' – organizes the national road-race championships, but also a separate time-trial national championship over a different course and distance each year. Both British Cycling events award the winner of each competition the national champion's jersey – white with a red and blue band – which the rider then wears in place of their usual team jersey for the next 12 months.

It's confusing having two different types of time-trial national championships, but it works, and no one's angry at anyone any more. In fact, that the battle between the NCU and the BLRC continued for so long seems astounding now, but fully explains why Britain has produced so many fine track riders and time triallists over the years. The 'new breed' of road racers – your Wigginses and Froomes – really only have a heritage of 'proper' road racing since after the war, compared to the eighty-odd-year head start enjoyed by the rest of the world. But one could say that Britain has caught up rather well.

4

1955 AND ALL THAT

Although Bill Burl and Charles Holland had been the first British riders to take part in the Tour de France, in 1937, no Briton started the race again until 1955.

Due to the Second World War there was no Tour between the 1939 and 1947 editions, but it was nevertheless a long wait for France's near neighbours to reappear at the race.

With the Tour de France starting in Yorkshire in 2014, local boy Brian Robinson was, quite rightly, in great demand during the build-up to the *Grand Départ* in Leeds. In 1955, Robinson was the first British rider to finish the Tour, in 29th place, while Tony Hoar was – in the same year – the second. Hoar rode just that one edition, finishing in last place: 69th out of 69 finishers, 130 having started in Le Havre on 7 July. Robinson would go on to become Britain's first Tour stage winner, too, in 1958, while Hoar, having completed the 1955 Tour, and riding, but not finishing, the Tour of Spain in 1956, retired from racing to live in British Columbia in Canada.

Fifty-seven years later, Hoar's still there, and it's from across the Atlantic, and from the far side of North America to boot, that he recounts his memories of that 1955 race – with what has become a gentle English-Canadian accent – and the story of how he got to the Tour in the first place.

Born in 1932, Tony Hoar grew up in Emsworth, near Portsmouth in Hampshire. As a child during the war, he was a good runner before turning to two wheels. 'I remember running this cross-country race, at the age of about thirteen, or something, and I won money!' Hoar laughs. 'We were just a bunch of kids, but we decided to start our own cycling club. We got bikes from some-where, and ex-army tents, and off we'd go on camping trips on the weekends.'

Sometimes the boys' trips – and their bikes – would take them to the Alexandra Park cycling track in Portsmouth, where they'd watch the racing.

'It was just spectacular to watch,' remembers Hoar, still now almost in wonder. They'd go to the smaller track in nearby Gosport, too, 'a quarter-miler' where they discovered you could enter the races on the line.

'I had a road bike, but we were riding fixed-wheel, so that was OK for the track,' says Hoar. 'I had touring tyres on my bike, so someone lent me a pair of Dunlop high-pressures, which were much faster than mine. And then they put me in a race against Gobber Fleming – the local sprint champion.'

As a result of watching the racing in Alexandra Park, Hoar had an idea of what the sprint races were about.

'Well, I knew you were supposed to hang around and then jump at the last minute,' he laughs, 'but that was about all I knew. So we were riding around – and why they put me up against Gobber, I'll never know – and I jumped him. I guess he thought he was going to be able to catch me, but he didn't. That was a little sensational, I can tell you!'

But Hoar then plays it down, saying that he managed to just

catch his opponent unawares, and that the two of them laughed about it afterwards. 'Our little club rode a time trial around the same time, too,' recalls Hoar. 'A kid at school gave us the entry forms, but we weren't members of the RTTC. We didn't even know it existed.'

What Hoar and his friends did know, however, was that you were supposed to wear black when you rode time trials.

'So we dyed these singlets black and just wore those. We turned up, and they said, "Hey! You've got to cover your arms up!" and asked us which club we were with. We told them the Emsworth Cycling and Camping Club. When they realized that we weren't members of the RTTC, they were very kind, despite everything being very official in those days. They told us that if we were going to join that they'd let us ride. So we did, although my bottom bracket came loose and I did about a "12" [one hour and 12 minutes] for the 25 miles.'

The next time, Hoar won the handicap, which made it a rather decent start to his racing career. Bitten by the bug, Hoar and his pals would ride as far as Southampton to do time trials, carrying their camping equipment so that they could stay nearby overnight and then race early the next morning.

'We got into the massed-start racing, too, and I started winning, fairly early on,' says Hoar. 'And it was funny, but I found that I was an expert at grass-track racing. I could ride the grass way above my "standing". I just had this knack for it; don't ask me how come.

'You could win tons of stuff doing it, too: canteens of cutlery, watches . . . No money, though, so the routine afterwards was for all of the riders who'd won something to go to one corner of the track, which was well known amongst the spectators, and sell it all. It was fantastic, and I won tons of prizes back then.'

Hoar is a real proponent of grass-track racing, and bemoans the fact that it isn't as popular as it once was, pointing out that it's a relatively cheap cycling discipline, only requiring a grass running track to put on meets.

It may not be such a big discipline these days, but it was never-theless the way that Britain's track-cycling golden girl Victoria Pendleton got into racing at the age of nine. Grass-track racing was a compromise the future Olympic individual-sprint champion's mum was willing to make until Pendleton turned sixteen and hit the 'real' track, and the ideal environment in which to learn to ride fixed-wheel and develop bike-handling skills.

When Hoar started racing after the war, he and many of his contemporaries progressed to riding custom-built steel frames.

'Around our way,' says Hoar, 'everyone bought custom frames from Bill Harvell's shop – or bought them "on tick" for 2/6 a week, or something like that – and then you'd get it built up with the components you wanted, or could afford.'

Bill Harvell had won a bronze medal in the team pursuit at the 1932 Olympic Games in Los Angeles, riding with Ernest Johnson, who won bronze again in the team pursuit in Berlin four years later, and Charles Holland: the same Charles Holland who, with Bill Burl, would go on to become Britain's first participant in the Tour de France in 1937.

The fourth member of that LA squad was Frank Southall, who in the lead-up to those Games had represented Great Britain in every world championships and Olympics since 1925, and who won the British Best All-Rounder competition four times on the trot, from its inception in 1930 until 1933, riding for the Norwood Paragon club. Southall later became champion time triallist Eileen Sheridan's manager when she turned professional and was sponsored by Hercules Cycles just after the Second World War.

Although cycling had become hugely popular in the years after the war, cyclists weren't always quite so popular at the café stops on club runs, Hoar recalls.

'Even a small club like ours from the little village of Emsworth would have three groups out sometimes,' he says. 'They'd each do different distances, and then we'd meet up for tea at some place that would let us all in. It was all quite high-spirited! They didn't actually ban you, but the spoons were chained to the tables – stuff like that!'

With hardly any cars on the roads, it was a cyclist's utopia, and Hoar finds it hard to quantify just how big cycling was then when the car wasn't the star. Fuel rationing ended in May 1950, but people were selling their cars because of the price of petrol.

'I remember once seeing a Morgan 3-Wheeler for ten quid!' says Hoar. 'And some of my mates bought this beautiful big limousine; you've never seen such a big car. It did about five miles to the gallon, though, so they couldn't really afford to run it, but on weekends we'd all chip in and go to dances in this bloody great thing!

'So the roads were for cycling; you hardly ever saw a car. And the clubs! You'd pass big clubs going the other way, and, if they were going the same way as you, there was always a bit of a dust-up, you know. It was a really good time for cycling – probably the best it's ever been.'

Once Hoar had begun to get more serious about cycling, he was racing almost every day.

'You could, back then. There were always midweek time trials, and lots of circuit races – tons of circuit races – at Brands Hatch and Goodwood. They were big fields, too – 250 riders – and the first prize was always three guineas. I won a few of those! And then there was all the track racing, at Gosport, Portsmouth, Southampton, Poole Park – near Bournemouth – and Brighton.'

He laughs at the thought of the Preston Park track in Brighton, which is still popular today. 'That one's from the old penny-farthing days, with its little bit of banking on the last corner. Whoever designed it didn't know what the hell they were doing!'

he laughs. 'We used to joke about it having a feeding station in the back straight because it's so big! It's something like 630 yards long.'

Hoar raced them all, and the race meetings pulled in big crowds in those days, too. 'But then there wasn't really much else for people to do in the early fifties, I guess,' he says.

As Hoar started to rack up the wins and augment his reputation, he began getting his bikes from frame builder Freddy Prince in Southampton.

'Freddy made me road frames and track frames, and I was always interested in the design, so I would talk about how it could be faster or better,' Hoar recalls. 'You had to give them back at the end of the season – they weren't yours to keep – and there was no written publicity, but people got to see the name on the frame.

'And then we used to write what we called "begging letters" to Dunlop. At the beginning of the year, you'd list how many races you'd won the year before, and they'd give you stuff. All illegal, but it was done, and everyone did it.'

There were also racing trips across to the Isle of Wight, which Hoar remembers fondly.

'Jack Gay was the promoter in Pompey,' Hoar recalls, employing the locals' vernacular for Portsmouth, 'and he put on the racing on the promenade at Ryde, I guess it was. He organized sprints, with people running alongside you at the end to take your hand and slow you down before you dropped into the ocean! The things we used to do!'

Those Isle of Wight races came early in the season, says Hoar, and so weren't taken as seriously as those that came later on. 'We'd still be partying and having club dinners, and stuff like that; the social and racing seasons often overlapped!'

Not that Hoar and his mates would even consider drinking alcohol during the season; save for the odd one or two. The off-season proper was a different matter, though.

'I drank and really smoked in the winter . . . Bloody idiot!' Hoar says, chastising himself. 'Bunch of idiots, we were! But it was great: every club had a big dinner, and they were great affairs. They gave the prizes out, and everybody had a good time. It was really a good scene, cycling.'

Hoar worked for the British Admiralty, in Portsmouth Dockyard, in the early fifties. They were very strict about how many days off could be taken each year, but when Hoar started getting sent to ride various races in Belgium for the national team, they were prepared to bend the rules to allow him a bit more time off, albeit unpaid.

'You didn't win any money at British races,' Hoar explains, 'but they gave you vouchers for, say, ten quid, which you could redeem at your local bike shop. But the good bike shops would give you the money for it – full face-value.'

Bike equipment was expensive to buy, but if the riders could convert their vouchers to hard cash, and then get some free equipment via their 'begging letters', there was the potential to make even more money.

'So you'd get sent the odd thing: Dunlop might give you a few tubulars, Brooks would give you a few saddles, and Airlite would give you a few hubs. And then we could sell some of those to the eastern nations when we rode internationally!'

Hoar got to race in Belgium on a number of occasions.

'We'd stay on there longer to do more racing if we could – depending on our jobs,' he explains. 'You could race every day there in those days; there were at least ten or twenty races every day, which sounds crazy. Then at the weekend there were thousands of bloody races!' And, most importantly, 'You got paid in cash – right down to 20th place.'

While Hoar's employers made allowances for his racing sorties abroad, in 1954 Hoar totalled an extraordinary thirteen weeks off work, at no pay, in order to represent England at the British

Empire and Commonwealth Games, as they were called then.

'The Games were in Vancouver, here in Canada,' says Hoar. 'The national team didn't give you anything, though. Other teams were getting a bit of pocket money, but not the good ol' Brits. We got bugger all!'

But if money wasn't on offer, the English team enjoyed an excellent medal haul on the track: Cyril Peacock's gold in the sprint, Norman Sheil's gold and Peter Brotherton's silver in the individual pursuit, and Keith Harrison's silver and bronze medals in the scratch race and 1-kilometre time trial, respectively.

Hoar finished mid-pack in the road race, helping teammate Eric Thompson to the gold medal and Bernard Pusey – Hoar's team-mate the following year at Hercules, and on the Tour de France squad – to bronze.

And Canada made such a good impression on Hoar that he'd be back there – for good – just a couple of years later.

In the meantime, there was the small matter of becoming one of the two first British riders to complete the Tour de France.

'At the start of the 1955 season, I rode the Tour of Egypt as part of a four-man British team,' Hoar explains. 'It was funny, really, being in Egypt at that time as the Suez Crisis was about to start. But they sent us idiots over there anyway, and I won a few stages. The race was run by the army, and we stayed in various types of accommodation, as hardly any of the cities had hotels at that stage. It was kind of rough.'

One of the places the team stayed at, though, was decidedly un-rough, which turned out to be rather lucky, as it happened.

'We got an invite to stop with a British cotton-mill owner in one of the cities, and of course our team manager jumped at the chance. We ended up in this nice house with servants and nice beds and food, although I think the owner may have been a little peeved to find out that we were a bunch of wharf rats rather than some nice British team from Oxford or Cambridge! But he kept a stiff upper lip and made us welcome.

'But I woke up the next morning with a temperature of 104°F,' continues Hoar. 'This guy called his doctor, who gave me a shot of atropine, and – Christ! – I was able to get up and walk around. And then I rode that day. What else was I going to do? You were never going to get home if you tried to get home on your own from where we were!'

Hoar recalls the effects of the atropine he was given: 'It totally dries your saliva glands, which made it impossible to eat anything. I was trying to, but it was like eating mouthfuls of sand. It was the weirdest thing.'

He survived the day by trying to take it as easy as possible in the bunch, and began to feel better in the days that followed, to the point that he was winning stages again towards the end of the race.

'It was lucky that we were staying at that guy's house, though, as otherwise I would have got some army doctor, and God knows what they would have done,' he laughs.

Some years later, Hoar was having some dental work done in Canada, which naturally included having a tube stuck in his mouth to suck up the saliva.

'I told them afterwards that they should try giving patients a shot of atropine, like I'd had in Egypt. Funnily enough, they knew what it was, and told me that Cleopatra had apparently also used it to put a blush in her cheeks!'

The race had been quite the Egyptian experience for Hoar, then, in more ways than one.

On his return to England he found that his stage wins hadn't gone unnoticed, and he was given the opportunity to turn pro with the British Hercules team. Hercules Cycles had already sponsored individual British time triallists, such as Eileen Sheridan, but this was a first toe-dipping into the water of road racing for them.

After signing the contract in Birmingham, Hoar flew down to

the Hercules training camp in the south of France to meet his new teammates.

'Some of them I knew already – like Bernard Pusey – but a lot of them I didn't know, although I'd raced against some of them.'

Members of the team that year included Dave Bedwell, Stan Jones, Austrian-born Fred Krebs, Brian Robinson and Derek Buttle: Buttle having been the man who had persuaded Hercules Cycles to sponsor a pro team for the 1953 season, and had therefore instigated the rapid growth it had experienced from then on.

At that point, says Hoar, there was still no talk of anyone riding the Tour de France, but they went to the Paris–Nice stage race in March, where Robinson finished eighth and Bob Maitland was 14th. It was a good performance, although Hoar reveals that the whole team finished outside the time limit on one stage: 'But they put us back in!'

Hoar's knowledge of the big European races was limited to what he'd read in British magazines like *Cycling* and *The Bicycle*.

'I never got the French magazines like some people did,' he says. 'I guess I was too busy doing it to be reading about it, racing several times a week, doing time trials, track racing and grass-track racing. And then the circuit races at the weekends. I was in the League, but I don't think I ever rode an open road race in Britain that I can think of – only circuit races – although when we were abroad in Belgium and Egypt we raced on the roads.'

But Hoar knew about the Tour de France, of course. Its reputation preceded it.

'Well, I knew it was the biggest, toughest event – that it was *the* race – and once there was talk about us doing it, I knew that it was likely to be bloody hard.'

The Tour organizers were keen to have a British team riding – the first since the mixed GB/Canada team in 1937.

'But it wasn't really a British national team – it was Hercules,' Hoar points out. It had been Hercules Cycles' aim to ride the Tour ever since the formation of its pro team, but the race just happened to be contested by national teams from 1930 until 1962 (and again in 1967 and 1968).

To help make up the numbers for the ten-man team, Hercules brought in a few other riders from rival British domestic teams: Ian Steel, who had won the Peace Race in 1952, from the Viking Cycles squad, and his teammate Bevis Wood, as well as Ken Mitchell from the Wearwell Cycles team.

'Ken was really more of a track man,' says Hoar. 'Neat guy, and still alive and living in Australia, I think.'

Hoar and his teammates turned up in Normandy in early July ready to race.

'And it was no big deal, really,' he says, 'because we knew that there were also five regional French teams that year – a lot of riders – which meant that the standard wasn't going to be killer, like it is now. We'd ridden against a lot of those riders, and had met a couple of brothers who rode for one of those regional teams when we'd been down in the south of France. They were just riders, not big stars. I think that made the whole make-up of the Tour look a bit less threatening. Today it's totally different!'

Hoar says he doesn't remember any fuss about there being a British team racing that year, and that no one paid them much attention. For Hoar, that would come later in the race.

The team – Hoar, Robinson, Bedwell, Maitland, Pusey, Krebs and Stan Jones, all from the original Hercules squad, plus Steel and Wood from Viking, and Mitchell, on loan from Wearwell Cycles – set off from Le Havre on 7 July. By the start of stage 12, they were down to just Hoar and Robinson.

'We had so many punctures in those first few days – it was incredible,' remembers Hoar. 'That meant that you were always having to wait for your buddies, and then it was a lot of work getting back to the bunch, which really sapped everyone's energy early on.'

Like most of the others, the British team were riding on Dunlop tubular tyres.

'But you don't ride them fresh; you need to mature them, age them, for at least six months, so we asked them to make sure that our "new" ones for the Tour were pre-aged,' Hoar explains.

But after all the flat tyres they'd had in the first week, Hoar and his teammates had become suspicious, and one night, at the hotel, they cut one open to look at the manufacturing date inside.

'They hadn't been matured after all, so the team had to rush around and get hold of some Italian tubulars: good ones, with a good reputation for being decent. And we chucked all our Dunlop ones away!'

Not that the British team announced that they'd swapped tyres.

'We were worried that we wouldn't get our bonus from Dunlop if we said anything, so they still paid us!' Hoar laughs.

And while it looked from the outside as though the Hercules men all rode Hercules bicycles, the truth, says Hoar, was quite different.

'We didn't ride their bikes – we all used custom frame builders, and they just painted their name on the frames,' says Hoar. 'Most of the guys rode stuff that wasn't provided by their sponsors back then. For example, everybody rode Airlite hubs, everybody used Reynolds 531 tubing and everybody rode Brooks saddles. The Brooks B17 was highly prized. And everybody used Dunlop No. 3 tubulars, I think they were – a good 10oz road tub that everyone rode. So you rode whatever you thought was best for you.'

Today's riders sometimes do, too.

The British team at the 1955 Tour were also sponsored by Ribena blackcurrant juice.

'But that was all right, because I used to drink it anyway,' laughs Hoar.

He and Robinson were left with just one team car, and a relaxed team manager in Syd Cozens.

'Cozens never suggested any tactics or anything that I remember, but then he was a track rider, and quite a good one.'

Indeed, Cozens had represented Great Britain in the sprint at the 1928 Olympic Games in Amsterdam, and was one of the big stars of Six-Day racing in London of the thirties.

'So Robbo and I just rode our own race and tried to get to the finish inside the time limit, which was very strict,' says Hoar. 'It was mostly just a matter of survival.'

Each day, Hoar would find himself within the same group of riders: *domestiques* together, just trying to make it through to the next day, the race falling into a kind of pattern.

The British team had little experience of riding in the mountains, although Robinson had ridden in the Pyrenees and the Alps during the 1952 Route de France stage race, which was an amateur version of the Tour de France. Hoar soon found out that safety in numbers was again the best way to make it to the finish inside the time limit each day. Making friends could be to your advantage, too.

'I was quite a good climber, but only on British hills, and there was quite a difference between them and the Alps and the Pyrenees! And you'd find yourself on the climbs with riders you'd got to know during the race. One of those was Bernard Gauthier from the French national team – a big, big guy who was in the race to help his team on the flat. We'd often find ourselves riding together on the climbs, and you'd get the odd spectator on the way up; most of them would be up nearer the top. Gauthier would shout, "*Poussez-moi!*" at them, and they'd come running alongside him, and he'd turn around and say, "*Et l'Anglais aussi!*" – "The Englishman as well!" – and they'd push us for 20 yards or so.

'He was shameless!' Hoar laughs. 'I'd always try to find him somewhere on the slope, and we'd ride, and get pushed, together.'

Going down the other side of each mountain came with its own problems, too. The British riders had limited experience of descending at such breakneck speeds.

'You would have thought that we might have been given some kind of coaching or training beforehand, but there was nothing. We figured we were pretty good bike riders, but it was certainly hairy.'

Hoar refuses to say that he was ever scared, but leaving too much of a gap to the rider in front would risk you feeling the wrath of the others.

'You just had to follow the rider ahead of you, and hope they knew what they were doing. And once you did it enough times, you started getting the hang of it, but there were riders actually breaking away on descents – experts at descending – so it was a different experience for us.'

Stage 11, which saw Fred Krebs and Ken Mitchell abandon, leaving just Hoar and Robinson, was from Marseille to Avignon, via the climb of Mont Ventoux. The Ventoux would later be seared into cycling fans' minds as the desolate scene of British rider Tom Simpson's untimely death during the 1967 Tour, but in a frightening foreshadowing of what was to come, in 1955 it was the scene of another infamous incident.

'I remember going past Jean Malléjac,' Hoar says, referring to the rider from the French national squad who had collapsed with about 10 kilometres of the 21-kilometre climb to go. 'The ambulance was there, and Dr Dumas was there with him. They only had one doctor on the race in those days, and I used to joke that to keep his job he had to drive the ambulance as well, which may not have been far from the truth.'

It was poor Dumas who would have to attempt mouth-to-mouth resuscitation on Simpson a few kilometres further up the mountain twelve years later.

'I saw Malléjac's eyes,' Hoar recalls, 'and his pupils were dilated – a telltale sign of amphetamines. You used to see guys with these big eyeballs, and it was the amphetamines that did it, I was told.

'Beyond him, up the road, I could see this group of riders. I was on my own, but I was catching up with them, and I remember thinking how strange that was. There were about ten of them – climbers and a whole bunch of top names – and I put two and two together: they were on the same stuff as Malléjac. Perhaps it wasn't good in the hot temperatures, or was a bad batch, but these guys couldn't even ride straight. It was really weird, but I went past them, literally looking the other way.'

Doping, says Hoar, was never openly discussed, but you'd see riders routinely reaching into their back pockets for various things whenever the mountains approached.

'Some of them even used suppositories. And the German team used to actually stop next to their team car!' he laughs, in-credulous. 'Whenever we saw them doing that, we'd look at each other and say, "Oh Christ, here we go again!" We were riding on fresh air, we used to say.'

It wasn't just at the Tour, either, according to Hoar.

'It was happening at every event. I did some criterium races after that Tour, and, at one of them, Steenbergen came up . . .'

Hoar calls him Steenbergen, simply – not Van Steenbergen. Belgium's Rik Van Steenbergen was a two-time winner of both Paris–Roubaix and the Tour of Flanders, and the 1949 world champion – a title he'd win twice more, in 1956 and 1957. Later, the Belgian would admit to having doped, although it's unlikely he'd ever done much to hide it. He was also notoriously tight with his money, and in retirement would struggle with a penchant for gambling.

'I was trying to get a *prime*,' remembers Hoar, referring to the French term for a mid-race cash prize, 'and to just put on a bit of a show. Steenbergen rode up to me, looked at me, and then just rode away from me. I tried to get on his wheel, and it was impossible – like trying to get behind a car, or something. It was crazy; this just for a little *prime*. I wasn't that weak, but it really was like trying to keep up with a train. It was a bit of an eye-opener.'

On 'bread and water' (cyclists' slang for riding dope-free) at the 1955 Tour, the race became a fight for survival for Hoar. By the final week, however, his efforts had garnered plenty of media attention. He couldn't understand why at first, but soon realized that it was because he was in last place – the Tour's *lanterne rouge*, named after the red lanterns that used to hang on the last carriages of trains.

Rather than fans and the media viewing the rider at the bottom of the general classification simply as 'last', the *lanterne rouge* has always enjoyed celebrity status. 'Losing' is quitting the race; still being in it and pluckily battling your way towards the finish of the world's toughest cycling event is something to be greatly admired and celebrated – so much so that riders are thought to have 'fought' to finish last, although there seems to be little evidence of that, as the risk of finishing outside the time limit on each stage is too great.

But Hoar was far from impressed by any prestige attached to being the *lanterne rouge* as he struggled through the last few stages to Paris.

'I was in last place on and off for the last six days or so,' he remembers, 'but I certainly wasn't trying to finish last. The press was trying to make out that there was a big fight between me and Henri Sitek, from one of the French regional teams, for last place, but that couldn't have been further from the truth. In fact, the photographers used to have the two of us drop off the back of the bunch so that they could take pictures of us fooling around with this paper lantern, which then meant that we had to struggle to get back up to the bunch, which both of us could have done without! I thought it was just weird, and never thought that it could be to my advantage in any way.'

He was told that some people liked to bet on who the first and last rider would be at the Tour, which he thinks may have accounted for some of the hysteria, but at the finish in Paris, where Hoar was confirmed as the *lanterne rouge*, finishing 69th out of 69 finishers, people were cheering for him and chanting his name. And only then did he see how beneficial battling on to finish the race could be: 51 riders had dropped off along the way.

'I got offered all these contracts for criterium races over the course of the next seven days. They were all over Belgium, and I was paid really well. And I was very popular! But it was at those crits that a lot of the guys made their money.'

It's a tradition that continues to this day, mostly still in France, Belgium and the Netherlands, where local fans pay an entry fee to get on to a circuit in their towns. Throughout the rest of the year, watching professional bike races is free, but these circus-like events give people the opportunity to watch the stars of the Tour de France – stage winners, jersey winners, the *lanterne rouge* – battle it out in their own backyard. While the races tend to be fixed (the star name might just pip the local hero on the line, perhaps) families head home happy, having seen their heroes up close.

Brian Robinson would later credit Hoar with having helped him get through the 1955 Tour, thanks to his good humour.

'I don't know about that,' says Hoar, 'but I've had mates who've come over to visit me here in Canada, and seen me doing work for the homeless and stuff, and they say, "Holy Christ! You've sure changed! You didn't used to give a shit about anything!"'

He laughs at his friends' reactions, and admits he probably has changed a bit.

'But back then at the Tour it was all quite relaxed and good fun, really; I was only twenty-three or something, so I didn't take any-thing too seriously.'

Today, Hoar's help for the homeless includes providing trailers that fold out into a one-man tent, all built by him in his workshop in Mill Bay on Vancouver Island, where through his business, Tony's Trailers, he also makes the most amazing bike trailers for carrying dogs, kayaks, other people, luggage, or anything else that you feel like ferrying around on two wheels.

After the 1955 Tour de France, Hoar rode the Tour of Britain for Hercules.

'Robbo [Robinson] didn't want to ride it, which should have left me as the team leader, but I wasn't,' he says, clearly still disap-pointed. 'On the first day, one of my teammates, Dennis Talbot, got a flat, and so I waited for him. But we had trouble getting back to the bunch and lost twenty minutes, so that was me finished for the overall classification anyway.'

Hoar did win a stage, however: stage four, between Filey and Sheffield.

'There were four or five of us in a break, and they were working me over like hell, so I made sure I outsprinted them all,' Hoar says with a laugh, enjoying the memory of the win. 'There was a good picture in *The Bicycle* of me flicking open my toeclips as I crossed the finish line in Sheffield, just to rub it in!'

But at the end of the season, the team was disbanded: a victim of declining bike sales as the new rise of the car began, and, says Hoar, as a result of the continued fighting between the NCU and the BLRC, with riders continuing to be banned and penalized for their affiliation with one or the other. Many of the Hercules riders, including Talbot and the team's founder member, Derek Buttle, simply retired; the process of reverting to amateurism after having been a professional was lengthy, bordering on the impossible.

In 1956, in late April, Hoar rode the Tour of Spain as part of a 'mixed team' – a mix of nationalities – that included Robinson, Glasgow's Ian Steel, and 1952 world champion Heinz Müller of Germany. The team was led by the Swiss Hugo Koblet (nicknamed *Le Pédaleur du Charme* thanks to his tendency to carry a comb in his jersey pocket to help keep him looking his best).

'We had no manager, no sponsor, no masseur, and the Tour of Spain wasn't as well organized as the Tour de France,' explains Hoar. 'And although we had a contract with the race organizers for them to pay our lodging, food and expenses, after ten days I thought, "Bugger this," and packed it in.'

Robinson finished eighth at that Tour of Spain – and was, incidentally, the first British rider to finish the race (a six-man British team, which included Ian Steel and Ken Mitchell, had failed to finish any men in 1955). That eighth place would remain the best British finish at the Vuelta until 1969, when Michael Wright, riding for the Bic team (yep – the biro, lighter and disposable-razor lot) finished fifth. In 1985, Scotland's Robert Millar became the first British rider to make the podium when he finished runner-up after the Spanish riders had ganged up against him to ensure that one of their own, Pedro Delgado, took the win. In 2011, before either of them stood on the top step at the Tour de France, Team Sky duo Chris Froome and Bradley Wiggins gallantly battled with Spain's Juan José Cobo – a surprise eventual winner – to stand on the podium in Madrid, in second and third place, respectively. A British rider has yet to win the Vuelta.

But in 1956, Hoar had had enough of the European scene, and that November he was off in search of pastures new. He'd fallen in love with Canada during the '54 Empire Games, and knew that was where he wanted to go.

'When I was there the first time, I'd spent a whole month in Vancouver, and it was the best weather I'd ever seen in my life, which made me think, "Right – I'm going to come back here!"'

So that's what he did, and he's been there ever since, today happily building bike trailers in Mill Bay.

As a footnote, Hoar later became president of the International BMX Federation (IBMXF), helping to organize four world championships in the mid-1980s.

'I'd been going down to California on business, which was where BMX had all started, and when I saw what was happening, with tracks springing up everywhere, I thought it was fantastic. I was on the board of the Canadian cycling association at the time, and I told my colleagues there that I thought we should get involved.

'They just saw all these kids as wannabe motorcyclists – that was the attitude of a lot of people – but the trouble was that if all these kids wanted to race, they had to join an association, and there were about a dozen associations at the time, and the whole thing just seemed like a big racket to rip these kids off.'

Hoar was only too aware of the youngsters' desire to race bikes, and had been party to that kind of overt bureaucracy with the NCU and BLRC in Britain in the fifties. With others, he was a founder member of the IBMXF in 1981.

'BMX is a great success story, really, which I'm pleased to have played a part in,' Hoar says, proudly, 'because in only twenty-five years it made it as an Olympic sport – although the UCI had muscled in and taken it from us by the mid-nineties.'

'In fact,' he laughs, as he prepares for another day in his trailer workshop, 'I only just sold my 24-inch wheel cruisers the other day.'

As for Hoar's former Tour teammate, Brian Robinson, he was the lone British representative at the 1956 Tour de France, competing as part of a 'Luxembourg mixed' squad, made up, quite rightly, of mostly Luxembourgers (including the famous climber Charly Gaul, who would go on to win the Tour in 1958) plus an Italian and a Portuguese rider. The British rider held his own, though: he finished an excellent 14th overall, and was there on his own the following year again, although a crash on the fifth stage forced him to abandon.

At the 1958 Tour, compatriots Stan Brittain and Ron Coe joined Robinson, who became the first British rider to win a Tour stage, taking victory on the seventh stage from Saint Brieuc to Brest, although he'd actually crossed the line in second place before Italy's Arrigo Padovan was relegated for having impeded the Yorkshireman in the sprint. Robinson, Coe and Brittain had taken part in that 1958 race as part of a mixed team of nations, which also included Austrian, Danish and Portuguese riders, as well as Ireland's Shay Elliott, who in 1963 became the first Irishman to wear the Tour's yellow jersey.

Robinson won again in 1959, beating second-placed Arrigo Padovan of Italy by more than 20 minutes on stage 20 from Annecy to Chalon-sur-Saône, and taking 19th place overall.

Robinson was joined that year – again in an international team – by Britons John 'Jock' Andrews, Vic Sutton and Tony Hewson, who had won the 1955 Tour of Britain. But it was a bleak existence as a Brit abroad, and Hewson, whose European adventures are told in his book, *In Pursuit of Stardom*, even had to live in a converted ambulance – with Sutton and Andrews – in order to make ends meet on the Continent.

It would have been much easier to have stayed at home in Britain and survived on a diet of time trialling and circuit racing, but, thanks to Britain's 1950s adventurers, the door had been opened – just a crack – to the possibilities in Europe.

5

EILEEN, EILEEN AND BERYL

The late 1950s saw the emergence of Britain's greatest-ever racing cyclist.

Her name? Beryl Burton.

Burton's list of race wins and titles is phenomenal: achieved during a racing career that spanned four decades, they were won on both the track and road – the latter in both road racing and time trialling. A seven-time world champion, Burton was a true all-rounder, and a true one-off, unlikely ever to be matched for that triumvirate – that cyclist's holy grail – of strength, stamina and speed. An all-rounder she may have been, but she definitely specialized in time trialling. In all, Burton won 96 RTTC (now CTT) titles across the distances of 10, 15, 25, 30, 50 and 100 miles, and for 12 hours.

In 2014, the name 'Beryl Burton' remains in the top five for all the CTT distances bar the 24-hour 'distance', which was the only title and record to elude her. It's a considerable achievement when you remember that she had no recourse to today's aerodynamic aids such as aero handlebars and helmets, and her times were only beaten relatively recently across the various distances by time-trial talents such as Maxine Johnson, Jill Reames, Yvonne McGregor, Sue Wright, Sharon Lowther and Jenny Derham in the 1990s, Wendy Houvenaghel in the 2000s and Julia Shaw in the 2010s.

Extraordinarily, Burton still holds the CTT record for 12 hours – 277.25 miles, set in 1967. Her 250-mile effort of eight years previous to that puts her in second place on the all-time 12-hour list, too.

Most extraordinarily of all, she won the women's BBAR title twenty-five times in a row between 1959 and 1983 – a record highly unlikely ever to be beaten, or to even come close to being beaten.

On the track, Burton was national pursuit champion thirteen times, and in 1959 won the first of her five world-championship gold medals in the individual pursuit. She also won the women's road-race world championships twice, in Germany in 1960, and again in the Netherlands in 1967. No man or woman has ever dominated the sport quite so completely, either on a national or an international level.

So strong was Burton, in fact, that the 12-hour record that she set in 1967 was also, unofficially, of course, a new men's record.

As favourite for the men's competition at the Otley '12' in West Yorkshire – and favourite to take that year's BBAR title – Mike 'Mac' McNamara would set off as the field's last man. The women's competition would then start after him.

What happened next, as Burton has reluctantly acknowledged herself, has 'passed into cycling legend', or into British time-trialling legend at least. Like all the best stories, it seems to be told a little differently each time you hear it. The 'punchline' is that it's always a liquorice allsort, though, and we can assume that Burton is one of two people who tells it most truthfully.

Eleven hours into the 12-hour event, Burton realized that she was catching McNamara, and she didn't really know what to do.

'"Mac" raised his head slightly and looked at me,' Burton recalls in her 1986 autobiography *Personal Best*. 'Goodness knows what was going on in his mind, but I thought some gesture was required on my part. I was carrying a bag of liquorice allsorts in the pocket of my jersey and on impulse I groped into the bag and pulled one out. I can still remember that it was one of those swiss-roll-shaped ones, white with a coating of black liquorice. "Liquorice allsort, 'Mac'?" I shouted, and held it toward him. He gave a wan smile. "Ta, love," he said, popping the sweet into his mouth. I put my head down and drew away.'

When the 12 hours was up, Burton had recorded a new women's record of 277.25 miles. It was a new British record, too – for men. It was, and still is, the one and only time that a CTT women's record has exceeded that of the men. That remained the case for two years, until the Clifton Cycling Club's John Watson beat it with 281.87 miles in 1969. Burton's 277.25 remains the women's record.

McNamara had taken it with good grace – both having been beaten and his liquorice allsort – but the sixties were different times, and in his excellent book *Cycling Heroes*, of which Burton is of course one, Les Woodland quotes McNamara at the RTTC champions' night dinner at the end of the season as feeling compelled to say, 'I've right let myself down,' accent an' all.

It should be said that McNamara was at the dinner to collect his BBAR trophy, as was Burton, and that his 276.52 miles at the Otley '12' had nevertheless given him the new men's record, officially. It was just that Beryl's ride had beaten it.

It's fun to imagine what Burton could have done if today's technologies – slippery carbon-fibre frames, skinsuits and aero helmets – had been at her disposal, or to wonder how many women's world-championship time-trial titles she could have won, if the category had existed in her lifetime. (It wasn't introduced until 1994 – two years before she died.)

Burton's (perhaps unintentional) confectionery-based humour did at times crack, however, when she felt that things weren't going her way.

Burton's daughter, Denise, followed her mother into competitive cycling, and soon found that she'd inherited a good dose of her mother's ability. Beryl had won the road-race national championships twelve times since they were first held in 1959, and now, aged thirty-nine, she was up against her own daughter in the 1976 Nationals.

Out on the road, though, it was every woman for herself, and on the last lap of the Harrogate course the title was going to go to one of three riders: the Long Eaton Paragon club's Carol Barton, or one of the Morley Cycling Club's mother–daughter duo of Beryl and Denise Burton. The Burtons had the beating of Barton, who came third, but as two matching Morley CC jerseys lunged for the line, only one of the Burtons was going to come out on top in this generation game.

The decision went in favour of Denise, and Beryl was furious, feeling that her daughter hadn't contributed enough in trying to distance themselves from the peloton, and had instead 'saved her legs' for the finish.

'I stood on the podium and refused to shake hands with my own daughter,' she wrote, which reads like some kind of confessional. 'It was not a sporting thing to do. I did our sport a disservice in allowing personal acrimony to intervene, and I can only plead that I was not myself at the time.'

Burton's 'excuse', it turns out, stemmed from problems at home – with her daughter, rather than with her husband, Charlie, although it was apparently nothing more serious than the standard teenage ailment (although Denise had just turned twenty) of being unable to help more around the house. In the heat of competition, however, it was perhaps entirely irrelevant that Beryl was trying to beat her own flesh and blood (who may or may not have done the washing-up the night before); Denise was just another competitor, and the guilt Burton had to carry after the incident seems almost unjust when you consider her immense competitive drive.

But before Burton came two other extraordinary British women – both called Eileen.

Eileen Sheridan was a true star of her time; or at least she was until her near-contemporary Burton burst on to the scene. Burton's twenty-five-straight BBAR titles are hard to match, but many of Sheridan's Women's Road Records Association (WRRA) 'place-to-place' records appear equally out of reach.

Sheridan and her husband Ken had met in Coventry during the Second World War, and enjoyed each other's company on leisurely bike rides in the surrounding countryside. Sheridan began racing only after she and Ken joined the Coventry Cycling Club in 1944, and decided to ride the 'club 10' (10-mile time trial). Not only did Sheridan win: she set a new club record.

She'd been bitten by the racing bug, and, back then, more than now, the talented racing members at cycling clubs would enjoy the weekend touring trips away and 'club runs' just as much as the non-racing members, and Eileen and Ken continued to take part in the social side of cycling. Sheridan just happened to be good at racing. Very, very good at racing, and she enjoyed it, too.

'I loved the thrill of chasing,' Sheridan explained in a 2012 interview with *Rouleur* magazine. 'I just had to try hard and win. It was just in me to chase; I think you're born with that.'

In 1951, having won the women's BBAR in both 1949 and 1950, Sheridan's obvious talent was rewarded with a professional contract from Hercules Cycles, which later 'sponsored' – or at least formed – the British national team for the 1955 Tour de France. But just like the British team at the Tour, Sheridan never actually rode Hercules bikes; like most top riders, she had her frames custom-made and simply badged up with Hercules logos. Everyone was happy, and standard Hercules bikes flew off the shelves thanks to her and her teammate Ken Joy's achievements.

Managed by four-time BBAR champion and 1932 Olympic team-pursuit bronze medallist Frank Southall, Sheridan went about setting new standards at the WRRA distance, time/distance (12 hours and 24 hours) and place-to-place records. Her distance records have long been superseded, but the five place-to-place records she still holds may remain unbeaten for some time yet, if not for ever.

London to Edinburgh (set in 1954), York to Edinburgh (1953), London to Liverpool (1952), 'London to Bath and back' (1952) and 'London to Portsmouth and back' (1954) are all difficult routes thanks to the proliferation of traffic lights and traffic-calming measures, as well as the ever-present danger of riding on such busy roads, which all combine in fact to make most RRA records more difficult to beat than ever these days.

For forty-eight years, Sheridan also held the women's record for the prestigious Land's End to John O'Groats – two days, 11 hours and seven minutes, set in 1954 – until it was finally beaten in 2002 by Lynne Taylor, whose record of two days, four hours and 45 minutes still stands.

After the birth of her daughter in 1955, Sheridan retired, totally dominant in her field, and the holder of all twenty WRRA records.

There's another Eileen who has loomed large in the history of British cycling. Eileen Gray was already an accomplished track rider when in 1946 she was invited to take part in a women's race at the Ordrup track in Copenhagen, as part of a three-woman British team: Britain's first ever women's national squad. The race was just one in a programme otherwise made up of men's events – just a bit of a novelty, it turned out – but Joan Simmons,

Stella Farrell and Gray took it as an opportunity not to be missed, thrashing the opposition.

'They just wanted us there as a sideshow, but what they didn't realize was that they'd given us a platform, visibility, and a chance to show what we could do,' Gray explained in an interview with British Cycling in 2010. Only later did she discover that their Danish opposition were women who were part of a theatre group, tasked with just trying to put on a show. Not that it really mattered. 'Other women saw us, too, and must have thought, "If they can do it, so can I," and from that point on, something started that they couldn't stop.'

By 'they' she means the opposition to women's cycling that Gray spent much of her career battling against. She became president of the Women's Cycle Racing Association in 1963, and Burton remembers Gray fighting the WCRA's corner when it came to finances after it had been discovered that invitations to the women's national team from foreign race organizers and other national federations were simply being made to disappear at the BCF headquarters in the 1960s.

'Any team would, of course, have had to meet its own travelling expenses and, no doubt, the BCF felt unwilling to meet such expenditure,' Burton wrote in her autobiography. 'As it was one of the poor relations of the sporting life of this country, this was understandable but, as the WCRA would probably have been willing to go a long way to finding the cash, it would have been nice if we had been given the chance, at least, to do something about it.'

Burton adds that she and her husband Charlie got on well with the Russian officials they'd met at various competitions, and says it's one of her regrets in her racing life that she didn't get to race in Russia.

Gray remained in her post as president of the WCRA until 1976, when she became president of the BCF. During her time at the head of the British federation – she remained in the post until

1986 – Gray was instrumental in getting women's cycling added to the Olympic Games programme, campaigning successfully to get a women's road race included at the 1984 Los Angeles Games. A single track event, the women's sprint, was added to the programme for Seoul in 1988, and it seems almost unthinkable now that women's cycling wasn't included before then. Women like Eileen Gray, though, are the ones who ensure that such things happen.

'There have been few harder workers for the sport, and women's bike-racing worldwide owes her a debt of gratitude for the way she has always fought for the girls at the highest level,' Burton said of Gray, who she also credits with having introduced her to opera, which became a lifelong love.

Gray was awarded an OBE in 1978, and then became mayor of the Royal Borough of Kingston upon Thames in 1990, a post she kept until 1999, receiving a CBE in 1997.

'I think I was quite a good mayor,' she says in her British Cycling interview. 'I hope I was. I made it my business to get out and about and talk to people, help them get their ideas heard, and I tried to encourage them to do things that they wanted to do.'

Doing what Eileen Gray always did best, then. But perhaps the ultimate recognition of her selfless serving of women's cycling, British cycling and the good people of Kingston upon Thames was when Gray was chosen as an Olympic torchbearer for the borough ahead of the 2012 London Games.

Both Gray and Burton were included in British Cycling's new Hall of Fame in 2010, which celebrates fifty years of the federation with fifty names who have made outstanding contributions to cycling in Britain. Eileen Sheridan is, surely, a glaring omission.

What also seems to be total injustice is that Burton never won the BBC Sports Personality of the Year Award, which would have illuminated her star even more. Perhaps it wouldn't have been what she'd have wanted, but the fact that Tom Simpson was recognized for his road-race world championships win in 1965 yet in 1967, after her second road-race world championships victory, Burton could only come second (missing out on the BBC prize to boxer Henry Cooper that year) seems a little unjust – and that's without reeling off all her other achievements. Simpson and Burton were, incidentally, great friends.

She was awarded an MBE in 1964 and an OBE in 1968, as well as the Sports Writers' Award, now the Sports Journalists' Association awards, and the title of *Daily Express* Sportswoman of the Year in 1967. But it's clear that a little more recognition wouldn't have gone amiss, for in *Personal Best* Burton writes: 'I think that my world championship successes might well have had more attention paid to them in this country if I had won Olympic rather than world medals.'

She died on 8 May 1996, aged fifty-eight, while out on her bike delivering invitations to her 59th birthday party a few days later.

But Burton and fellow Yorkshireman Brian Robinson were well remembered during the Tour de France's 2014 *Grand Départ* in the county. And Burton was the subject of a 2012 BBC Radio 4 play, called *Beryl*, written by Maxine Peake, whom those who watched the original UK version of television comedy-drama *Shameless* will know as the Gallaghers' next-door neighbour Veronica. *Beryl* was adapted for the stage in 2014, and played at the West Yorkshire Playhouse in Leeds throughout July in honour of Yorkshire's – and Britain's – greatest-ever cyclist.

6

THE SUMMER OF '67

In 1965, he was fêted as the UK's top sportsman, winning the BBC Sports Personality of the Year Award thanks to his victory at the professional road-race world championships in September – the first male British rider to win the title.

But by the summer of 1967, Tom Simpson was no longer with us.

The Englishman's death during the Tour de France sent shock waves through cycling and the wider sporting world. Doping in the professional peloton was rife, and many riders considered it 'professional' to do it, but no one was supposed to die. Only the year before, during the 1966 Tour, cycling's world governing body, the UCI, had implemented its first drug tests, which led to strikes and protests by riders concerned about samples potentially not being sealed properly; not to mention the fact that many saw 'medicating' as necessary if they were to do their job.

Pierre Dumas, the Tour's race doctor, had led the calls for routine drug testing at the race, and in all sports at the Olympic Games, ever since the 1955 episode on Mont Ventoux when French rider Jean Malléjac had collapsed, wild-eyed and frothing

73

at the mouth, and been attended to by Dumas before being taken away in an ambulance. Malléjac later made a full recovery, but always insisted that he must have been drugged by one of his team's *soigneurs*, rather than having willingly taken anything. Dumas retorted that this *soigneur* should therefore be charged with attempted murder.

Twelve years later, after more than a decade of campaigning for dope testing, it would again be Dumas who, on the scree slopes of the upper section of the Ventoux – that mountain again – would have the responsibility of trying to save a British sporting super-star's life.

The autopsy on Simpson's body revealed that he'd died of a heart attack caused by extreme exertion on what was a stiflingly hot day, while drugs were found in his bloodstream. More were in his jersey pockets; Simpson had pushed himself beyond his limits.

Inspired by the foreign adventures of the likes of Brian Robinson and the two Tonys – Hoar and Hewson – Simpson had made the Continent home, and Ghent, in Belgium, in particular, where he enjoyed life as 'Mister Tom', hamming up his Britishness for the foreign press while at the same time conscientiously adopting the different languages and cultures of Europe in order to fit in with what continued to be an extremely European sport at the top level.

Unfortunately, that included adopting the doping culture.

Simpson's room-mate at that 1967 Tour de France was Welshman Colin Lewis. It's late morning when, after a long drive from London, I arrive in the small, sleepy Devon town of Bovey Tracey, where Lewis lives: 'the gateway to the moor', on the edge of Dartmoor National Park, ten miles inland from Torbay.

It's a drive that former pro Lewis knows only too well. Once retired from racing in the mid-1970s, the Welshman took a job as the manager of the then-new Eastway road-racing circuit, later commuting home from the capital to Devon every fourth weekend. The bike shop he'd opened in Preston, next to Paignton, was left in good hands while he managed Eastway, but after a couple of years away, he returned to Devon for good, running his successful bike-shop business for the next three decades. Although Colin Lewis Cycles still bears his name, he handed over the reins to one of his employees, Simon Aske, in the mid-2000s, and it's Aske who arrives with Lewis in a 'Colin Lewis Cycles' emblazoned van, and who later tells me about building bikes and forks for Chris Boardman and Graeme Obree. But first, Lewis humbly holds court with his take on that fateful summer when cycling lost Tom Simpson.

'I was terrified – *terrified*,' Lewis reiterates, remembering how he felt in the lead-up to the start of the '67 Tour. Fyffes, the banana company, had come in as a sponsor of the national team in the month before the race, which paid for a month's training in Belgium, helping to get the domestic pros up to speed ahead of what would be the biggest race of their lives. But nothing was truly going to prepare them for what was to come.

Lewis arrived at the team's hotel in Angers ahead of some of his teammates, and was already in bed when his room-mate, Vin Denson, arrived at about a quarter past nine with three Italian riders in tow, who all seemed more than a little animated.

'They had this tiny little battery-powered drill,' Lewis recalls, 'and went over to the wall and drilled a hole! Then one of them had this optical-glass thing that he put in the hole, which they could look through, and they went crazy.'

Lewis does a rather entertaining impression of the Italians in rapturous excitement before revealing the reason for their behaviour: 'It turned out that there was this honeymooning couple next door.'

Lewis complained to the team manager the next morning. This wasn't exactly how he wanted to prepare for the Tour.

'Colin, I'll tell you what I'll do,' Alec Taylor said. 'I'll put you in with the best guy. I'll put you in with Tom Simpson.'

'So that's how I got to be sharing a room with Tom at that Tour,' says Lewis. 'He had been in a room by himself, but he was OK about me rooming with him.'

Simpson and Lewis were two of a ten-man British squad, along with Peter Chisman and Albert Hitchen, who both abandoned the race early on, followed by Peter Hill and Bill Lawrie, the latter an Australian 'guesting' on the British squad. Michael Wright was next to go, abandoning on stage 11 – but not before taking the first of two British stage wins that year, on stage seven in Strasbourg. Lewis's old room-mate, Denson, quit on stage 17, broken by his friend Simpson's death, while Barry Hoban and Arthur Metcalfe, like Lewis, made it all the way to Paris.

It was the first time the Tour had been contested by national teams since 1961, and the 1967 British squad wore identical white jerseys with Union flags on the shoulders, but with each rider's trade-team name – Mackeson, Peugeot, Bic – printed on the front, with their own black trade-team shorts.

Simpson was the undoubted star of the squad: winner of the Tour of Flanders one-day Classic in 1961 at the age of twenty-two, Milan–San Remo in 1964 and the road-race world championships in '65. And as early on as day two of the Tour, Simpson had the occasion to call upon his younger room-mate.

'One of my most prized possessions was a hat – a Great Britain cycling cap – which I wore proudly perched on the top of my head, because we didn't have crash hats in those days,' Lewis recalls. 'Tom came up alongside me in the bunch, and said, "Give me your hat!" and ripped it off my head. I said, "Tom, what do you want that for?" and he said, "I want to wipe my arse on it," and promptly stopped at the side of the road and used my freshly laundered hat to wipe his bum!

'But that was life as a *domestique*,' Lewis laughs, 'and we got on all right, because Tom was a grafter.'

In the 1960s, café raids still existed at the Tour: unofficial refreshment stops that entailed the different teams' *domestiques* throwing their bikes down at the side of the road and bursting into cafés and restaurants to grab bottles of whatever they could get their hands on from the shelves, all without losing too much ground to the rest of the peloton, which they then had a mad dash to catch up with. Café owners were usually reimbursed later by the Tour organization.

Lewis recalls one day when he and some fellow riders spotted the perfect-looking café at which to 'steal' some refreshment.

'We had to run about a hundred metres down through these woods to get to this place – there were about four of us – and when we got inside we found that it was a bordello full of scantily clad ladies,' Lewis says, deadpan, before dishing out the punchline. 'There was one French rider who took just over an hour to get back to the race!'

But Lewis remembers the café raid he was part of on 13 July 1967 rather more sombrely. Two weeks into the Tour, the climb of Mont Ventoux featured on stage 13's 211.5-kilometre route between Marseille and Carpentras. 'You could see the Ventoux from 40 kilometres away, and a frisson of nervousness had gone through the peloton,' Lewis remembers. With 20 kilometres to go before the start of the climb, a suitable café was spotted for plunder.

'I came out with four bottles, and quickly got going again. What everyone really wanted was Coke: that was highly prized. I rode straight up to Tom, and pulled the first bottle out of my pocket.'

It was brandy, Lewis realized. In cold weather, a lot of pros back then would carry a *petit bidon* (a small hip flask) filled with black coffee with a dash of brandy, he explains. But no one wanted brandy on a stinking-hot day at the Tour.

'You'll never believe what I've got, Tom,' Lewis told his team leader, and went to throw it away. 'But he grabbed it before I could throw it. "No," he said. "Give us that. My guts is a bit queer." Those were his exact words, and he took one swig of this brandy before throwing it into a cornfield.'

The town of Bédoin came and went, signalling the start of the climb, which quickly ramps up through the forest.

'The race soon split because the Spanish rider, Julio Jiménez, had attacked, and Roger Pingeon and a couple of the other guys went after him,' explains Lewis. Simpson was lying in around sixth or seventh place, trying his best to give chase. 'And I was on a good day, and second [from the team] on the road.

'It was windy, and the roads were twisty, so you couldn't see much up ahead,' Lewis continues. 'But once we got to Chalet Reynard, and out of the trees, you could see the summit again.'

If this was a documentary, images of the colour, noise and sheer chaos of the 1967 Tour de France would flash up in between contrastingly quiet footage of Lewis drinking his cup of coffee in the calm environs of the Brookside tea rooms in peaceful Bovey Tracey. A clock would probably tick.

At the side of the road up ahead, Lewis says, softly, he could see that someone had fallen off their bike.

'As I got closer, I could see that it was Tom.'

At that point, Lewis wasn't overly worried. Spectators would often give their favourites a helping hand by pushing them on climbs, and he thought an over-zealous fan must have pushed Simpson right off. 'The French riders really had it worked out, because they'd get pushed from one guy to the next. The problem was, though, that a lot of those spectators had usually been drinking all day.'

'Quick, quick, quick – carry on!' Lewis remembers the team manager, Alec Taylor, saying to him. 'Tom's OK, so just keep going and keep looking back.' The plan was that Lewis, riding well, was to keep going so that he could help Simpson chase the leaders further on once he'd caught up with Lewis again.

'I was three minutes and 10 seconds behind the leaders at the summit,' Lewis says, in a way that shows he'll never forget the smallest details of that day. 'All the way down the other side of the Ventoux, towards Malaucène, I kept looking behind to see where Tom was. He never arrived, and I didn't know what had happened; I thought maybe because he'd fallen off he'd been injured or something.'

At the finish, a Dutch *soigneur* told Lewis that his teammate had died. Lewis went to bed that night, alone in his room, 'crying my eyes out'.

'I was twenty-two years old, and was left pinching myself because I thought it couldn't happen, because Tom had been so full of life.'

The next day, at breakfast, Lewis announced that he wanted to quit the race. His teammate, Arthur Metcalfe, felt the same way. How could they possibly carry on when a member of their team was dead? But the manager, Taylor, intervened, asking them what they thought Simpson would have wanted them to do.

'He would have wanted you to finish the race,' Taylor told them, and in addition decided to take a vote on what to do next. Barry Hoban and Vin Denson, the only two other members of the team left in the race by that point, raised their hands, wanting to continue; Lewis and Metcalfe wanted to go home. Taylor had the casting vote.

On the start line of the 14th stage in Carpentras, the race took a moment to remember Simpson, and it was a difficult, sombre day for everyone involved. Later, some said Denson was supposed to win that stage between Carpentras and Sète. Lewis understood that the team was meant to cross the line together, but admits that because of the distress he was feeling that day he was happy to be told what to do.

Jean Stablinski was Denson's Bic teammate at all races other than the Tour and the world championships, and, says Lewis, the Frenchman was also very much '*Monsieur Le Patron*', the unofficial leader and spokesman of the bunch, at that Tour. So when Hoban rode off the front of the bunch, Stablinski took action, remembers Lewis.

'"Hey – what's going on?" he asked Vin, and Vin, who was as cut up as I was about it all, replied, "He's just going to piss. He'll be back." But he'd bloody well cleared off, hadn't he?'

When the peloton arrived in Sète, Hoban had been there for almost four minutes already, having taken the stage win alone. Back at the hotel afterwards, there was what Lewis calls 'an almighty bust-up'. Taylor, the manager, decided to take Hoban's prize money off him.

'It was £800,' explains Lewis, 'so a lot of money, but, as a Tour stage winner, Hoban was going to be offered lucrative criterium appearance fees anyway.'

Later, says Lewis, Hoban came out with a number of platitudes and protestations: that he was a victim of circumstance, that he'd looked round and found himself on his own.

By stage 17, Denson had quit, too, and Hoban, Metcalfe and Lewis were the only ones to finish in Paris. Lewis says he's been to visit Hoban since, but doesn't elaborate on how well they get along these days.

Hoban went on to achieve a phenomenal eight Tour stage victories during his career – a record eventually beaten only by Mark Cavendish. Hoban also scored a rare one-day Classic win for a British rider, when in 1974 he became the first, and still the only, Briton to win the men's version of Ghent–Wevelgem; Lizzie Armitstead kept the British connection with the race by winning the first women's edition of the race, in 2012. Denson, a faithful lieutenant to France's Jacques Anquetil and Belgium's Rik Van Looy earlier in his career, and a stage winner at the Tour of Italy in 1966, retired two years later having seen out his career with the British domestic outfit Bantel. Metcalfe – who, outside of the national team, rode for the Carlton Cycles team, which was owned by Raleigh – is still the only rider to have won both the road-race national championships and the BBAR in the same season, in 1966. He died in 2002 following a battle with cancer.

Simpson is still remembered fondly. For many years, no one wanted to admit that doping had played a part in his death, yet today's acknowledgement of doping as a blight on the sport, before and since Simpson died, has transformed matters into a kind of hope, perhaps, that today's riders don't need to turn to drugs as readily as many did before.

Now, whenever the Ventoux features on the Tour, British riders taking part, such as Bradley Wiggins, David Millar and Mark Cavendish, can be seen doffing imaginary caps in the direction of the memorial that stands in the spot where Simpson collapsed. Visit it yourself, and you'll find that it's draped with cycling caps, water bottles and even tyres and inner tubes – items left as marks of respect by the cycling community who've suffered in climbing the Ventoux themselves.

And Lewis? He continued racing for the Mackeson-Condor team, swapping their iconic purple and white jersey for the white jersey with red-and-blue bands of national champion in both 1967 and 1968.

He went to the Tour again in '68, too, which didn't end in quite the way he would have liked. He arrived at the start in Vittel that year refreshed and ready to try to do something on one of the stages, determined to make an impression. He'd trained hard in the lead-up to the race, but, on stage 3b – between Forest, in Belgium, and the famous velodrome in Roubaix, where the one-day Classic Paris–Roubaix finishes – Lewis crashed hard on a section of cobbles, snapping his frame in two. By the time he'd got a replacement bike it would be a race against the clock to make it home before the cut-off time, 'which was always very strict'.

Going hell for leather, he caught up with three German riders, who he hoped would ride with him but who, Lewis recalls, muttered something about being *en vacances*: French for 'on holiday', i.e. taking it easy. But as Lewis got closer to the velodrome, alone, the three Germans suddenly flew past him, hanging on to their team car. Lewis, by association of proximity, got chucked off the race with them. Furious, he appealed, but the Tour organizers were having none of it. It was the end of the line for Lewis.

'And do you know what? After that, for the next three weeks, I rode the same distances as the stages in training, as if I'd still been on the race, out of sheer anger.'

Lewis never got the chance to ride the Tour again, and he was the last Welshman to ride it until 2007, when Geraint Thomas took part, riding for the Barloworld squad. But Lewis gives the impression that he still doesn't quite believe that he got the opportunity to ride the Tour in the first place. Indeed, his journey there was really quite extraordinary.

As in all the best stories, Colin Lewis's route to the top began with a bet. 'I got drunk one night and had this bet with a chum of mine,' he explains. 'He decided that he was one day going to play football for Torquay United, while it looked as though I was going to do nothing, because I was just smoking and drinking and all the rest of it.'

When the same friend came round to his house at midday the next day, Lewis was still in bed. The friend hadn't forgotten about the bet they'd made the night before, and asked again what Lewis was going to do.

'I said, "Well, I don't do sport, do I?" But he said he'd seen me ride a bike. Which was true – but only if I was late for work down on the Strand in Torquay. It was three miles away, downhill, so if

I did that I'd then leave the bike at work and get the bus home!'

Lewis's mate suggested that his new thing could be cycling, which Lewis agreed to. 'But only because he was irritating me and I wanted to get rid of him, so I said, "All right – I'll take up cycling. Now bugger off."'

His friend still needed something to put his money on, so, with the 12-inch black-and-white television downstairs in his mum and dad's lounge blaring out the 1960 Rome Olympics as inspiration, Lewis said he'd make it to the next Games in four years' time. He probably rolled over and went back to sleep after his friend had left, and dreamed of . . . anything but taking part in the next Olympics.

'It was perhaps later that day, though, that I got the bike out of the garage and rode from Torquay to Shaldon to Teignmouth and back to Torquay, which is 18 miles, although I had to walk up the last two hills,' admits Lewis. 'But I made this resolution that I'd stick with it, and so every day I started riding to work, and would sometimes ride that 18-mile circuit twice.'

The day things really changed, however, was when another cyclist caught up with Lewis one night – or eventually did after a chase through the roads around Torquay.

'This guy called Rex Godfrey finally got me at some traffic lights,' says Lewis, who'd been doing his best to hold him off. 'He said, "You're quite good, aren't you? Which club are you with?" I wasn't a member of a club, but because I'd recently been living in London for 12 months – having run away from home – I knew of the Catford Wheelers, and fibbed I was with them.'

Then came the inevitable question as to what his best time for a 25-mile time trial was. Lewis had never ridden a time trial, but knew from reading cycling magazines that the fastest riders could go under the hour, so he fibbed again that his best was one hour, two minutes and 22 seconds.

'1–2–22?' Rex Godfrey repeated, impressed, and promptly

persuaded Lewis to come along to the Mid Devon Cycling Club's clubroom the following week.

'So I went along, and sat there for ages while everyone ignored me, of course,' Lewis remembers, encapsulating the practice of cycling clubs past and present, at times, to treat new members a little too warily. 'Eventually, this bloke Rex came over and said that some of them were riding back to Torquay, and asked whether I wanted to ride with them. So for the seven miles from Newton Abbot to Torquay, they spent the whole time trying to get rid of me! "What kind of bloody club is this?" I asked myself. But I survived, and was then asked to go out with them again on Tuesday: "We do a *proper* ride on Tuesdays . . ."'

By then, Lewis was riding a second-hand, fixed-wheel Carlton, and, try as they might, his new Mid Devon CC teammates couldn't drop him. There was one race left that season, they told him – a 25-mile time trial, appropriately enough.

'And what time do you think I did?' Lewis asks, teasingly.

You already know his answer: '1–2–22.'

Ahead of the 1963 Milk Race, Mid Devon CC's Roy Hopkins, Lewis's club-mate, was selected for one of the British squads.

'The race started on the May Bank Holiday,' Lewis recalls, 'and on the Wednesday before I got a phone call from the organizer, Chas Messenger, who told me that the Romanian team couldn't get over for the race because of visa problems. Roy had told him that he thought I had a bit of talent, so Chas was inviting me to take part as part of a hastily put together Commonwealth team.'

Feeling totally overawed at the task ahead of him, Lewis caught the train to Blackpool for the start of the race. Would he sink or swim at the 14-stage and almost two-week-long event?

As it turned out, as early as the first stage, from Blackpool to Nottingham, Lewis was involved in the action. 'I was in a break of about eighteen guys, chasing this one guy, Peter Chisman, who'd

Above: The opening of Herne Hill Velodrome in south London in 1891 brought bicycle racing to a British public eager to see the sport.

Right: Tricycle racing was another popular event, and one which required a deft technique when cornering at speed. This was Mr J. Rowley on his machine in 1895.

Below: The penny-farthing remained popular for several decades after its invention, albeit partly for its novelty value.

Above: The 1908 London Olympics proved to be another landmark occasion, with huge crowds at White City for the cycling events.

Left: Charles Bartlett comes home to win the 100-kilometre track race, out-sprinting his compatriot Charles Denny.

Benjamin Jones took two of Britain's five gold medals, in the 5,000 metres and team pursuit.

Left: Another early Olympian, Bill Bailey, at a National Cyclists' Union amateur meeting at Herne Hill in 1929.

Below: The actress Gracie Fields was there to present the trophy to the winner of the Cycle Championship for Young Ladies.

Below: The Brooklands track in Surrey was another popular venue for cycle racing throughout the 1930s.

Left: Reg Harris crosses the line to win the sprint at the world championships in Paris in 1947. A year later, when the Olympics returned to London, he won two of Great Britain's three silver medals, to go with two bronzes, including the team pursuit (**above**).

A telling image from the Good Friday Festival of International Cycling, also held at Herne Hill in 1948. The sport enjoyed a post-war boom in popularity and participation.

Above: Ladies in swimwear at a publicity stunt for the latest Raleigh bicycles in 1951, at the British Sports and Games Fair.

Right: The 1950s saw the emergence of Britain's greatest ever racing cyclist – Beryl Burton. Her achievements are simply phenomenal.

Above left: In 1955, Brian Robinson became the first British cyclist to finish the Tour de France, and finished an impressive 14th overall in 1956, the same year that Tom Simpson first came to the general public's notice, at the Olympics in Melbourne. Here he is (**above**) on his way to Australia with Don Burgess, with whom he would win bronze in the team pursuit.

Left: Robinson also recorded Britain's first stage win in the Tour de France in 1958.

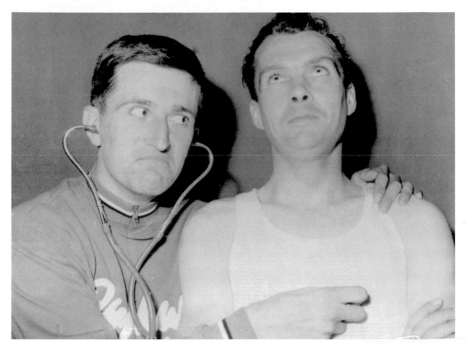

Above: Simpson and Robinson fool around for the cameras ahead of the 1961 Tour de France. Simpson would become the first British rider to wear the yellow jersey the following year, then in 1965 (**below**) won both the world road race championships and BBC Sports Personality of the Year.

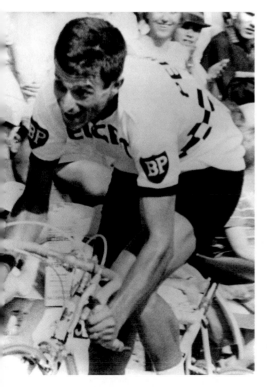

Above: Simpson proudly sports the rainbow stripes. Cycling was the height of fashion.

Right: His life came to a tragic end on Mont Ventoux in 1967, however.

Below: Cyclists pay homage to their hero at Simpson's funeral in the Yorkshire village of Haworth.

gone away at the start. We had to wait at the Manchester Ship Canal – the gates went down – so he won by six minutes, or something. Towards the end, I blew up, badly, and had to sit on the back of the group, grovelling. But, after eating a banana, I came good again, and got fourth on the stage.'

It was an impressive début, and Lewis's result on the second stage between Nottingham and Cheltenham was almost as impressive again.

'I was seventh, and so after the stage they called me to the podium and gave me a jersey – the points jersey – but I didn't even know what a points jersey was!'

It was a steep learning curve for Lewis in every way, and, although he later lost the jersey, he found himself getting stronger as the race went on, eventually finishing the race, back in Blackpool, ninth overall.

Lewis continued his climb up the British-racing pecking order during the 1964 season, and finished fourth at the national championships, which was enough to be selected for the Milk Race again: and this time as part of the Great Britain national team. After an opening 10-kilometre team time trial around Blackpool, won by Switzerland, Lewis won stage 1b that same afternoon, edging out Spain's Vicente Lopez, which was enough to give him the leader's yellow jersey.

'But the next day, I got "done",' Lewis says. 'I'd lost three of my teammates, so didn't really have much of a team around me to look after me. The Spaniards were trying to put me in the gutter because I had the jersey, so I shouted at some of them, and the organizers fined me £10 for swearing, and also docked me two minutes.'

Furious, and no doubt swearing a bit more, Lewis appealed the decision, and, although he was let off the £10 fine, the two-minute time penalty remained, which meant he lost the race lead.

Lewis's teammate, Arthur Metcalfe – who would later be

Lewis's teammate at the 1967 Tour de France – won the third stage, between Aberystwyth and Cardiff, alone, by almost four minutes, and so the team worked after that for Metcalfe, who won the race overall.

'Peter Chisman was fourth, I was fifth, despite the two-minute penalty, and we won all the categories: points, mountains, overall and team.'

Following the race, the BCF selected their teams for the amateur world championships and that year's Olympic Games, in Tokyo. And although Lewis was selected for the Worlds, taking place in Sallanches in the southern Alps, he didn't make it into the Olympic squad, which was a real disappointment. Regardless, he showed his good form in the world-championship road race, and made it into the front group that looked set to battle it out between them for the rainbow jersey.

'We'd been out there all day, in the pouring rain, and on the last lap, with 22 kilometres to go, at the foot of the final climb, I looked back and could see the peloton. Just then, the guy next to me decided to go. I could have gone with him – without a shadow of a doubt – but I thought he'd gone too early. It was Eddy Merckx, and he won by 27 seconds.'

Lewis finished 22nd, but the team manager, Chas Messenger, who was also the organizer of the Milk Race, had some good news for him. 'He said he had a surprise for me – that I was going to the Olympic Games after all,' says Lewis. 'It was because the British national champion, Pete Gordon, had packed after 40 kilometres.'

Lewis would go to the 1964 Tokyo Games in his place, where he finished as the best British rider, in 25th, after being in the mix for the gold medal, which went to Italy's Mario Zanin in a bunch sprint.

'I was beaten by the distance from here to that table,' Lewis says, pointing to the next one over from us in the café.

But there was another prize at stake, too: did his friend – the one he'd made the £10 bet with about making it to the next Olympics – pay up in the end?

'He'd got married and had three kids by then!' Lewis smiles. 'But we had a night out on it, yes – a mellow one anyway, because I was an athlete by then, having given up all the smoking and drinking I'd been doing back when we'd made that bet.'

Lewis was ready for the next step in his career, which meant trying his luck on the Continent. So he wrote to the French newspaper, *La Voix du Nord* (in English, as he didn't speak French) and they helped to place him at a club in Brittany, where he raced for two seasons.

He was then approached by the ACBB: the Athletic Club de Boulogne-Billancourt, which is a sports club based in the western suburbs of Paris. Its cycling section became *the* destination for English-speaking amateur riders in the 1960s, '70s and '80s, serving as a feeder team to the Peugeot professional team.

'They sent me this contract, and I was on the cusp of making some good money in France,' Lewis remembers. 'But the professional class was just starting in the UK, and Whitbread – the brewery – got in touch and asked if I wanted to join their team.'

The team was Mackeson-Condor: sponsored by Mackeson stout and the famous London bicycle shop and frame builder, Condor Cycles. But financially, Lewis says, it was the biggest mistake he ever made: 'I turned pro in 1967 for just ten quid a week. Had I stayed in France and gone to the ACBB, I'd perhaps have been in the Peugeot team the following year.'

Lewis nevertheless competed at the highest level in the UK, and his results were the stepping stone to the British squad at the '67 Tour de France, and, unfortunately, to his ill-fated ride with Simpson.

'I'd met Tom a few times before that Tour, and I remember the last stage of the 1964 Milk Race, when he was there at Crystal

Palace with Jacques Anquetil doing some celebrity thing or other,' says Lewis. 'It was a terrible day – pouring it down with rain for 110 miles from Bournemouth to London, and I remember him saying to someone: "Look at that peloton. They look like a bunch of old men . . ."

'I really didn't like him saying that, as he hadn't seen what we'd been through that day.'

In 1969, Lewis moved to the Holdsworth-Campagnolo team, with which he saw out his career, retiring in 1975, having taken 38 professional victories.

If Herne Hill is the British track cyclist's spiritual home, then Eastway was its road-circuit church – at least, for London-based cyclists. While road racing often took place on motor-racing circuits, the iconic east London venue was opened in 1975 and, between then and its closure in November 2006, when it was razed, ironically enough, to make way for the London Olympic Velodrome, it played host to thousands of races for riders of every age and ability, from schoolchildren to professionals. And as if having been one of the nation's top pro racers during the 1960s and early '70s wasn't enough, Colin Lewis was also Eastway's first manager, taking the job soon after the end of his riding career.

'I'd retired as a pro at the request of my first wife, which was a mistake. She told me I was sick to death of travelling the length and breadth of the UK to race, and of always being the last person home on a Saturday or Sunday night,' Lewis explains, which makes the rest of us feel a little awkward. It's almost imperceptible exactly how he's worded it.

'So I decided to open my own bike shop,' he continues. 'I found a shop in Preston – near Paignton, here in Devon – for £8 a week, which had been a greengrocer's. I've still got the scales at home.' The business blossomed from as soon as he opened the doors, he says. 'It was ever so popular. But six months after I'd moved into

Preston, I was reading *Cycling* magazine, and there was a quarter-page advert for a prospective manager at a new cycling centre, which hadn't yet been built, so I went up to Enfield for an interview, and two weeks later was told I'd got the job. "Now you've done it," I thought, as what about the shop? But the business was growing all the time, and I'd got a guy to come and work for me – a local lad, and a mechanic – so I thought I'd give it a try, leaving him in charge.'

Lewis travelled up to Hackney for his first look at the proposed site for the cycling circuit, and was shown a rubbish tip with a gypsy encampment next to it. He admits he had second thoughts then, but decided to give it a shot.

'They allotted me this bungalow in Eaton Park, nearby, which I had to paint myself, as no one had lived there for so long, and on the third day my car was stolen,' remembers Lewis. His wife came up to stay, and was horrified, but eventually she moved up there as well, and got a job in nearby Newham. 'She had this flash BMW sports car, which someone vandalized with a key.'

But the circuit soon began to take shape – although it would have been completely flat had Lewis not been keeping his eye on it.

'While it was being built, I was mainly at the main headquarters in Enfield, going through facts and figures, basically. The high-light of my day was the tea and coffee at 10 a.m. and 3 p.m.,' says Lewis. 'But I also got to sometimes go down and have a look at the progress of Eastway, and if it hadn't been for that, there wouldn't have been a hill on it!'

Don Wiseman was the architect; he and Lewis got on well, so plans were made to include a climb.

'Oxo Hill, as it came to be known, which came just after Clarey's Corner – so called because John Clarey was the first professional to fall off on it!' Lewis smiles.

Clarey was, incidentally, also Britain's second and last *lanterne rouge* at the Tour de France in 1968, thirteen years after Tony Hoar had finished last in the race.

The Eastway circuit was an immediate hit; so much so that a previously unplanned pavilion, containing changing rooms, was soon built.

'We organized for these eight-foot-tall speakers to go on the roof, which took four guys two days to get up there. They were superb. But they didn't last the night. When I got there the next morning, someone had nicked them. Who would have wanted four bloody speakers that size?' Lewis bellows, but can't help laughing. 'And how on earth did they get them down?'

There's a bit of a theme to Eastway's early life. Bikes, wheels and other equipment often went missing. 'I left the office there one night, and locked the door, but then remembered something I'd left behind, and had to go back in,' says Lewis. 'I left my briefcase by the door, went back inside for a few seconds, and when I came back, it was gone.'

In June 1977, Eastway played host to a raft of domestic and international superstars for a race called the Glenryck Cup, among them Eddy Merckx, Luis Ocaña, Phil Bayton, Lewis's 1967 Tour teammate Barry Hoban, Sid Barras and eventual winner Dietrich 'Didi' Thurau. It had been organized by boxing promoter Mike Barrett, and drew a good crowd.

'Before that, I held the course record for Eastway,' Lewis says, 'which was two minutes 12 seconds. But then Didi Thurau, who came second at the world championships a couple of months later, came along and put four seconds into it! I'm curious to find out what the course record ended up being, if his time was ever beaten.'

It was, and got trimmed right down to two minutes and one second by the late Ray Eden of the Eagle Road Club – the 1995 RTTC national 100-mile champion – which was apparently still the best time when the Eastway circuit closed in 2006.

After nearly two years in east London, Lewis's wife decided she wanted to move back to Devon, so Lewis then had every fourth weekend off to go back home, which included a long drive through the night on a Sunday evening. Soon he, too, decided to return to Devon for good.

'I spent two years of my life as the manager of Eastway, but they were two years I really enjoyed,' says Lewis, who settled down to growing his eponymous bike-shop business, later moving it to larger premises in Paignton.

Today, Simon Aske owns Colin Lewis Cycles, although Lewis, now in his seventies, is still very much involved. And it's Lewis who recalls meeting Aske for the first time.

'It was a Saturday afternoon in the shop, and we were busy, as we always are on Saturdays. I saw this guy come in, and he was a bit sort of hesitant, and I remember thinking, "I hope he's not trying to nick something..." You've got to keep an eye on people!

'Under his arm, he was clutching this big brown paper package. We were serving customers, but I soon realized that this guy was looking for a quiet moment to speak with me.'

When that quiet moment came, Aske opened up the package to reveal a balsa-wood mock-up of a bike frame. 'That was in 1992,' adds Aske, picking up the story, 'and I needed some parts to complete the bike. At that time, I was working for a company called Carbon Infinity, which made medium-format cameras. We used carbon-fibre for the cases, which was what gave me the idea of making a bicycle out of the stuff.'

Aske commuted to work by bike, and was in need of a new one but didn't have the money. As a trained engineer, he thought he'd make his own. Through connections in the car industry, in which he had worked before, he managed to pull together the funding to form Hotta.

'I started the first bike in about May 1992, and had finished it by September,' he says. 'But I hadn't heard of Mike Burrows until the '92 Olympics, and was quite surprised when I saw his bike, as I thought, "Blimey – he's copied me!" But he'd been designing it from years before.'

Burrows was the engineer and bike designer who'd created Chris Boardman's LotusSport super-bike on which he won gold at the Barcelona Games: a similarly shaped, one-piece monocoque design, built at a time when there were few UCI rules governing bike design.

'After the Olympics,' continues Aske, 'Boardman actually came down and rode our bike, and liked it, but said there was an element of it that was a bit too flexible for him, and so he didn't take it on.'

That was the last Aske heard from Boardman until around 1995 or 1996, by which time Hotta were also making special carbon forks with really thin, narrow blades. 'Chris had seen someone at the Manchester Velodrome with a pair, and asked where he'd got them from.'

And so came the second bite of the Boardman cherry. By then a professional with the French Gan team, Boardman was mainly racing on the road, and called Aske up to see if he could get some forks for himself.

'He first used them on his bike to win the time-trial stage in the 1996 Paris–Nice,' says Aske – a race at which Boardman rode consistently all week, finishing third overall behind Laurent Jalabert and Lance Armstrong. 'Then he used the forks again at the '96 Atlanta Olympics, on what was probably a Terry Dolan bike.'

It was indeed a Terry Dolan bike, albeit designed by Boardman himself, and badged up as an Eddy Merckx frame, as Merckx was Boardman's Gan team bike supplier that year.

Dolan, the famed Liverpudlian frame builder, had learned his trade in the seventies under the tutelage of another master frame builder from Liverpool, Harry Quinn, at whose shop he'd regularly come into contact with top British riders like Sid Barras and Reg Harris. Colin Sturgess rode Harry Quinn frames for years, winning the 1989 professional individual pursuit championships in Lyon on one. Dolan went on to open his own shop and build his own frames, and has become a long-time supplier of track bikes to British Cycling and the Manchester Velodrome, while the list of riders he's built frames for reads like a who's who of British riders, and includes Chris Hoy, Rob Hayles, Yvonne McGregor, David Millar, Craig MacLean, Bradley Wiggins and Chris Boardman.

'It was awful,' Boardman later told me, referring to his own bike design for the Atlanta Games. 'But that's why I worked with Terry for nearly twenty years: he gave me free rein to make my own mistakes. He would feed in his input: "Oh, that bottom bracket's going to flex like mad, that,"' says Boardman, affecting his best Liverpudlian accent. 'And I'd go: "Yeah, but I'm going to do this," and he'd go, "OK!" But he'd always warn you . . .'

'Chris never believed me until he saw it,' Dolan told me when visiting him for *Procycling* magazine in 2006, rolling his eyes while showing me Boardman's original drawings for that particular bike.

'You know the worst part of it, though?' Dolan asked me. 'Just before the race started, a brake cable, which we had painstakingly threaded through the length of the frame, broke, and the mechanic had to just tape a new one on to the outside of the frame, with black tape!'

The beautiful all-white frame – with Simon Aske's black Hotta forks up front – nevertheless worked well enough to carry Boardman to the bronze medal in Atlanta. 'The handlebars were attached to the top of the fork crown, which was Chris's design, too,' remembers Aske. 'And then he also used our forks when he broke the Hour record in 1996 – the one in the "Superman position" – on what I believe was a Lotus frame, again badged up as an Eddy Merckx.'

It wasn't only Boardman that Aske supplied forks to, either. 'We made them for Lance Armstrong and most of the Motorola team, as well as Laurent Dufaux and Richard Virenque, and they were all buying them – we weren't giving them away!' Aske says.

'And it was £2,500 a go for those forks,' chips in Lewis.

Armstrong, Dufaux and Virenque may have all been using a little extra help of another sort, but there was no doubting the quality of their forks. 'I've still got the videos at home,' Aske laughs, 'and I can still watch them and point out the forks that I'd made.'

Later on, though, when it all went a bit 'Pete Tong', says Aske, he went to work for Lewis.

'Somebody had to,' Lewis grins. The two of them are clearly on the same wavelength and enjoy each other's company, and, aside from shop matters, they work together on the organization of the Dartmoor Classic sportive: one of Britain's biggest and best mass-participation rides, which attracts 3,200 riders.

Hotta bikes, though, have become a cult time-trial bike – although they're as impressive now as they were when time triallists like Richard Prebble was riding them to victory at the 10-, 25- and 50-mile championships in the mid-1990s, and it's not uncommon to spot one or two at club time trials across the country today. And you don't get much more cult than everyone's favourite British time triallist, Graeme Obree. With Chris Boardman – everyone's other favourite time triallist – having also ridden Aske's forks and bikes, Hotta have been on hand to supply machines for arguably the two greatest time triallists Britain has ever produced.

'Graeme's manager rang us up to ask if we could make him some bikes for the '96 Atlanta Olympics. They wanted one TT bike and two track bikes, built for Graeme's "Superman position",' explains Aske, referring to the radical, outstretched, arms-extended position that Obree had developed.

Having built them to Obree's exacting specifications, Aske then tested the time-trial bike himself. 'And it absolutely flew! It was just so stiff and fast.'

Obree won the British individual pursuit national championships that year, but it had been a difficult period for him, following the death of his brother in a car accident in 1994. He'd gone into the '96 Games suffering from a virus, unable to fire on all cylinders in the pursuit. He headed home instead of taking part in the time trial, where Boardman won bronze.

'You went training with Graeme once, didn't you?' Lewis reminds Aske, as we drain our coffee cups. 'You on a Hotta and him on his mountain bike.'

'Yeah, that's right,' laughs Aske, who's no slouch on a bike himself, grinning at the memory. 'He was on a Specialized Stumpjumper and I was on my Hotta, and we got to the bottom of this hill just outside Torquay. Graeme simply rode away from me – on a mountain bike, with off-road tyres on it. It really was rather impressive . . .'

7

BRITAIN'S 'MR CYCLING'

These days, being a two-time Olympic team pursuit bronze-medallist would hardly raise an eyebrow in the world of British cycling, but, back in the seventies, it was quite something for the likes of Ian Hallam and Mick Bennett.

Hallam and Bennett drilled it around the track to win bronze at the 1972 Munich Games, together with Willi Moore and Brian Smith's now father-in-law, Ron Keeble, for the first cycling medal of any hue since the 1956 Melbourne Games. Four years later, in Montreal, Hallam was again joined on his bronze-medal ride by Bennett, plus Robin Croker and Ian Banbury this time.

Mick Bennett these days has a lot on his plate, deftly juggling his roles as race director on each of the Tour of Britain, the Tour Series criterium races, and the new Women's Tour, which took place for the first time in May 2014. But he remembers arriving at those '72 Games in Munich in nothing short of a total daze.

'I was twenty-three years old, from Sparkbrook, in Birmingham, where I had to keep my bikes outside under a sheet in the yard of a house with no bathroom and no running hot water, so to find myself in this amazing Olympic village, surrounded by all these amazing athletes, was just a complete shock,' he says.

The pursuit team had been put together by the national coach and 1955 world amateur pursuit champion Norman Sheil, and although Bennett had ridden before with Keeble, Hallam and Moore on the road, he says he doesn't remember the quartet having raced together on the track before 1972.

And this meant that Bennett had to pinch himself as they made progress through the early rounds of the competition and the reality started to dawn that an Olympic medal was within the team's grasp. A puncture for Moore, however, in the semi-final against West Germany, put paid to the squad riding for gold in the final – which West Germany went on to win. But beating Poland in the bronze-medal ride-off nevertheless meant that Bennett headed home to Birmingham after what had been an unforgettable experience with an Olympic medal around his neck.

'I slept wearing it the night I won it; it had been such a surprise to everybody as it had been so long since we'd won a cycling medal as a nation,' says Bennett.

The homecomings of Britain's medal heroes from the Olympics these days usually attract huge media attention, with people greeting them at the airport, banners in the streets in their home towns, and golden postboxes.

Bennett, though, had to take the bus home from the airport in 1972. 'I had to get on one with a road bike, a track bike and my wheels,' he laughs. 'And there was no one home when I got there, and I didn't have a key to get in!'

Bennett also rode the 1-kilometre time trial at the Munich Games, finishing 17th. 'No one else wanted to do it!' he explains.

He might have done better if he hadn't been told that he had to take his cling-film off, too.

'I'd stretched cling-film across my helmet to cover the vents,' Bennett explains, which had been an effort to improve aero-dynamics, proving that there's nothing new under the sun; today's pros favour slipperiness over ventilation when it comes to their helmets, both on the track and, increasingly, on the road.

'But I got to the start, and they told me to remove it! I really don't know if other people had done it before; I don't know where I'd got the idea from, but I must have done it before.'

Between the Munich and Montreal Games, Bennett and his gradually changing band of pursuiting brothers repeatedly came painfully close to adding the world title to their *palmarès*, and at the 1973 track world championships in San Sebastián, in Spain, Bennett, Moore, Hallam and Rick Evans beat their West German rivals in the final seemingly to become the team-pursuit world champions.

'I always say we were world champions for half an hour,' Bennett laughs. But the British team had won by virtue of the West German quartet crashing inside the final 100 metres, when they were certain of victory. 'We crossed the line first, and were given the world title, but we decided we couldn't accept it, and gave it to them,' explains Bennett, although he's happy to admit that he was the one who had to be cajoled into doing so by the other three.

And he was pleased he was talked around, too: later that year, the riders were invited to receive the World Fair Play Award, in Paris. As Bennett was living and racing in the Netherlands at the time, he was picked up on the way at Amsterdam's Schiphol airport.

'There was a gold Learjet waiting for me, sponsored by Mercedes-Benz, and I flew the rest of the way there with Bobby Charlton,' says Bennett, almost matter-of-factly, but with a hint of knowing how impressive it sounds. 'He was given a medal as well for "inventing" a gesture, which has become standard practice now, of passing the ball back to the other team if they'd kicked it out to stop play so that an injured player could be tended to.'

The pursuit team was also invited to Germany's Sports

Personality of the Year awards, where they were presented with Omega watches in honour of their gesture.

And, almost thirty years later, when Bennett was part of the organization for the 2000 track world championships in Manchester, the old West German team presented him and his teammates with replica gold medals of the ones they'd given up in 1973, 'and a book of press cuttings from the time'.

Bennett was thrilled.

At the '76 Games in Montreal, the team pursuit squad could 'only' manage bronze again, but as a group they were more tightly knit than ever.

'What I think we pioneered then was a kind of togetherness,' says Bennett. 'We warmed up together, we got off the rollers together, put our shoes on together, put our helmets on together, went to the line together . . . Before, we'd been four random guys, all with different coaches, all joining up at championships, hoping it would all come together. I think we probably set a new standard in doing that, if you like.

'It was a period when we had such a sense of humour and morale, which I'm not sure exists in quite the same way today. Even through the bad times, when things went wrong, we still had such a good unity between the four of us.' In addition to Willi Moore's unfortunate puncture in Munich in 1972, there was the time when they again lost out on the world title, this time at the 1974 Worlds in Montreal, two years before the Olympics in the same city, when Hallam's wheel collapsed.

He remembers cycling in Britain in the 1970s as a time when there was an abundance of outdoor tracks, when track racing was hugely popular both in terms of participation and spectators.

'These were the days when there was a hard straight and an easy straight,' laughs Bennett, referring to the wind, as there were very few indoor tracks back then. He remembers Eileen Gray becoming president of the British Cycling Federation, in 1976, and says that there was very much a 'club atmosphere', as he describes it, at that time. 'And I still went away youth-hostelling with my saddlebag on my bike. I loved cycling for cycling's sake, not just for winning or performing.'

But when it came to the competitive side of things, Bennett was coached by Tommy Godwin. As ITV cycling reporter Ned Boulting points out in his book, *On the Road Bike*, there were two Tommy Godwins in British cycling's history: 'Tommy Godwin 1', born in 1912 and famous for his long-distance riding, and 'Tommy Godwin 2', who was born in 1920 and was an accomplished track rider.

Bennett's coach was the second Tommy Godwin, who died in November 2012, having enjoyed that year's London Olympics, in the city where he'd won bronze medals at the 1948 Games at Herne Hill in both the team pursuit – as Bennett would later do – and in the 1-kilometre time trial.

'There was no real science to my training in the seventies, though,' admits Bennett. 'You didn't know if you'd "overtrained"; you just felt tired!

'I can remember there was a book out then: *The Italian Coaching Handbook*, I think it was called. It was full of useful advice, like, "If your urine's cloudy, you're overtrained," which must have meant I was permanently overtrained then!' he laughs. And he'd warned me at the start of our conversation that he wasn't sure he'd be able to remember anything.

'Another sign that you'd overtrained, according to the book, was if your blood pressure was up,' explains Bennett, as the book's advice begins to come flooding back. 'I just remember thinking, "Well, how am I supposed to test my blood pressure?" We were so into it, though – we just loved it! It was the book everyone wanted a copy of. I think it might have been sponsored by Campag [Campagnolo].'

*

In 1984, Bennett's pro career was ended by a car accident in France in which his fiancée was killed.

'It took me about eighteen months to recover from that, and I moved down to London and went into sports promotional work, working on the Kellogg's city-centre racing series, and later the Kellogg's Tour of Britain.'

At that time, Ever Ready batteries were keen to get involved with cycling, and it was Bennett who became the Ever Ready team manager: a modest squad, which raced a domestic programme.

'I needed a sprinter for the team, and found out that Gary Sutton, an Aussie rider who rode the track, had a brother called Shane back in Australia, who Gary thought might be interested in riding for us.'

Shane flew to the UK, and lived in Bennett's house in Birmingham; Bennett stayed down in London during the week, heading home to Birmingham at the weekend.

'We were like the odd couple,' remembers Bennett, fondly, of that time. 'I'd just lost my fiancée in that motor accident, but Shane helped me through what was a very difficult time in my life.'

Bennett's new sprinter was quite handy to have around, too. 'I'd get home on a Friday night, and Shane would have cooked my dinner for me, presenting it on a little tray with a cloth on it, and a flower in a pot!' Bennett laughs. 'And he used to do the house-work with an apron on!'

But he was a brilliant rider, continues Bennett, and wasn't the only Australian to pass through his house back then. Another Aussie – Neil Stephens – came over and lived there, too, riding for Bennett's Ever Ready team in 1987.

'Of course, Neil went on to ride for the ONCE team and Festina and all that in those troubled years.' Bennett trails off, just about referring to the Festina team in which Stephens was riding at the 1998 Tour de France, when one of the team's *soigneurs* was stopped at the Belgian/French border, on his way to the start of the race, in Dublin that year, with a car boot full of doping products intended for the team.

But back to 'Hotel Bennett', where Gary Sutton lived for a while, too.

'It's funny, because Gary is completely the opposite of Shane,' says Bennett. 'You used to have to drag Shane out of the pub. I'm not sure how they came out of the same womb.'

They must have a funny relationship, I suggest: Sutton now working for British Cycling and Gary working with the Australian federation.

'Yes,' he agrees, 'but you can often see them at track world championships or track World Cups, with the British team on one side and the Australian team on the other, and then the two of them conferring in the middle.'

Today, Shane Sutton is arguably the most important man working at British Cycling, having been named technical director following Dave Brailsford's decision in April 2014 to step down as BC's performance director in order to concentrate fully on his role as team manager at Team Sky – the team Sutton was also instrumental in setting up ahead of its launch in 2010.

The sports promotional work Bennett became involved with while also running the Ever Ready team was, initially, for a company called Sports Plus, run by Alan Rushton. It later became Sport for Television, and Irishman Pat McQuaid, who would later become president of the UCI from 2006 to 2013, was also involved. 'Pat and I worked together for years,' says Bennett. 'We'd been on the same pro team – Viking – in 1979, and were very close. Still are.'

Alan Rushton was very much Britain's 'Mr Cycling' in the 1980s and '90s, responsible as he was for running, and securing television coverage for, events like the Kellogg's city-centre cycling series (or the Kellogg's Cycling Championship, as it was officially called) in the mid-1980s, and the Kellogg's Tour of Britain in the late 1980s and early '90s, and for bringing the Tour de France to Britain in 1994.

'When I became interested in working in cycling, I found that there were a lot of people who knew a lot about cycling but nothing about advertising, marketing and PR, and a lot of people who knew a lot about advertising, marketing and PR who knew nothing about cycling,' Rushton explains. 'I found myself in the middle, and thought there was an interesting opportunity.'

He was one of the founders of *BMX Action Bike* in the early 1980s, and was instrumental in building 62 BMX tracks around Britain, at a time when the new sport was huge. 'We were selling 80,000 copies of this magazine, and I remember that Raleigh watched their market share drop from 70 per cent to 40 per cent, because they didn't go into BMXing at first.'

Eventually, they had to join the growing craze, and Rushton helped Raleigh set up their own team, which included British star Andy Ruffell who, says Rushton, was Chris Hoy's hero when he was growing up. Hoy started out racing BMX, as did a number of other road and track stars, including the recently retired Australian sprinter Robbie McEwen, Rushton reminds me. 'In fact, I'm working with Robbie at the moment on some criterium races in Singapore,' Rushton says.

Rushton also set about promoting, and doing the publicity for, a number of different cycling events, including the now defunct London–Holyhead alongside organizer Stan Kite.

London–Holyhead was another race that had been started by BLRC founder Percy Stallard, in 1951, at the height of the battle between the NCU and the BLRC. As well as being such a proponent of stage racing, Stallard had also been inspired by the Continent's big-mileage one-day events, like Bordeaux–Paris. The inaugural London–Holyhead took place just two months before the first edition of the *Daily-Express*-sponsored Tour of Britain. The race started at Marble Arch in the centre of London, with 28 riders taking part. Les Scales won that first edition, out-sprinting Geoff Clark in Holyhead after a leg-sapping 267-mile race.

When he came to work on London–Holyhead three decades later, Rushton pushed hard to garner television coverage, but was always up against it, in that the one-day race always fell on the same day as the FA Cup Final. 'It was explained very clearly to me that it was at the wrong time, that there were no cameras available, and that in fact there was no interest in it,' remembers Rushton. 'That's when I decided that perhaps a different concept would work better for television.'

Criteriums – races around laps of a road circuit – always attracted large crowds, were relatively easy to organize and wouldn't have to be done on weekends, Rushton decided. His initial plan had been for a much bigger, 40-event 'racing league', but that idea was pared down to a five-week series of city-centre races around major cities in the summer of 1983, with rounds in Bristol, Glasgow, Nottingham, Manchester and Birmingham. The series title went to Falcon-Campagnolo's Phil Thomas.

Adrian Metcalfe – who had brought basketball to Channel 4, which had just started the year before – agreed to broadcast the races, which took place on Monday nights and were sponsored by Kellogg's. 'And television, when you get to know it, is full of technical guys who are always looking to put a camera where a camera's never been before,' laughs Rushton. 'I knew that already, and I also knew that the best pictures for bike racing came from a motorbike.

'But you couldn't really put a motorbike in a criterium, as it could take everybody off, so we came up with the idea of a "film lane", which was a coned lane inside the criterium barriers, with the riders on one side and the camera bike on the other.'

Next, Rushton got ex-riders to pilot the motorbikes, as they were capable of reading the race and would be able to guide the cameramen as to what was likely to happen and when. 'So it was a case of, "Watch Sid Barras!" or "Look out for Phil Bayton!" – something like that,' explains Rushton, 'which meant you could get the "lion leaping", so to speak. We got some great footage, really close-up.'

Rushton also managed to bring in 'guest riders' to 'liven things up', such as Australian star Phil Anderson.

It was massively popular: the Channel 4 programmes got audiences of between 2 and 2.5 million, and the number of rounds was bumped up to six for the following year.

In 1987, Rushton persuaded Kellogg's to back a professional Tour of Britain, rivalling the already well-established, and well-loved, Milk Race, which had been the domain of amateurs for so long, but which had opened its doors to the pros, too, in 1985.

'The Milk Race tended to finish outside of the city centres, in parks, not really penetrating the centre of towns like the Kellogg's Tour stages did,' explains Rushton. It was a more commercial answer to the Milk Race, and a city-centre series continued, too, sponsored by insurance company Scottish Provident.

For a few short years, bike racing was riding the crest of a wave. Many will remember the Kellogg's Tour fondly, both for its racing and its King of the Mountains jersey – mimicking the Tour de France version with red Kellogg's 'K' polka dots.

The first edition – a five-stage race between Edinburgh and London, taking in Newcastle, Manchester, Birmingham and Cardiff along the way – was won by Liverpool's Joey McLoughlin.

Massive crowds on the climbs on stage two in the Yorkshire Moors showed a real appetite for European-style bike racing. This was the stage on which McLoughlin put in a blistering finish to win in Manchester from a five-man breakaway, which included

Dutch star Steven Rooks and Frenchman Denis Roux, who would finish in the top 10 at the following year's Tour de France.

Despite Rooks and McLoughlin being equal on accumulated time overall, Rooks – of the Dutch PDM team – took the yellow leader's jersey by virtue of having finished better than McLoughlin the day before. 'Everything went to plan,' McLoughlin said after the stage. 'I'm afraid I haven't got the jersey, but there are still another two [in fact, three] days to go, so we'll see what happens.'

Rooks was already well aware of the young British rider's ability. At the Dutch one-day Classic Amstel Gold in 1986, which Rooks won in a two-man sprint from world champion Joop Zoetemelk, McLoughlin had finished fourth, just 37 seconds down. It was an extraordinary result for the then 21-year-old, the last decent British performance in a Classic before that having been Graham Jones's second place at Het Volk (now Het Nieuwsblad) four years earlier.

The next day at the 1987 Kellogg's Tour, through the Peak District, the status quo was maintained, with McLoughlin and Rooks locked together on equal time, and the Dutchman still in yellow.

But on stage four – Birmingham to Cardiff – the peloton tackled the climb of The Tumble, just outside Abergavenny in South Wales, and McLoughlin, in that iconic white jersey covered in red K-for-Kellogg's polka dots as King of the Mountains, ironically lost contact with Rooks, and was in very real danger of watching the race slip away from him on the six-kilometre climb.

With The Tumble also featuring on the route of the 2014 Tour of Britain – providing a 'summit finish' to stage three – expect more of the same as the climb does its 'level' best to test the best riders in the world on its slopes in September.

However, in 1987, the riders also descended the climb –

destination Cardiff – and it gave McLoughlin the opportunity to get back on terms with his Dutch rival.

There were two riders clear by the finish, but the American 7-Eleven team's Bob Roll was left fuming after pulling his foot out of the pedal just metres from taking the stage win, handing it instead to Belgium's Paul Haghedooren from the Sigma team. A recovered McLoughlin, meanwhile, was given the perfect lead-out by his ANC-Halfords teammate Malcolm Elliott (who would win the 1988 edition of the race, riding for the Fagor team), and McLoughlin's third place – thanks to the bonus seconds awarded on the line for the top three finishers – gave him the yellow jersey from Rooks that evening by five seconds.

On the Westminster circuit for the final stage, it was 'just' a case of keeping an eye on Rooks, and the job was done. 'Fantastic tour,' McLoughlin told Channel 4 afterwards, having achieved his goal. 'I said in Manchester I was going to win this jersey for the people in Britain, and I'm really pleased I have done.'

McLoughlin had already won the 1986 Milk Race; now he could add Britain's newest stage race to his *palmarès*.

That well-taken 1987 Kellogg's Tour win – helped, no doubt, by his fourth place at Amstel Gold earlier in the season – earned McLoughlin a spot on the French Z-Peugeot team for the next two years, where he was teammates with Robert Millar for his second year there. But already his best years seemed to be behind him, and in his relatively short six-year pro career you were left with the feeling that McLoughlin could have won a lot more were it not for a series of injuries that blighted his time at the top.

Writing in the Kellogg's Tour souvenir guide, published by *Winning* magazine, previewing the second edition of the race in 1988, the then *Guardian* cycling correspondent Graham Snowdon heralded the first edition of the event as a huge leap forward for the sport.

'To lift cycle racing in Britain from its Cinderella status into a mass spectator sport has been a long, hard struggle. And make no mistake, the battle is by no means won. But there can be little doubt that, in terms of public acceptance of the sport in the UK, the biggest step forward yet came with last year's introduction of the Kellogg's Tour,' he wrote. 'It was from the sheer volume of spectators – on remote mountain climbs as well as in the city centres – and from the following generated by the superb Channel 4 television coverage, that those of us on the race knew we were witnessing the dawn of a new era.'

The truth is, the sport's popularity only slowly wound up from the mid-1980s to the mid-2000s, but progressed nonetheless – in fits and starts in the face of the fickle nature of team and race sponsors – thanks in no small part to the efforts of men like Rushton and Bennett.

The Kellogg's Tour of Britain ran concurrently with the Milk Race between 1987 and 1993, at which point the Milk Marketing Board was essentially scrapped, and the Milk Race was no more after a nevertheless rather decent 35-year run. The following year, 1994, was to be the Kellogg's Tour's last edition, too, when the sponsor pulled out. There's probably some kind of clever joke there somewhere about not being able to have cereal without milk.

Four years later, Rushton was able to revive the Tour of Britain with title sponsorship from the Prudential insurance company, and the race became known as the PruTour. But when the sponsor again pulled the plug after just two editions, Britain was without a tour of itself again – until yet again it was resurrected in 2004. This time, there was a fresh approach by new organizers SweetSpot Group, using funding from the (in fact now defunct) regional development agencies (RDAs) rather than a precarious lone race sponsor, and the Tour organization worked closely with the RDAs to extol the virtues of exercise, awareness of the environment and the commercial benefits to businesses when the race came to town.

Later, as the 'new' Tour of Britain became more established, a number of smaller commercial partners did combine to plug the financial shortfall in light of the RDAs' disappearance when the government scrapped them in March 2012. But the load is now spread, as opposed to the 'all or nothing' nature of a single head-line sponsor.

Mick Bennett – now employed by SweetSpot – is at the helm of the latest incarnation of the Tour of Britain, but he and Rushton worked together throughout the 1980s, '90s and until 2000, their relationship ending that year following their organization of the track cycling world championships in Manchester, where Bennett had received his honorary medal from the West German team pursuit squad.

'You go through peaks and troughs,' says Rushton, 'and, when you get a trough, you have to look out for whether you can pay people. Unfortunately, we hit a big trough, and Mick was made redundant as a result, which was a shame, as he was very good at what he did.'

'It was the best thing that ever happened to me,' says Bennett, in a separate conversation. He went on to bring the Tour de France to London in 2007.

Besides the Kellogg's-sponsored events, between 1989 and 1997 Rushton and Bennett had worked together to host a round of the UCI World Cup: the now defunct season-long competition that awarded points for placings in the major one-day races, crowning a winner at the end of the season. 'There was an opportunity for a British round of the competition, so we started it in Newcastle, where the circuit wasn't great,' admits Rushton. It was moved to Brighton for the following year, where it remained for two editions.

'We then took a big offer to take it to Leeds, in 1992, who really wanted it, for four years, and it became the Leeds Classic, where it went over much of the same route of the 2014 Tour de France.'

In 1997, it moved to Rochester – to be known as the Rochester International Classic – which was the last time the men's World Cup was held in the UK.

Bennett and Rushton had also worked together to bring the Tour de France to British shores in 1994, and this was a great success.

The 1994 Tour had already started with a huge British victory as early as the prologue in Lille, where Chris Boardman – riding the Tour for the first time – blasted around the 7.2-kilometre time-trial course to beat the defending Tour champion, Miguel Indurain, of Spain, by 15 seconds, with Switzerland's Tony Rominger a further four seconds back.

It was a hefty margin for a Tour rookie over such a short course, but, arguably more important, even, than the stage win was the fact that it put Boardman into the yellow jersey, which made him the first Briton (and only the second of all time) to wear the *maillot jaune* since Tom Simpson wore it for a day in 1962.

Boardman went one better, too, by holding on to it for two days longer than Simpson did, but had to hand the race lead to Johan Museeuw after the Belgian's GB-MG Technogym team won the stage-three team time trial in Calais, while a lack of discipline at Boardman's Gan team saw them fall to pieces on what was a shambolic stage for the French outfit, who lost a minute and 17 seconds to the winning Italian squad.

For Anglophile race director Jean-Marie Leblanc, taking the Tour to the UK was a dream come true. The occasion also commemorated fifty years since D-Day, as well as celebrating the opening, just two months earlier, of the Channel Tunnel.

Leblanc and co. were immediately dazzled by the enthusiasm and warm welcome that their race received. Three million people were said to have lined the routes of stage four between Dover and Brighton, and stage five, which started and finished in Portsmouth. For the first of the two stages, the peloton was trumpeted on its way by the Prince of Wales Royal Regiment from the ramparts of Dover Castle, with a 204.5-kilometre stage ahead of them that would take in Canterbury (which would host a stage finish when the Tour visited again thirteen years later), Ashdown Forest and the climb of Ditchling Beacon before finishing on the seafront in Brighton.

Boardman and Sean Yates were the only two British riders taking part in the '94 Tour, and seeing as the stage passed through Yates's home in Ashdown Forest, race leader Museeuw allowed him to go ahead of the race and greet his family at the side of the road, which Yates describes as 'a big highlight'. This was despite the fact that a two-man breakaway had escaped from the peloton's clutches after just 20 kilometres. Spain's Francesco Cabello from Kelme and Emmanuel Magnien of the Castorama team built up an early lead of over five minutes, but by the foot of Ditchling Beacon, with the run-in to Brighton to come once the riders had got to the top, their lead was down to just over three minutes.

I was on the Beacon that day; as a Sussex local, how could I not be? The crowd was three and four deep in places, and more than that if you counted the people who were lined up on the grassy banks that tower over the road in places, hoping to get a better view.

As we waited for the riders to arrive, with the buzz-buzzing of the camera helicopters getting ever closer, it felt like the excitable, building atmosphere you'd get in the Alps or the Pyrenees, rather than on the South Downs a few miles north of Brighton. At least, that's how I liked to imagine it felt in the mountains; this was my first 'live' experience of the Tour de France, and it turned out to be every bit as thrilling as I'd hoped it would be.

Among the pro riders making short work of what is considered to be a pretty tough climb – as anyone who's ridden the annual London to Brighton bike ride will attest – was the late Marco Pantani, making his Tour début. Miguel Indurain would later take the race by the scruff of the neck a few days after it returned to French soil, and go on to win his third-straight title, but Pantani did enough to take third place in Paris, behind Piotr Ugrumov, and was also the race's 'best young rider'.

After the speed bump that was Ditchling Beacon, there was still the climb of Elm Grove, in Brighton itself, which was tackled twice on two 8.5-kilometre laps of a Brighton town-centre circuit.

Up at the front of the race, on Elm Grove for the second time, Cabello attacked, shedding Magnien. Behind them came lone chaser Flavio Vanzella, while Boardman himself decided to escape the main field with just over a lap to go.

Cabello finished alone on Madeira Drive as the day's stage winner, and, while Vanzella caught Magnien, it was the Frenchman who came out on top for second spot. The Italian, however, had done enough to take the yellow jersey from the shoulders of his GB–MG teammate Museeuw.

Boardman stayed clear to take fourth, and celebrated the result in front of the huge crowd almost as though he'd won the stage.

'It was just insane how many people there were; I just wasn't expecting it, and remember just being blown away,' Yates says of the day he got to ride the Tour de France on his home roads.

There was more of the same the next day, too, when large crowds enjoyed a 187-kilometre fifth stage that started and finished in Portsmouth, with a loop taking in Basingstoke, Andover and Winchester. This time, however, it came down to a bunch sprint, in which Italian Nicola Minali took the win from Germany's Olaf Ludwig and Italian Silvio Martinello. Vanzella, meanwhile, kept hold of the yellow jersey.

But there was an odd, almost symmetrical, 'book-ending' to the two Tour stages in the UK. Boardman had lost his yellow jersey the day before the race arrived in Britain, and then Yates took the yellow jersey on the day that the race returned to France. And they were the only two British riders in the race, remember.

On stage six, from Cherbourg (where the ferry had arrived from Portsmouth) to Rennes, Yates, riding for the Motorola team, finished sixth as part of a seven-man breakaway. The stage was won by Gianluca Bortolami, of Italy, but, as the best-placed rider overall in the group, the leader's yellow jersey was Yates's. It was only his for a day – not that he really minded. The intermediate sprints on the flatter stages offered 'bonus seconds' to help keep things interesting: to try to shake things up as often as possible, and ideally help the yellow jersey to change hands as frequently as possible.

On stage seven, it worked out exactly as the organizers would have liked, as Museeuw, with more than a little help from his team-mates – Rolf Sørensen in particular – took back the yellow jersey for the first time since having it on stage four.

'We were going for this bonus sprint, and there was a little bit of argy-bargy,' remembers Yates, which you can imagine might well have been a bit stronger than he makes out. 'Phil Anderson, who was on my team, was kind of doing a bit of pushing, and Rolf saw that, and thought, "I'll have some of that," and just slung me back.'

The TV cameras caught Sørensen in the act, pulling on Yates's jersey to prevent him from contesting the sprint for the bonus seconds on offer. But Yates was never overly bothered; it was just the kind of thing that went on in sprinting – and still does – and admitting now that his own Motorola teammate, Anderson, had also been involved may well absolve Sørensen from being seen as the pantomime villain that I, and no doubt plenty of other British fans, thought he was at the time.

'One day or two days in yellow didn't really make much difference to me,' Yates says. 'I knew Museeuw could outsprint me, so I wasn't going to start crying about it. I was just happy to get the jersey for one day.

'And it's still the only time that two Brits have worn the jersey in the same year,' he adds, proudly. 'Good memories.'

The 1994 stages of the Tour weren't the first time the race had been brought to British shores. In 1974 the race had started in Brest, in Brittany, a standard-enough start. But then on stage two it suddenly diverted north, via ferry, across the English Channel to Plymouth. There was a reason behind the Tour's first overseas sojourn: to promote the new Plymouth–Roscoff ferry route, and the opportunity, thanks to the new route, for Breton farmers to peddle their wares in Britain.

Once in Devon, the 164-kilometre stage consisted of a decidedly uninspiring gallop up and down the new Plympton bypass – which was new, yes, but still had to be closed for the stage, as former *Cycling Weekly* journalist Keith Bingham makes clear in his piece about that 1974 Tour stage for volume 4 of *The Cycling Anthology*.

'It was not an "unopened stretch of highway", as people say, but it had been operational for several months,' Alf Palmer, who was secretary to Plymouth's Lord Mayor, a keen club cyclist and part of the organizing committee, told Bingham. 'Although it is now the main trunk road link between Devon and Cornwall, at the time it was probably felt that its closure for the day would not be of enormous inconvenience to traffic bypassing Plymouth because it was comparatively new and people were still familiar with the roads they had used before it was opened.'

Palmer also reveals that the stage had a simple format so that the Tour organizers could simply get in and out again as quickly and with as little trouble as possible.

Barry Hoban was the only British participant riding that year for the crowd to cheer on, and the smattering of spectators – said to be in the vicinity of 15,000 – 'enjoyed' the 'spectacle' about as much as the riders, by all accounts.

The Dutch Frisol team would have enjoyed it, at least. Their man Henk Poppe won the day by leading home a bunch sprint.

*

Alan Rushton still runs Sport for Television, but now mainly promotes races in Asia, including the Tour of Beijing (a UCI ProTour event) and the Tour of Korea. After leaving Sport for Television, Bennett applied for a job as 'director of cycling' with Transport for London (TfL).

He realized in the interview that the job wasn't really what he thought it was going to be: 'It was more of a highways engineer role, managing the cycle network.' However, one of the questions he was asked was how he'd promote cycling in the capital. 'I said I'd bring the Tour de France to London,' says Bennett, 'which would have that "Wimbledon effect", put cycling on the map and spark a revolution.'

Around the same time, he was interviewed for another job with Upper Street Events, which organized exhibitions at the Business Design Centre in Islington (just by chance, the venue for London's first Six-Day race in 1878). They wanted to start an annual cycle show, with Bennett at the helm. He took the job, and the Cycle Show is still running to this day, currently housed at Birmingham's NEC, with Bennett as its creative director.

'But two years after I started, I got a call from a guy called Mick Hickford, from TfL. "You once put an idea to us about bringing the Tour de France to London," he reminded me. "We'd like to do it; could you help us make it happen?"'

Bennett agreed to meet them, and was asked to put a proposal together.

'This was around early 2004, when I was also working as the UCI women's World Cup road coordinator,' explains Bennett. 'But I put this idea to them, and, that weekend, Mick called me at home and said that TfL had the budget, and asked what we needed to do next.

'So I said, "If you just hang on . . ." And this is true, this: I called Pat McQuaid on my mobile, who was in the car with the

Tour director, Jean-Marie Leblanc, at the Flèche Wallonne race that weekend, and he was talking to Jean-Marie in French, who was talking to Pat in French, who was translating it back to me, and I was talking back to Mick on the other phone . . .'

The upshot of the four-way conversation was that if Mayor of London Ken Livingstone wrote to Leblanc in the next two weeks, Leblanc would make sure that London's request to host the Tour went forward favourably.

The rest is history, except Bennett also got another job out of it, when TfL offered him a consultancy job with them for three days a week. 'So I went back to Upper Street Events and said that this was my passion, and they said that they still wanted me to work for them for two days a week, and could I still do it, and I said yes. And I'm still doing it, but I'm now doing one day a week. I know what I'm doing now.'

And in 2007, the Tour start in London happened – on the most perfect summer's day, with blue skies and huge crowds.

Bradley Wiggins – the individual and team pursuit world champion, having taken the titles at that year's track Worlds in Mallorca in March, and the winner of the prologue time trial at the Dauphiné Libéré stage race just a few weeks ahead of the Tour – was the home-town favourite for the 8-kilometre prologue time trial.

'Kids from Kilburn aren't supposed to win the Tour,' Wiggins told the *Guardian* in an interview a few months after his 2012 Tour de France victory. But in 2007, the kid from Kilburn was thrilled to be racing through the streets of the city he'd grown up in.

Wiggins was born on 28 April 1980, in Ghent, Belgium, where his Australian father, Gary, was based while racing Belgian *kermesse* (circuit) races and European Six-Day events. But, after his parents split up, a two-year-old Bradley and his mother moved to Kilburn in north-west London to live with her parents.

Although Wiggins grew up not knowing his father, he followed him into cycling, racing as a twelve-year-old at venues such as the Herne Hill Velodrome in south London. Racing on the familiar roads of Whitehall, Birdcage Walk, Constitution Hill and The Mall were a thrill for him, therefore, and although the fairytale result would have been victory in the opening time trial at what was only his second Tour de France, Wiggins's fourth place – behind winner Fabian Cancellara, Andreas Klöden and George Hincapie – was an excellent, crowd-pleasing result nonetheless. Little did the British public know that they were watching their Tour-winner-in-waiting, five years before his overall victory. Wiggins himself had no idea at that stage, either; he was a time-trial specialist, aiming for the kind of success on the road that would match what he'd achieved on the track, which also included Olympic gold in the individual pursuit at the 2004 Athens Games.

David Millar was another British TT specialist at that 2007 Tour, and finished a very respectable 13th in the prologue. The next day – the second and final stage in the UK, from London to Canterbury – Millar went on the attack, thrilling the huge road-side crowds with his solo breakaway. He was never going to stay away all the way to Canterbury, but by virtue of the points taken on the small climbs of Kent along the way, he earned the right to wear the polka-dot King of the Mountains jersey on the following day's stage, becoming the first Briton in twenty-one years to wear the climber's jersey since Britain's other great cycling Millar (Robert) wore it in 1986, having also worn it and won it for keeps in Paris in 1984.

According to a Transport for London document produced following the 2007 *Grand Départ* in the UK, an estimated three million people watched the racing across both days, 900,000 of those having been packed around the prologue circuit in central London.

It was nothing short of a massive success.

*

But Bennett's story doesn't end with the organization of that 2007 Tour *Grand Départ* – not by any stretch.

'In 2004, a guy called Hugh Roberts rang me, around the same time as we'd started planning for the 2007 Tour, and said he wanted to bring the Tour of Britain back, with the regional development agencies sponsoring it.' Roberts was in charge of organizing a golf tournament called the Mobile Cup for Carphone Warehouse, but brought in Bennett and former individual pursuit world champion Tony Doyle to resurrect the Tour of Britain.

'And we had about four months to organize it!' says Bennett. 'We went to see the Minister for Sport, who at that time was Richard Caborn, and it was thanks to him that we got coverage of the Tour of Britain on the BBC. I remember him saying that if we don't do more to get more people cycling, then the NHS was going to self-destruct, and so he contacted the BBC on our behalf.'

Next came what Bennett describes as 'the tidal surge'; British success began to come on both the track and the road, and the 'new' Tour of Britain went from strength to strength, with the announcement in February 2014 that it was to be awarded 2.HC category – the second-highest category below the very top-tier UCI ProTour level.

Hugh Roberts's SweetSpot company is also behind the Tour Series, of which Bennett is also the race director: a televised series of city-centre races that conjure up the magical summer evenings of those 1980s Kellogg's city-centre races, but with a twist: the races are entirely team-oriented. Yes, there's literally an individual winner on the night – the rider who crosses the line first – but it's largely irrelevant; it's all about where the three best-placed members of your team finish.

And with the addition to the calendar of May's inaugural – and hugely successful – Friends-Life-sponsored Women's Tour, which enjoyed an hour-long highlights programme on ITV4 each evening, SweetSpot and Britain's current 'Mr Cycling', Mick Bennett, have been instrumental in helping to create what looks like a very bright future for the sport indeed.

8

A TALE OF TWO TONYS

In December 2009, fifty names were unveiled to celebrate British Cycling's 50th anniversary. Formed as the British Cycling Federation (BCF) in 1959 following the merger of the National Cyclists' Union (NCU) and the British League of Racing Cyclists (BLRC), British Cycling ended their long-running feud over massed-start racing on public roads.

The names chosen for British Cycling's first Hall of Fame included athletes, organizers, administrators and volunteers, and represented the federation's growth and achievements in more than just racing. There were two Tonys included on the list: Tony Yorke and Tony Doyle. Both happened to have ties to racing, and they knew each other well, too – a story about handlebar tape being the link that lasted longest.

Tony Doyle was a two-time individual pursuit world champion, and a prolific winner of Six-Day events on the Continent throughout the 1980s and '90s. Following his retirement in the mid-nineties, he was briefly president of the BCF, and later one of the founding directors of the modern, resurrected Tour of Britain, along with Mick Bennett.

'I went out to the Olympic Games in Sydney in 2000, and took Hugh Roberts [now head of Tour of Britain organizers SweetSpot] to watch the road racing and track racing,' Doyle explains, 'which sowed a seed in his mind about bringing back the Tour of Britain.'

Doyle could help him get it off the ground, and Bennett, who'd worked on the previous iterations of the event, was brought in, too. Roberts was commercial director, Bennett was technical director and Doyle was events director.

I covered that first 2004 race for both *The Times* and *Procycling* magazine, and while the Tour of Britain has grown to become one of the premier stage races on the international calendar over the ten years since the event returned, the opening stage of the then-new race – a 207-kilometre loop from Manchester back to Manchester, via Blackpool and Preston – was beset by problems. Indeed, at times it even conjured up thoughts of when the NCU and the BLRC had battled over the NCU's insistence that road racing on the public highway was simply too dangerous, while the BLRC had insisted that road closures weren't necessary.

The number of cars on the road had increased somewhat by 2004 compared to the 1940s, however, and as I weaved my way through the busy traffic in a press car alongside Irish journalist Shane Stokes, Bennett was losing his cool over the race radio. Things had become very dangerous as rush-hour traffic poured in between the peloton and Scotland's Duncan Urquhart and South African Rodney Green of the Barloworld squad in the two-man breakaway.

'I could give you chapter and verse on that day,' Bennett, who remains the race director, says now. 'We had to use different police forces for each stage back then whenever we crossed over from one county to another. That day, we had a police inspector who refused to move his riders from the front of the break to the middle, and we had all this traffic in between. It was awful, and we had to go back to the drawing board for the next day.'

For my piece in *The Times*, I wanted to concentrate on the stage – won by Quick Step-Davitamon's Italian sprinter Stefano Zanini – but felt obliged to mention the traffic problems, which were particularly dangerous going through Blackpool.

'We are aware of what was happening, so rest assured we're going to do everything in our power to improve the situation,' Doyle told me at the time. 'We're aware that the riders' safety is paramount,' he added for William Fotheringham's piece for the *Guardian*. 'We've been assured that steps will be taken to solve the problems there were today.'

Voicing the riders' concerns, Charly Wegelius said, 'Most of the pros didn't want to race, because they just weren't safe conditions to work in. The situation seemed to be too much for the marshals. My livelihood is at stake, but I'm a British pro and I want racing in Britain to be successful, something I can be proud of.'

Thankfully, nobody was hurt, which tragically wasn't the case at the 1998 PruTour when one of the police motorbike outriders, PC Dave Hopkins, was killed in a collision with a car, near Worcester, on stage five between Birmingham and Cardiff. The race was stopped, and the rest of the stage cancelled, before the race resumed the next day. PC Hopkins was part of the advance party employed to temporarily halt traffic while the race passed through: a system known as a 'rolling road closure', which differs from the methods used at larger events such as the Tour de France, where the roads are closed along the entirety of the route for the whole day.

Tragedy was avoided – by luck more than anything else – at the Kellogg's Tour of Britain in 1994, when, on stage two, from Carlisle to Blackpool, the driver of a car failed to adhere to the demands to stop made by the police outriders controlling the rolling road closure, and drove headlong into the peloton at the start of the climb of Kirkstone Pass near Ambleside. This took down several riders, including Dutch rider Adri van der Poel, defending Kellogg's Tour champion Phil Anderson and his Motorola teammate – and British road-race champion – Brian Smith. Smith hurt his arm badly, but was able to continue, while Van der Poel's injuries forced him out of the race.

Soon after that, the riders themselves neutralized the race in protest against the danger, stopping with around 30 miles of the stage to go; the experienced Anderson, having caught up with the peloton after a lonely and painful climb up Kirkstone Pass, acted as spokesman.

'An oncoming car swung into the peloton,' Anderson explained to Channel 4. 'Luckily it didn't hit anyone, but it caused quite a swerve in the bunch, and we were travelling at quite a high speed at one of the most crucial points of the day – ahead of the crucial mountain of the day – and I was one of the victims of the crash.

'I think the organization has to take some responsibility,' the Australian continued, 'and maybe increase the amount of policing at the race, to make sure this kind of problem doesn't happen. If racing at this level is going to continue in Britain, I think we have to increase the number of police [officers] controlling this race.'

Both accidents were contributing factors when Kellogg's and PruTour sponsors Prudential decided to end support of their respective races. That 1994 edition of the Kellogg's Tour was its last, while the PruTour lasted for only two editions, in 1998 and 1999. In light of such incidents, and after the problems on the first day of the 2004 Tour of Britain, the organizers of the revived event have worked hard to safeguard everyone involved with, and watching, the race, and things have improved dramatically – the quality of policing at British cycling events having grown in parallel with the popularity of the sport in the UK.

'Our events have got to be immaculate. The safety of the spectators and the riders is absolutely paramount,' says Bennett, who today also organizes the Women's Tour and the Tour Series, and echoes Doyle's comments of 2004.

Doyle understood the riders' worries perfectly, having ridden on the road as a pro, but the track had always been where his heart was. Like Bennett before him, Doyle was a pursuit specialist, and was British amateur pursuit champion in 1977, '78 and '79, before becoming professional individual pursuit world champion for the first time in 1980. That world title came just weeks after the Moscow Olympic Games, from which Doyle had returned frustrated and angry.

The Olympics were solely the domain of amateur riders in 1980; only in 1996, when they were held in Atlanta, were they opened to professionals.

Doyle had already had offers to turn pro, but retained his amateur status in order to go for Olympic gold in Russia. He was up against a twenty-year-old called Sean Yates for the sole British place in the event, although both riders already knew that they were in for the team pursuit, alongside Glenn Mitchell and a nineteen-year-old Malcolm Elliott.

'Sean and I always got along fine, but in Moscow the national coach couldn't decide which of us should ride the individual pursuit, so it was decided that we'd have a four-kilometre pursuit under race conditions, and I won by nearly 2.5 seconds,' explains Doyle.

Doyle had understood that it would show who had the best form, but the BCF's director of racing at the time, Jim Hendry, told *Cycling Weekly* that it wasn't a selection race. 'I made it clear that it would not necessarily be a case of the winner being selected,' he said, and explained that he'd told pursuit coach Willi Moore – the bronze medal winner in the 1972 Olympic team pursuit with Mick Bennett, Ron Keeble and Ian Hallam – that he 'would want to see a big difference between the two to change my mind'.

He already had Yates in mind as the best man for the individual event.

'Back at the Olympic Village later on, Jim called me into his room and said that we were both going well, but that he'd decided that Sean was riding, which was a total surprise to me,' says Doyle. 'Sean then got to the quarter-finals, where he was beaten, so he'd done relatively well, but I was very frustrated and annoyed.'

How things then went in the team pursuit did little to placate him.

'After his first turn on the front, Sean got dropped, and we lost in the quarter-finals, and we were out,' Doyle says. 'Not only did the decision [to pick Sean for the individual pursuit] cost me a medal; I'm convinced it also cost us a medal in the team pursuit.'

Doyle returned to the UK and promptly turned pro with the KP Crisps–Viscount team, joining Ian Hallam and Phil Bayton on the squad. 'My first race as a pro was the British pursuit championships, which I won,' says Doyle. 'Then, a couple of weeks later, I went to Besançon, in France, for the world pursuit championships, and I won there, too, beating Hans-Henrik Ørsted, who'd been third at the Olympics.'

Doyle finished second to Ørsted at the world championships in both 1984 and 1985, but then beat the Dane again to become individual-pursuit world champion for a second time in Colorado Springs in 1986.

By the mid-1980s Doyle had begun to use the services of both a sports scientist and a sports psychologist.

'I found out about the performance laboratory down at Bishop Otter College in Chichester [in West Sussex; now the University of Chichester], and so I went down to meet Tudor Hale, who was head of the department,' explains Doyle. 'I said that I was after some sports science support, and that I was prepared to pay for it, and that I was wondering if there was any help he and his department could give. And he said: "I'll tell you what: we've got a young student who's recently started here called Peter Keen, and he's keen on cycling." So I started working with Peter Keen, in 1984. I was the original guinea pig.'

With Keen, Doyle started using the Kingcycle – the forerunner of today's complex measuring computers and stationary bicycle systems used by British Cycling to analyse riders' 'numbers', including power produced and heart rate. Doyle also met Ian Maynard, a psychologist who also worked with Robert Millar and the British sailing team, and who now heads the sports psychology department at Sheffield Hallam University.

After third place in 1987 – the year when Ørsted took his third world title in Vienna – Doyle saw the 1988 Worlds as a chance to win his own third title, on the outdoor track in Ghent, in front of what he knew would be good support from British spectators, for whom it was easily accessible.

'I was fastest in qualifying, and through every round up to the final,' says Doyle. 'I was always very methodical in my build-up to the Worlds, and each year had a good team of people around me.' The BCF, he says, offered minimal support, so Doyle would take his own mechanic, his own masseur, his own psychologist – Maynard – and his own physiologist, Peter Keen. Mick Bennett was team manager.

'Each day, we'd run through a timetable of what was happening when: what time we were going on the track, what time we'd go out on the road, and everything, so that everyone knew what was going on. Mick had set the schedule for the day of the final, and he'd put it together from the race manual, which had been printed some time before the event, so there were also updated daily communiqués . . . Mick had planned that there were two and a half hours between the semi-final and the final – whereas in fact it had been changed so that it was only an hour and a quarter.'

The massage cabin, explains Doyle, was about a kilometre away from the track, in a completely separate complex.

'I was there relaxing, and hadn't yet begun my mental or

physical preparation to get ready for the final, and I got a knock on the door saying that I was on next!' Doyle says, almost reliving the panic he felt. 'I was using one of those rubberized skinsuits, which you can't just climb into at the last second; you have to use talcum powder to help you get into it, and in the panic and confusion my *soigneur* and Mick broke the zip! This was a very, very expensive suit, and we had to stick safety pins through it to do it up.'

Doyle had been the hot favourite to take the title, but hadn't time to do any kind of warm-up.

'I was up against Lech Piasecki, the Polish rider, who had a pedigree on the road, but I just wasn't warmed up enough, and he ended up beating me by a couple of seconds,' says Doyle. 'Given another kilometre or a kilometre and a half, I probably would have been OK.

'There's something about winning a hat-trick of victories, so I was devastated, and left very disappointed with another silver.'

Tony Yorke – the 'other Tony' in British Cycling's Hall of Fame – was the national junior coach between 1979 and 1984, and went on to hold a number of posts at the BCF, including that of national coaching development officer from 1988 to 1995. In 1998, Yorke became the GB Paralympic team manager, and worked tirelessly to get para-cycling accepted under the UCI's umbrella, which he achieved in 2007.

In 2006, Yorke had already received the UCI Merit Award for services to international cycling, and in 2009 his services to cycling were recognized at the highest level when he was awarded an OBE. A year later, he was named on the list for BC's Hall of Fame.

Sadly, after battling cancer, Yorke passed away in November 2012, but he had enjoyed the British Paralympic cycling team's phenomenal performance at London 2012, where they topped the medals table with eight golds, nine silvers and five bronzes across all classifications.

Yorke was also active in his – and my – local track league, at Preston Park in Brighton, for many years, and it was he who put me forward as a junior rider to go and ride at the then new Manchester Velodrome, for which I'll always be grateful. Today, he would have had more than a few stories to tell about his time with the BCF and working with the UCI, but his wife, Gretel, was there to experience much of it, helping him out along the way, and I sit down with Gretel at her home in Lancing, in West Sussex, to hear more about the work he did for the development of cycling and para-cycling.

But first the Tony Yorke/Tony Doyle connection. Shortly after Yorke passed away, Gretel and their son David were going through what was rather a large collection of cycling paraphernalia in the garage, and happened across a box of roll upon roll of handlebar tape.

'David said, "Oh, this is the stuff off Tony Doyle's bikes!"' says Gretel. 'Tony Doyle always changed his handlebar tape for every race, and my Tony, being what he was – waste not, want not – wasn't going to throw it away, and he kept it all, rolled up, and would then use it on other people's bikes.

'I was very fond of Tony Doyle,' she continues, 'but he was very fussy – about how he looked, how his bike was set up; everything had to be just right. But then you've got to be tunnel-visioned when you're going to be a champion, and he was.'

Yorke would help Doyle out at track events, pumping up tyres, checking the bikes. Changing handlebar tape, too, perhaps.

'I remember Tony being the team manager at my first international race – a three-day race in Germany – in 1976,' says Doyle. 'It was the first time I'd ever been abroad.'

Doyle later got his own manager, and Yorke started to help a promising youngster by the name of Sean Yates.

'It was just psyching him up, really,' remembers Gretel. 'Sean never had much confidence in himself, and Sean's father was always getting in touch with Tony to help Sean. In fact, I remember a time when he wanted to pay for Tony to go to a world championship, which Tony couldn't do, because he was working in those days as well. But Sean was so shy and retiring back then, and just didn't have faith in himself half the time. He's very shy, you know. He doesn't like to be the centre of attention. Never did.'

'I often stayed round at Gretel and Tony's,' Yates later tells me. 'Tony would give us lifts up to the track at Leicester. He was extremely passionate about cycling and put a lot of time into it: because he loved it, rather than to gain anything out of it. And then what came later with the Paralympics and everything really told that story. It was his love. It's guys like him who help keep the sport going: one of those guys who dedicates their lives to it – after their families – just helping steer riders who've got ambition in the right direction.'

Yates attended Yorke's funeral in December 2012.

'When they read out all the stuff he'd done, it made me realize, "Wow, he's a real unsung hero," you know? Luckily, there are others like him, in lots of other sports, but you perhaps don't always realize everything they've done until much later.'

Gretel never got a chance to speak to Yates at the funeral, and found that she didn't have his latest address to thank him for coming. So she simply wrote on the envelope: 'Sean Yates, Forest Row'.

It found him easily at his home in East Sussex.

Yates remembers meeting Tony for the first time in, he thinks, 1978, in Cuckfield, not far from Forest Row. 'That must have been my first ever fitness test,' Yates says. 'I'd just started cycling and just did what my dad told me. It must have been some kind of ramp test, on a Kingcycle.'

'I took our old Kingcycle up to the dump only last week,' Gretel says, which would probably horrify some students and historians of the sport.

Yorke had worked closely with national coach Doug Dailey and a young Peter Keen to devise methods to test riders' capabilities.

'Both Sean and Tony Doyle would have been tested on a Kingcycle,' remembers Gretel. 'And they probably would have been there at the Nuffield hospital in Birmingham, too.'

Each year, Gretel explains, her husband used to arrange for elite cyclists to come to the hospital in Birmingham for an assessment by doctors, dentists, opticians and dieticians. 'This is going back to the 1970s and '80s, through the BCF, before there was any money in cycling,' says Gretel. 'The doctors and everyone were all interested in cycling, but gave their services free, and if the riders needed any further treatment, it was organized. Again, I can imagine Tony Doyle was one of them, and Sean Yates must have been there.'

Yates remembers it well. 'Yes, it was one of those things that people didn't hear so much about back then,' he says. 'It was a support structure, really.'

Later, as Yates's career took off, he made sure he dropped in to visit the Yorkes whenever he was out training and came past their house.

Both men were named in the Hall of Fame, and, fittingly – even though it's really down to their surnames – Yates and Yorke sit next to each other on the list: Yates for being 'an outstanding pro and highly valued team rider', and for having won a stage of the Tour de France and worn the yellow jersey, and Yorke for his 'huge contribution to the development of para-cycling' and as a 'well-respected coach'. And neither man is less or more important than the other for having helped to push the sport forward, in all its guises.

'Tony was more pleased to be in the Hall of Fame than he was to get his OBE,' says Gretel. 'He was thrilled with being named in the Hall of Fame, and I remember there being a huge dinner for that in Manchester – a wonderful dinner.'

The 1982 road-race world championships at the Goodwood motor circuit, near Chichester, in West Sussex, were no exception when it came to wonderful dinners. As somewhat of a local, Gretel was roped in to help organize a special dinner at Goodwood House.

'Back at our house, we had various people who were staying with us for the world championships, while I was over at a hotel near Goodwood,' she explains. 'We had this caravanette at the time, which was good for carrying bikes and lots of people, but I begged Tony not to turn up at this dinner in it, having told him that there were butlers who were going out the front and opening the doors for people. So I was humiliated when he turned up in this ruddy caravanette and people virtually fell out. I was so cross. But it was another wonderful meal.'

When people refer to Mark Cavendish's 2011 Worlds road-race win as the first since Tom Simpson's in 1965, it's a little like calling Andy Murray the first Wimbledon champion since Fred Perry in 1936, and forgetting Virginia Wade in 1977. In the women's cycling world championships, there were wins for both Beryl Burton in 1967, and then Mandy Jones on home soil there at Goodwood in 1982, who won alone by 10 seconds from second-placed Maria Canins of Italy and Belgium's Gerda Sierens in third.

'There were big crowds,' says Gretel, 'and you were supposed to pay to get on the circuit, but people were arriving from all directions, over the fields, and there were people put in prison overnight for writing on the roads. The police here didn't know it was allowed on the Continent!'

Gretel always attended the track national championships, too, 'which were always held at Leicester back then, organized by Benny Foster.'

Just twelve years before the Goodwood road Worlds, Foster had organized the world championships in Leicester, in 1970, which in those days had the road and track events at the same venue. The road race was held at the Mallory Park motor circuit, while the track events were at Saffron Lane.

If Mick Bennett and Alan Rushton are considered the 'Mr Cyclings' of recent times, Benny Foster was the original holder of the title before them. In his autobiography, *The Benny Foster Story*, it's clear how proud he was to bring such an important event to Leicester – the first time the Worlds had been held in Britain since 1922, when they were in Liverpool – even if he went a tad over budget.

'Sure I get worried about the cost . . . but in this game you've got to have the courage of your convictions,' he told the *Sheffield Morning Telegraph*, according to his book. He was eight times over budget, spending £1.5 million rather than the projected £186,000.

Like Tony Yorke, Benny Foster is named in the Hall of Fame, and received an OBE, too.

'We got a letter around June 2009 saying that Tony was being considered for an OBE, and would he accept it, and at first he said no,' says Gretel. 'I told him that he had to be joking, but, well, he was a socialist, wasn't he?'

Gretel persuaded him to accept it, but as there were only three 'guest' tickets, a tough decision had to be made.

Their son, David, had to be there, Gretel decided, as he'd helped his father with the Paralympic teams, and there was no way she was going to go in place of either of her daughters. 'Plus they'd all have longer to remember it than me anyway,' Gretel smiles.

Not that she stayed away entirely: 'I was at the gates of Buckingham Palace with other family members, and the police were trying to stop us coming in, but they couldn't control us!' she laughs. 'It was a lovely day.'

Yorke's work in para-cycling came about quite unexpectedly.

'He got a call from a lad called Nigel Capewell, who asked him why there were no disabled people in cycling, and Tony said that it was a good question, and set up a meeting with him,' explains Gretel. 'From that meeting, Tony and my son David set up the first disabled cycling team in this country and, every month I think it was, Tony used to write a report for the BCF, and started adding a paragraph about disabled cycling, although they weren't so interested in it then. Tony used to go abroad with them, and they all used to have to pay their own way in those days to go to world championships and things.'

When the possibility of Lottery funding came along in the late 1990s, however, 'Tony was the next best thing to sliced bread, because to get Lottery money you had to include the disabled'.

Yorke was officially made the manager of the para-cycling team, and suddenly there was money in the sport.

At that time, although para-cycling was part of British Cycling, internationally it came under the International Paralympic Committee (IPC), explains Gretel. Yorke soon became chairman of the IPC Cycling Committee, and began to push for change.

'His one aim in life became to take it out of the IPC's auspices and put it with the UCI, as he felt that it should be under the same umbrella as cycling,' says Gretel. 'He resigned from being GB manager, and for six years threw everything at trying to get them into the UCI. Once he did, in 2007, he retired. But it was Nigel Capewell, who's now a cycling coach [with Lichfield CCC, having represented the GB para-cycling team for thirteen years] who instigated the whole thing.'

Her husband simply threw himself wholeheartedly into everything he did. 'And I was just there to do all the back-room organizing!'

But I'm left with the distinct impression that she wouldn't have wanted it any other way.

Tony Doyle was also a passionate advocate of Six-Day racing. This had become a hugely popular spectator sport in the last decade or so of the nineteenth century, with the first event of its kind held in 1878 at the Agricultural Hall in Islington, on Upper Street in north London, which is today the Business Design Centre.

Riders would race for a set time of between 14 and 18 hours per day, over six days, watched by enthusiastic crowds in the stands. Although riders could take regular breaks for food and rest, the 'clock' was always ticking, and the winning riders would have completed distances well into the thousands of miles by the time the six days were up.

Racing time was limited to 16 hours per day during that first Six in Islington, and the event was won by Sheffield's Bill Cann, who on his penny-farthing covered 1,060 miles.

Reports from the day show that it was as much about spectators and the media enjoying each competitor's riding style and handling of their bicycle, which in the early years were all penny-farthings, as it was about their out-and-out speed, although riders taking 'centuries' – milestone distances of 100 miles – were cheered as enthusiastically as when a cricketer scores 100 runs.

By 1879, Six-Days were being held in Birmingham and Hull as well as the capital, and by the following year had spread all over the country – to Dundee, Glasgow and Edinburgh, Leeds, Newcastle, Sunderland, Wolverhampton and York, to name just some of the cities hosting the events, which were usually held on temporary indoor tracks rather than exposed to the elements at one of the numerous outdoor velodromes.

This style of indoor racing died out in Britain during the first quarter of the twentieth century, but then returned to Wembley in the 1930s and again in the '60s and '70s as the beer-sponsored 'Skol Six'. As a child, Tony Doyle had been to watch the Skol Six at Wembley, and had wanted to race a Six-Day ever since. And in 1980, that's what he did, taking to the Wembley boards for what was Britain's last-ever Six. At that time, in the rest of Europe, the

Six-Day scene was in good shape, with money to be made, providing you were prepared to put up with tough working conditions.

'I was thrown in at the deep end, and that first winter I rode nine Sixes, so it was a real baptism of fire. It really was a tough apprenticeship for those first few years, as you weren't given any favours by "the establishment". It was really only when you started making their legs ache that they accepted you.'

But Doyle was prepared to test himself in the world of Six-Day racing; no British rider had ever given it a go over a number of seasons, and Doyle wanted to see how far he could progress. His main partner – the Six-Days are raced by teams of two – was Australian Danny Clark, but Doyle also rode what he thinks was around ten Sixes with Gary Wiggins – Bradley's father.

'Gary was a very tough Aussie who rode very hard, trying to break into the higher echelons of the Six-Day world, like me. We rode quite a bit together and won the Bremen Six in 1985,' says Doyle. 'There wasn't a Madison world championships then, but the unofficial world title was the European Championships, and we won that together, in 1984. Even though he was Australian, he was still allowed to ride!'

Doyle's 1988 winter season was his best so far.

'I rode five Six-Days with Danny, and we won each one!' says Doyle, who headed into the '89 season in excellent form, determined to do even better again, but crashed heavily on the fourth night of the Munich Six.

'I ended up on the concrete in the track centre, and was in a coma after that, with multiple fractures,' explains Doyle. 'But broken bones heal; it was the head injury that was most worrying, as they really didn't know what the outcome was going to be.'

Doyle remained in a coma for ten days, and was read the last rites. But, showing signs of recovery, he was then flown back to the UK, to RAF Northolt, and taken to Charing Cross Hospital in London. 'I spent six or seven weeks in a neurological ward, and then another two months in a rehabilitation centre, where I had to have speech therapy and learn to walk again.'

Doyle explains his story very matter-of-factly; clearly it was far from an easy time.

'I was very, very lucky,' he says.

Doyle returned to Munich, and visited the intensive-care unit at the hospital that had cared for him a year earlier. The head of the ward recognized his family, but not Doyle, as he looked so different compared to when he'd been fighting for his life in a coma.

'Once they saw it was me, they said, "Oh, it's so great to see you've come back from London to Munich to say hello to us!" And I said, "Well, I'm back here for the Six-Day." And they said, "Fantastic that you're back here to see your old teammates and comrades!" And I said, "No – I'm back here racing," and they couldn't believe it.'

And then he only went and won it, didn't he?

Although it was a fairytale ending in Munich, a crash at the Zurich Six in 1994 did it for Doyle.

'I was brought off by a couple of German riders – Uwe Messerschmidt and Markus Hess – and broke my back. I came back and rode a couple of races after that, but I was in too much pain when pushing hard, so I ended up retiring in 1995. I was thirty-six at the time, and I probably would have carried on for another five years given the choice, but I decided to stop rather than ending up a cripple.

'I'd had a very successful career, and a great time as a pro rider, but after my retirement I could see how out of touch the BCF was with their membership,' says Doyle. 'It was very much a blazer brigade at that time: a "them and us" situation. I was still young, and a club cyclist at heart, and had never lost touch with my roots. So, having realized what dissent and dissatisfaction there was amongst the membership, I decided I wanted to put something back into the sport, and put my name forward to become president of the British Cycling Federation.'

In late 1995, Doyle stood against incumbent president Ian Emmerson, who has been the organizer of the Lincoln Grand Prix since 1963 and who was also instrumental in getting the Manchester Velodrome built – and Doyle won.

'My first two letters of congratulations were from the then UCI president Hein Verbruggen, and from Tour de France director Jean-Marie Leblanc,' Doyle recalls. 'They thought it was fantastic that the job had gone to a pro rider who had just retired, and who was prepared to roll up his sleeves and get involved at the grass-roots level of the sport.'

It should have been the start of a new era.

'However, the old guard wouldn't accept the new guard,' Doyle says, diplomatically, remaining calm and measured throughout our conversation, despite talking about a period of his life that was clearly very traumatic.

The board opposed the new president, even though he'd been voted in by the membership. At the time of his election, Doyle did some consultancy work with Alan Rushton's company, Sport for Television, which was involved in the organization of various BCF races and championships at the time. It was used against Doyle – a supposed clash of interests. In turn, various board members' own companies had strong links with the federation. It was an almighty mess, and it dragged on through most of 1996.

Former *Cycling Weekly* journalist Keith Bingham remembers the time well.

'Doyle's ticket was to address those things that the BCF wasn't go-ahead enough to address,' says Bingham. 'The membership were fed up and wanted change, at a time when the membership was in decline. Doyle's election in '95 was the beginning of the end of the old BCF, but they decided they couldn't work with Doyle, for whatever reason, and they rejected him and wanted him removed.

Yet they were in breach of the BCF's own constitution because he'd been elected by the membership.'

Doyle continues his story: 'The board stood firm, and tried to oust me, but I wasn't moving. They tried to apply so much pressure that I'd walk away. The board said prior to an extraordinary general meeting that if I got reaffirmed they would all resign. So I got reaffirmed – I was there by the members' choice – but none of the board walked.'

Despite having stood his ground for so long, Doyle left his post of his own accord, pursued the case on a civil basis, and won.

The UK Sports Council, having been alerted to allegations of mismanagement, ordered an audit of the BCF's finances, the upshot of which was that the BCF board was changed. Peter King came in as chief executive – he was later awarded the CBE in the same Birthday Honours List as Tony Yorke was awarded his OBE, in June 2009 – and Brian Cookson became the new president, a role he remained in until leaving to become UCI president in 2013.

Bob Howden took the helm as president of British Cycling in late 2013. He had already been on the board for the previous thirteen years, and between 2005 and 2012 was the organizer of the Ryedale Grand Prix: part of BC's Premier Calendar race series (rechristened the Elite Road Series for 2014).

Ian Drake took over from Peter King as British Cycling's chief executive as of the 2009 season. Drake was a former teacher, and masterminded British Cycling's schools programme – a 'playground to podium pathway', introduced in 2000, which saw British Cycling coaches heading into schools and uncovering, and then developing, latent talent, such as 2012 Olympic team pursuit gold medallist Dani King, and 2008 and 2012 Olympic team pursuit gold medallist Ed Clancy.

Both Drake and Howden were able to take the reins of what had become a very successful sports federation, light years away from the turmoil of the mid- to late 1990s, when it was on the verge of collapse. No one will ever know whether it was the new 'blazers', the subsequent injection of Lottery funding, the new coaches and staff, or 'simply' a talented batch of athletes coming along at the right time that made all the difference to British Cycling's fortunes. One would suspect that it was a combination of everything, but British Cycling was changed for the better, and, whichever way you look at it, it was because Doyle had come along and shaken things up.

Doyle moved on to bigger and better things. Having helped to resurrect the Tour of Britain in 2004, in 2013 Doyle did the same for another institution of British bike-racing history: the Milk Race. He managed to secure the backing of the Dairy Council, having sold them on the legacy of the old Milk Race and cycling's elevated status in Britain since the last edition in 1993.

Although it's just a one-day race for now – with both a men's and women's race – the first edition was a great success, and it returned in May 2014 for its second edition, again in Nottingham, with its cycling heritage as the home of Raleigh bicycles.

Doyle's keen to bring Six-Day racing back to the UK, too, and clearly he'd be the man for the job. The format remains massively popular in Europe, and in Germany, Belgium and the Netherlands in particular. But despite Britain's recent track-racing successes, and the very well supported, and similar, Revolution track-racing series, Six-Day racing has yet to make a return to British shores. It can surely only be a matter of time before it does.

Doyle came close in 2008, but the economic climate meant he wasn't able to get it off the ground.

'Of course, we didn't have a permanent track in London then,' he points out, 'so the possibility of doing something is more realistic than ever.'

9

THROUGH PAUL WATSON'S EYES

While the Tour de France is, quite rightly, the focal point of the international cycling calendar, with supporting roles for the other two grand tours – of Italy and Spain – and for the end-of-season world championships, there are other races that attract a certain type of fan and rider: the one-day Classics.

These tend to be 'place-to-place' events, usually, although not always, linking two big cities, although traffic considerations mean that these days starts and finishes are often some distance outside a city, and sometimes in a completely different town or city altogether. Paris–Roubaix, for example, starts in Compiègne – about 50 miles north-east of Paris.

They're spread throughout the year, but the bulk of the main one-day races come in spring; and spring in the Netherlands, northern France and Belgium, where most of the events take place, can often be pretty punishing, weather-wise, only adding to the mystique and appeal. These are the races for the hard men – and indeed for the hardy spectator, although there seems to be no shortage of those in Belgium and the surrounding countries.

There have been mixed results for British riders at the Classics over the years. It all started so well with Paris–Rouen – the very first one-day race, and the first road race of any kind – in 1869, which was won by James Moore. George Pilkington Mills then won the first Bordeaux–Paris in 1891, and Arthur Linton won the same event in 1896. But it would be another sixty-five years until a Briton next won a Classic: 1961, when Tom Simpson won the Tour of Flanders, one of the five 'Monuments'.

Paris–Rouen and Bordeaux–Paris (which Simpson also won, in 1963) are now long gone, but the five Monuments are the biggest, best and most revered one-day Classics of them all. They start with Milan–San Remo in March, before the following month sees the back-to-back frenzy of the Tour of Flanders, Paris–Roubaix and Liège–Bastogne–Liège; Italy then rounds off the season with the Tour of Lombardy in October.

Brian Robinson's third place at the 1957 Milan–San Remo had been heralded by *Cycling* magazine as Britain's best Classics result since Linton's Bordeaux–Paris win, but then along came Simpson to win first Flanders, then Milan–San Remo in 1964, followed by the Tour of Lombardy in 1965.

When, in 2009, Mark Cavendish became only the second Briton to win Milan–San Remo – one of the longest, toughest Classics, with a series of climbs that come close to the finish in the Mediterranean resort – it had come off the back of both media and his fellow riders having written him off for such a race. That, however, had been part of the plan.

'At the Eroica [an Italian one-day race in early March, now called the Strade Bianche], I made sure I got dropped with a few teammates around me, and I made sure it was on TV,' Cavendish told *Cycle Sport* magazine after his victory. 'I knew people would look at it and say, "Well, he's not going to win Milan–San Remo climbing like that. People think I can't climb. Tom Boonen [a rival at the time, but a teammate at Omega Pharma-Quick Step in 2014] said I couldn't get over a railway bridge,' Cavendish said. 'I wanted them to keep thinking that. I needed them to keep thinking that.'

But following the attention heaped on Great Britain's track stars at the Beijing Olympics in 2008, suddenly here was Cavendish – already known as a Tour de France stage winner – joining the world of Tom Simpson as a Classics man. Simpson had been the last male British rider to win the road-race world championships, in 1965, the year after his Milan–San Remo victory. Would Cavendish now take aim at the world championships? We'd find out later that the Worlds road title was already in his sights.

After Simpson's death at the Tour de France in 1967, Barry Hoban took up the mantle as Britain's main hope in the Classics, finishing second at Paris–Tours later that year, third at Liège–Bastogne–Liège in 1969, and third at Paris–Roubaix in 1972. They were barren years, results-wise, following Hoban's win at Belgian one-day race Ghent–Wevelgem in 1974, but Graham Jones's excellent second place at Het Volk in 1982 was a much-needed British return to Classics form.

It would be another four years again before Joey McLoughlin's fourth place at Amstel Gold, in 1986, but then in 1987 came Paul Watson's sixth place at the Flèche Wallonne in Belgium, and less than two weeks later Malcolm Elliott took third at Amstel Gold: the first, and still the only, British podium finish at the Dutch Classic.

Scoring phenomenal results in such quick succession was a major milestone in British bicycle-racing history. But what made them extra special was that McLoughlin, Watson and Elliott had achieved them while riding for a British team.

ANC–Halfords – the little British team with the big heart – had come good, and suddenly appeared capable of keeping pace with the big boys. So when the team received an invite to the 1987 Tour de France, it looked as though their place in the big league was assured, and that a significant step forward had been made in British sport.

Team spirit was excellent; morale was a different matter. You didn't have to look far behind the curtain, or scratch very deeply below the veneer, to realize that this was a team run on a shoe-string, with wages going unpaid and riders not even having enough team kit.

Right from the beginning of the 1987 season, travel arrange-ments left a little to be desired, too, as Watson demonstrated – or, rather, the rest of his team demonstrated – when he was left standing at the services at Newport Pagnell on the M1, and they sailed on by. He swears to this day that he was there (the team said he wasn't) but, either way, Watson missed his lift down to the south of France, where ANC–Halfords were to kick off their season.

'This was before mobile phones, and I think they maybe just overshot – and then carried on,' he explains, laughing about it now.

Not that anyone was laughing at the time. 'Luckily' Shane Sutton's visa hadn't been up to date, so Watson met his Australian teammate in London, where he'd been sorting it out, and the two of them were able to share a car, and a drive through the night, to the south of France, arriving at three in the morning.

Team manager Phil Griffiths – a five-time winner of the British Best All-Rounder and a silver medallist at the 1974 Commonwealth Games road race – was still furious, and threw some kit at Watson.

'I'd been told that my race bike would be ready for me, but to bring my training bike, too, for some reason,' Watson says. 'They hadn't put my bike together, though, and so I had to use this old Motobécane training bike, which I'd at least removed the mudguards from.'

It wasn't the nicest bike ever, apparently.

'You wouldn't go to the shops on it today,' is how Watson describes it.

He was furious on the start line of their first race: a long drive through the night, bed at 3 a.m., up at 7 a.m., tired, on a rubbish bike . . . 'It was the worst start to the season, ever!'

So when a break went, Watson knew what to do.

'I just drove it. It was like hitting a punchbag, trying to get my anger out of my system,' he explains. 'Anyway, next thing I know we've got a five-minute lead, which meant that Griffo had to come up to me, and talk to me and be polite.

'"Would you like a drink, or something to eat?"

'I was just, like, "Fuck off!"' Watson laughs. 'But then we stayed away – and I got third!'

He's not even entirely sure which race it was now, but, looking at his results, it must have been the Grand Prix d'Ouverture La Marseillaise – the 'opening race' of the French season.

On the start line at the following race, probably the Etoile de Bessèges, a couple of days later, Watson could feel someone looking at him. 'It was [Dutch star and 1978 world champion] Gerrie Knetemann. He then looked at my bike – still my old one – and then looked at me again. And then at my bike again. All the paint was flaking off.'

Watson puts on his best Dutch accent.

'"You can't ride this, eh!" Knetemann said to me.

'I said: "Why?"

'He said: "Look at it! Seriously, you can't ride this!"

'And I said: "Mate, it's the only bike I've got."

'He and his other mates almost backed away; as a team, we were kind of there for their amusement anyway whenever we turned up. They didn't really know who we were.

'But, later in the race, Knetemann went off up the road, and I went storming up next to him, and I was smashing through, and he was going, "Strong boy, eh!? Strong boy, eh!? Who's the strong boy!?"

'That was pretty funny.'

*

Next up was Paris–Nice, in March. The races were coming thick and fast, and Watson was already beginning not to enjoy himself. 'The thing is, we were just so naïve,' he admits. 'We didn't know about all the different race programmes riders were on; we were just riding everything.'

At one point in the race, he found himself struggling to hold the wheel in front, and teetered on the edge of disappearing out of the back of the bunch entirely.

'No one had attacked or anything; the race was just getting faster and faster, and I was just in a spin. I looked over, and there was Malc, coming out of the back at the same time.'

Snap. The sound of the elastic going.

'We started working together, to try not to get eliminated, but luckily this police motorbike helped us out, and towed us a bit to help us keep inside the time limit, and we finished.'

Elliott told Watson that if they hadn't been together, he probably wouldn't have made it. 'And we thought, "Christ, what's going on?" I think I finished last and he finished second to last.'

But at least they finished – that was the main thing, and it would have been even more important had ANC–Halfords been a big enough team to own the latest form of team transport.

'The ADR team had turned up to Paris–Nice with this big bus, which was a new thing then,' says Watson. 'But as the race wore on, all their riders were packing, and in the end there was one rider left on this huge bus on his own.' Watson laughs at the memory; having a joke about things like that helped get him through the race.

Watson and his teammates may have been taking a hammering, 'but we got fitter and fitter, and sort of rose to the challenge'.

At Flèche Wallonne, in April, Watson managed to get into the decisive break.

'I was working my way up, and at one point the bunch just sort of moved across to one side, and left this opening, and, because I was coming through with quite a bit of speed, the next thing I knew I was off the front with Yvon Madiot and Eric Boyer.'

At first, Watson was just pleased simply to be there, animating the race.

'I was just thinking, "If I can stay away for the next lap, that will be good,"' he remembers. 'We had this Belgian guy, Eddy Wouters – we used to call him "Muddy Waters" – as our manager that day, and he came alongside me in the team car at one point, just laughing and shaking his head, wondering what on earth I was doing there.'

Nothing like a bit of faith from the management.

'But then we actually stayed away the next time up the Mur,' says Watson, referring to the Mur de Huy, Flèche Wallonne's iconic climb, which is tackled three times by the race, with the finish line, cruelly, at the top. 'And I'll tell you what: we were going at a right old speed, and we dropped Boyer, and I could tell Madiot was struggling a bit, too.'

However, they were joined on the last lap by Rolf Gölz, Claude Criquielion, Stephen Roche, and Jean-Claude Leclercq, who ended up winning the race.

'When Leclercq attacked, I went off the back, but then managed to get back to them,' says Watson. 'But then I broke a spoke, maybe five miles before the final climb, so I flicked the quick release on the brake open, to stop it hitting, and just carried on.'

Sixth place at Flèche Wallonne made Watson kind of a big deal.

'Everything changed a bit after that. Suddenly the bunch gave me a bit of respect,' he explains, 'and the team was looked at a bit differently – especially when a couple of weeks later Malc did what he did at Amstel Gold.'

The following year, when Watson signed with Criquielion's Hitachi squad, the Belgian asked if Watson had been working with Roche that day at Flèche.

'I said, "No, not at all," and he told me that he thought I had been, and that he would have paid me to try to pull back Declerq otherwise,' Watson laughs. 'And I told him that I would have gladly done that, but nobody had asked me!'

Watson admits that it was a pretty good programme of races that ANC–Halfords 'enjoyed' in 1987. 'And at one point, we were ranked the sixth-best team in the world because of me, Malc and Adrian [Timmis, who won a stage of the Midi Libre in June].'

The team rode the Milk Race in May, where Elliott won five stages and the overall, and Watson finished fourth. It was another hugely impressive result from Elliott, proving that he was ready for the next level. Until Watson and Elliott's ANC teammate Joey McLoughlin had won the 1986 Milk Race, it had been dominated by riders from the Soviet Union. The last Briton to win it had been Bill Nickson in 1976. Now Elliott was taking on the Soviet sprinters and winning, almost at will.

But despite his fourth place overall, Watson was struggling.

'The next day we had to go to this stage race in France, and I just didn't want to go,' he recalls. 'I was absolutely exhausted from all the racing and travelling we'd been doing, crammed into team cars – no buses for us!'

Having had a break of just a day between one race and the next, Watson admits that he completely lost it once he found out that the first stage was 220 kilometres.

'I was effing and blinding and asking myself what I was doing there,' Watson says. 'I rode up alongside Malc, and I started saying, "Get off! Get off! Please, Malc, get off!" And he told me, "No, no – we'll be fine." He wasn't as highly strung as me.

'I think we went through three stages, bless him, with me telling him to "get off" all the time. I don't know why I wouldn't just quit on my own, but for some reason I wanted him to stop with me, which he wouldn't. I'd be complaining that it was too hot, too fast, too hilly . . . "Come on, Malc – get off, get off!"'

Eventually, Elliott gave in, and Watson briefed him on the plan. 'I said to him, "Right, we're coming into the next town, and if it goes right, we go left, and if it goes left, we go right – right?"'

'So we came into this town, and the race turned right, so we turned left', laughs Watson. 'And the plan was to just keep riding – to get anywhere, go somewhere, just not be in the race any more. So, the race went right, we went left,' Watson reiterates. 'And it was a dead end!'

He's almost crying with laughter now and, thanks to the way he's told it, so am I.

'We'd gone about 100 metres, and all the race motorbikes had gone right, but then some of the spectators started saying, "Oh my God, they've gone the wrong way!" which caused some of the motorbikes to decide that they'd better come back to get us, because we'd gone the "wrong way".

'We thought, "Shit!" and hid behind these cars,' Watson explains through the laughter. 'We were off our bikes, hiding behind two parked cars, and six or seven race officials came and found Malc and me just cowering, like two naughty schoolboys, and they were saying, "What are you doing? What are you doing?" And we had to say that we were really sorry, and then the team car turned up, and they were furious at us.'

Watson takes a moment to compose himself, having explained exactly how not to quit a race.

'It was so embarrassing, but at least we were able to go home.'

While Watson would end up doing just one more pro season, with Hitachi in 1988, Malcolm Elliott's racing career continued on an upward trajectory. Riding for Fagor in '88, he won the Kellogg's Tour of Britain and a stage at the Tour of Spain, where he also won two stages and the points jersey the following year, having shifted to the Teka team.

British riders had won stages at the Tour of Spain, or the Vuelta a España, before Elliott – Hoban took two wins there in 1964, Simpson two in 1967, and Robert Millar had won a stage en route to his second place overall in 1986 – but in winning the points jersey in 1989, Elliott became the first Briton to win one of the Vuelta's three main jersey competitions. It was a feat eventually matched by Mark Cavendish in 2010, when he equalled Elliott's three stage wins and went home with the points jersey.

Elliott became road-race national champion in 1993, and in the same year he moved to the US, where he was handsomely paid, riding for the Chevrolet–L.A. Sheriffs squad until 1996. These days, he's almost as well known for having made a comeback to the sport at the age of forty-one, in 2003, and having been able to continue to win at the highest domestic level. In 2011 he retired from racing again, for good this time.

Both Elliott and Watson made it on to ANC–Halfords' Tour de France squad in July 1987.

'It was the last thing we needed,' says Watson, who was, like the others, still completely exhausted. 'It was the last thing anyone on that team needed.'

The announcement that the team had been selected was to be made live on children's TV show *Blue Peter*. 'Gloria Hunniford's daughter, Caron Keating, was the presenter who told us we were in, and we just all looked at each other and were, like, "Oh, for f . . ."'

Quite rightly, she'd thought it would have been a dream come true. And it was exactly that for the team's owner, Tony Capper.

Capper had sold his ANC company – a haulage firm – in 1986, but retained the right to use the name and had negotiated a budget for the cycling team with the new owners. The trouble was, there was no money left by the time the team started the Tour.

'I think I had about two jerseys left, or perhaps one skinsuit and one jersey,' recalls Watson. 'Part of me simply didn't want to go, but I suppose part of me thought, "Well, you might never get another chance to ride the Tour again."'

Watson quit the race, completely spent, on stage six. There turned out to be nothing about his Tour experience that he enjoyed.

'Well, there was this groupie who'd turned up, unannounced, at the start in Berlin,' Watson says. 'She was from Holland, and had been chasing me all over Europe. She just walked in when we were having dinner, which really wasn't the time . . . I was about to do the Tour de France!'

The race, though, had just been all too much, says Watson. 'I had one jersey, I hadn't been paid, I was ill, and I'd already had talks with Hitachi about joining them. Even at the pre-race medical, they'd asked me if I was OK. They could tell my readings weren't good before I'd even started. Although that was the day after the groupie had visited.'

As for Capper, he simply disappeared later on at that year's Tour, and the team later folded.

'But I don't think we should be too hard on him,' says Watson. 'He was genuinely passionate about getting his team to the Tour de France, and his heart was in the right place. I did write to him to say thank you. He meant well, and had only worked on the advice he'd been given, so I said thanks for everything he did do; without him we wouldn't have had the opportunity.

'It was a shame it ended like it did. It felt a bit like being in a rock band that had imploded, or something. It should have been something really special but it went horribly wrong.'

Watson went to Thailand after quitting the Tour, and says he spent his time lying on the beach, and didn't touch a bike for about three months.

While ANC–Halfords struggled at that 1987 Tour, Stephen Roche flew. The Irishman overcame Spanish challenger Pedro Delgado to win by just 40 seconds in Paris, and while Irish eyes were smiling, quite a few British ones were, too.

In the absence of a British contender – and while appreciating the efforts of Robert Millar and Sean Yates, and Watson, Elliott, Graham Jones and Adrian Timmis on the ANC team – cycling fans in Britain got behind Roche in his ding-dong battle with Delgado. Thanks to his regular interviews with Phil Liggett and Paul Sherwen during the Channel 4 coverage, it seemed only natural that British fans should warm to the English-speaker in with a shot of winning the world's biggest bike race.

Roche's compatriot Sean Kelly was equally loved by British fans, perhaps even more so than Roche, and had been for years. Despite being a Classics man at heart – twice winning each of Milan–San Remo, Paris–Roubaix and Liège–Bastogne–Liège, and the Tour of Lombardy three times – Kelly could win anywhere. He won Paris–Nice seven times in a row between 1982 and 1988, and the green points jersey at the Tour de France four times, along with five stages. And, in 1988, he won the Tour of Spain outright.

But in 1987 Roche was the one everyone was talking about. He'd already won the Tour of Italy earlier in the season, and winning the Tour de France in the same year put him in an elite club. Only four riders had done it before him (Fausto Coppi, Jacques Anquetil, Eddy Merckx and Hinault) and only two riders have done it since: Miguel Indurain, in both 1992 and 1993, and Marco Pantani in 1998.

Having won the Giro and the Tour, could Roche now win the 'triple crown'? The term describes winning the triumvirate of the Giro, the Tour and the world championships in the same season, and only one rider had ever done that before.

'When you have just won the Giro and the Tour de France, nobody expects another performance in the world champion-ships,' Paul Kimmage wrote in his 1990 book, *A Rough Ride*. Kimmage, Martin Earley, Kelly and Roche made up the four-man

Irish team for those Worlds in Villach, Austria – the self-styled 'fab four'.

And how fabulous they were. Earley and Kimmage worked hard to keep the race together for Roche and Kelly, and when the team's two leaders made it into the select group that would duke it out for the rainbow jersey and the world title, most people's money would have been on Kelly. But Roche slipped the clutches of the lead group in the closing kilometres, then attacked from the remaining group of five with less than half a kilometre to go to beat defending champion Moreno Argentin of Italy and Spain's Juan Fernández. Kelly was fifth.

'He looked resplendent in his new rainbow jersey, but the magnitude of his achievement had not yet sunk in,' wrote Kimmage of meeting up with his teammate after the finish. 'He had done something that only one other man in the whole world had done. In winning the Tour of Italy, the Tour de France and the world championships in the same year he had equalled Eddy Merckx.'

Roche's son, Nicolas, now rides as a professional, and chooses to represent Ireland, when he could have chosen France – his mother's home country.

Dan Martin wouldn't have remembered his uncle's Tour win in 1987; he wasn't even a year old. Martin's English father, Neil, was a professional rider in the 1980s, while his mother, Maria, is Stephen Roche's sister.

Despite having grown up in Birmingham, and having become British junior road-race national champion in 2004, Dan chose to represent Ireland on the international stage, and today he and his cousin Nicolas are a force to be reckoned with, enjoying as much British support as their fathers did.

Martin won the 2013 Liège–Bastogne–Liège, and later won a stage of that year's Tour de France. Roche won a stage of the 2013 Tour of Spain, and went on to finish fifth overall.

Cycling is a sport of peaks and troughs – as a professional rider from one season to the next, from one week to the next, and one day to the next. Even from one moment to the next in a single race. The same goes for a nation's dominance. British cycling is on the crest of a wave right now, but for a long time it wasn't. In France they're still waiting for their first Tour winner since Bernard Hinault's fifth victory in 1985, while Irish cycling, thanks mainly to Roche and Kelly, had its day in the 1980s, and will do again – perhaps via Roche junior and Martin.

In between whiles, it's only natural that fans from one struggling nation will get behind a rider or riders from another. It's a little like the Eurovision Song Contest, when support is transferred to nations that have a similar culture, history or, more often than not, language.

It happened at the 1986 Tour, during the epic battle between Hinault and American Greg LeMond, and again at the 1989 Tour, during the epic battle between LeMond and France's Laurent Fignon: Brits tended, on the whole, to side with the English-speaker. And it happened again during Lance Armstrong's seven-year reign; now known to have been achieved fraudulently, of course, but at that time he drew in many British fans who now have their own British team and British riders to get behind and support.

But for many years in Britain, 'European' bike racing was the domain of the nerdy, alternative kid who was fascinated by the foreignness of it all: the colours of the national jerseys, and subsequently the foreign sponsors, plastered liberally and boldly across their heroes' kits. And you could choose your own hero – one you'd read an interview with and liked, or who seemed to you to look particularly fluid on a bike. Nationality didn't have to come into it.

It's similar, in a lot of ways, to Formula One: you can support a Scandinavian on a British team, or a Brit on an Italian team; the mix-and-match aspect of it all creates a true circus of nations, languages and cultures, and sport is all the richer for it.

In 1988, Paul Watson returned to the Continent for the Hitachi team launch in Belgium. If ANC–Halfords had been shambolic, then his new team was considerably more professional – although not the kind of 'professional' Watson was hoping they'd be.

'There had been all these stories floating around about what people were taking in 1987, and I knew what the amateurs were up to from when I'd raced in France as an amateur myself,' says Watson. 'But you didn't realize the level of it until you turned pro, and started to realize what was needed. Luckily, at ANC–Halfords, we wouldn't have even known where to get anything from, which was a blessing, really.

'The thing is,' Watson continues, 'I'm still sure that, in '87, there was talk of EPO. I'm certain of it . . . I know that can't really have been the case, but I'm sure it had come up in conversation at the time. Unless I've got the years wrong, but then I wasn't really around much later.'

The general consensus is that the use of EPO – erythropoietin, the performance-enhancing drug – only became widespread in the early-to-mid-1990s. Still, there was plenty of other stuff going on in the late eighties.

'When some of my new Hitachi teammates realized I wasn't taking anything, they were looking at me like I had two heads,' says Watson. 'It was more out of curiosity on their part than anything else.'

One of the riders Watson shared a room with decided to open his attaché case, which a lot of the riders seemed to own in those days, to show him what was what. 'And it wasn't sandwiches and spreadsheets in there. He was pulling out some scary stuff: pre-prepped syringes and boxes of stuff that would have a skull and crossbones on the packet. I didn't want to know about it.'

The really scary part of it was that most of it was self-administered, with doses taken through guesswork.

His room-mate, perhaps concerned that the language barrier was preventing Watson from taking the plunge, decided on some charades.

'This guy's going, "Pauly, Pauly – this one, this one," pretending to inject this particular syringe he was holding, and trying to explain that it was like vintage champagne. The needle was like a bloody lance.

'Then this rider held up a different one, and was trying to explain that it was for when you were finished – too tired to carry on. He lay down on the floor, showing me what exhaustion looked like, and then he said, "Like this!" and pretended to inject himself. "You put this in," he said, and then jumped up, shouting, "You're good again! You're good again!"'

Was Watson ever tempted to dope?

'I was tempted, and if I wasn't still so exhausted from the previous year, and if I'd already had good form, and if it was administered by a doctor that I trusted, who did blood tests and showed me what was what, then almost certainly I would have done it,' he admits. 'But in terms of getting a syringe off someone who was lying on the floor and jumping up at me and saying, "You're good again!" then no.

'The *soigneurs* used to go round with a bin liner at races to collect all the wrappings, ampoules and syringes from the riders, and then they'd drive out of town and it would get lobbed in a skip or something, away from the hotel. If you were the last room, that bin liner was full; there weren't just a few things at the bottom; it was full.'

Watson also says that he witnessed riders using some kind of oil-based product, although he still doesn't know what it was. 'It used to bubble up under the skin on their arse cheek, and make them quite stiff, so you'd see riders going up and down the corridors, trying to walk it off.

'I'm not saying I had better morals than anyone else, because it was what it was,' he says. 'But it just wasn't like anything was going to help me win.'

Watson tells of another teammate he roomed with: a *domestique*, like him, who was just finishing races, just getting through.

'After breakfast, he put four syringes in. I asked him what he was doing, and he was, like, "It's my job, eh?" But I was worried for him, and, after that, he felt uncomfortable, I think, and it wasn't done in front of me any more.

'They were all great guys, and I'm not saying they were all doing it,' says Watson. 'But I got about halfway through the season and just thought, "I don't want to do it any more. I don't want to have to take drugs." I didn't like anything about it.'

Watson left the team, and later that year talked to a *Guardian* journalist about what he'd seen.

'I wasn't saying that I'd done anything – I hadn't – but the BCF response to the resulting newspaper piece was to refuse to give me a racing licence,' says Watson, still frustrated about what happened. 'They said I was bringing the sport into disrepute.'

The sport was certainly pretty disreputable, but Watson had recovered by that point – at the start of the 1989 season – and wanted to return to professional cycling, as there was a chance that he'd get a new contract with a different team.

'I was fit again, and was able to run a sub-32-minute 10K, and had even been British duathlon champion, as I'd done some duathlons that winter,' says Watson. 'But the federation wouldn't give me a licence, so I was stuffed.'

Watson raced mountain bikes in the USA for some years after that: the new sport wasn't part of the UCI at first, so he didn't need a licence. He rode for, and then managed, the Marin team.

'It was brilliant,' he says. 'They always had a party both before the races and afterwards.'

Watson now owns a hotel in his home town, Milton Keynes, and also does photography and videography for the Gulf Racing motorsport team. He says it's funny now to see his former ANC–Halfords teammate, Shane Sutton, heading up the racing side of things at British Cycling.

'But he's such a motivator, and so straight-talking – no messing, no hidden agenda, it is how it is – so he's perfect for that job,' Watson says. 'And what a job he and Brailsford have done. You pinch yourself, don't you?'

Looking back, Watson nevertheless thinks he and his old colleagues did pretty well with what they had.

'When we were racing, we'd look up at all the big foreign stars. We were on the back foot before we'd even started. But now we are the stars; as a nation, we're leading the sport, and it's hard to believe. Cav, Wiggo, Ian Stannard . . . He's from Milton Keynes, you know,' Watson says, name-checking Stannard, who won the Het Nieuwsblad one-day Classic in 2014.

If he had his time again, Watson says that, like Stannard, he would definitely specialize as a Classics man.

'Oh yeah – I could only ever really get it out in one day,' he says, then adds: 'The Tour wasn't my thing at all.'

10

HARRODS, HERETY AND EMERGENCY MEASURES

In 1982, two more British graduates of the legendary ACBB amateur club had joined the professional ranks in Europe: Sean Yates signed for Peugeot and John Herety went to Coop–Mercier.

But while Yates went on to ride for Fagor, 7-Eleven and Motorola, to wear the yellow jersey at the 1994 Tour de France, and to managerial stints at a slew of European pro teams, Herety's career in Europe was cut short in his third year when he began suffering from chronic fatigue syndrome.

'I was spending the best part of fifteen hours a day in bed,' Herety remembers, 'but no one really knew what was wrong with me in those days, and in fact these were the days of "yuppie flu", so it was kind of lumped in with that!'

The Coop–Mercier team was actually very understanding, though, says Herety, and manager Jean-Pierre Danguillaume – who had ridden as a pro for the Peugeot team in the seventies – in particular.

'He was a really nice guy, and I'd been living with his parents, which meant that I was just around the corner from him when he needed a replacement rider for Paris–Nice,' Herety explains. 'The French rider Jean-Louis Gauthier had perhaps broken his wrist, or broken something, so he couldn't start. I was a bit sick at the time, but Danguillaume didn't want to start the race a rider short, and asked me just to see how I got on, and said that I could get off after a couple of days if I needed to. But I carried on, like an idiot, and basically put myself into a box. Afterwards, Danguillaume kind of blamed himself for having got me to race while I wasn't feeling well, but it was partially self-inflicted.'

Today, as manager of the Rapha Condor JLT team, Herety says he takes the responsibility of making such decisions away from his riders. 'It's a lot easier for them, mentally, if you're the one who tells them to get off; it's not their fault if you tell them that that's enough, and try to safeguard them,' he says. 'So it was a lesson learned from when I was a pro – albeit a hard one.'

Herety returned to the UK racing scene the following season, and joined the Ever Ready squad, managed by Mick Bennett.

'The money was very good, but the standard of racing, compared to the Continent, was like dropping down a couple of divisions, in footballing terms, to be quite honest.'

In 1986, Herety signed for the Percy Bilton outfit, riding there alongside Bob Downs, who'd won gold for England in the team time trial at the 1982 Commonwealth Games, and Neil Martin, father of current Garmin pro Dan Martin.

'Len Willett was the manager, and what a great character he was,' laughs Herety. 'He was brilliant. And then the chief executive of Percy Bilton – a civil engineering firm – Ron Groom, was passionate about cycling. He ensured we always had the best equipment, as soon as it came out, by paying for it all himself. He was a very formidable character, and would chain-smoke Dunhill King Size cigarettes all day, lighting the next one with the one he was putting out.'

But Herety continued to get sick, and asked his GP, who was

also a cyclist, whether he thought he might be causing any long-term damage by continuing to race.

'"I won't tell you to retire," he told me, "but if you had an opportunity to do something else, then you should seriously consider it."'

It was around then that Willett, who also had a separate full-time job, got in touch and asked Herety whether he fancied being the team's rider-manager. 'And I told him, "No – just the manager bit!"' says Herety, who retired halfway through the 1988 season, and shadowed Willett at that year's Kellogg's Tour of Britain and for the rest of the year.

Herety was at the helm for the '89 season, but a number of sponsors pulled out at the end of the year, including Percy Bilton, so he kept his oar in by helping to manage a number of other teams in the years that followed, and also worked with Chris Boardman's business manager, Peter Woodworth, and his Adidas-SciCon team in the late 1990s, which included a young Bradley Wiggins, Paul Manning – who won Olympic gold as part of the team pursuit squad in Beijing, and is now a coach with British Cycling – and Yvonne McGregor.

Herety got to know Boardman's coach, Peter Keen, well during that period, which led to his becoming the national road-race team manager once Keen masterminded British Cycling's World Class Performance Plan (WCPP) in 1997, with funding coming via the National Lottery through UK Sport, which back then was known as the UK Sports Council.

According to UK Sport, British Cycling received £5.4 million ahead of the 2000 Sydney Olympics, which rose to £8.6 million for the Athens Games four years later, although this was only for the elite 'Podium'-level riders. The amount awarded then jumped to more than £22 million for the Beijing Games, where the GB team enjoyed unprecedented success on both the road and track, and that figure includes funding for the entire programme, including medical and sports-science support. Further funds were granted for the period 2009–13, when British Cycling received over £26 million, while the Paralympic funding for Beijing had been £1.8 million.

Such a large injection of cash into a sport that had pretty much been run on a shoestring prior to 1997 would soon see the sport reap the rewards, results-wise, but what was it like to be a part of the British Cycling set-up back in the late nineties when the money first rolled in?

'Not nice!' says Herety, surprisingly. He pauses for a moment, then says it again.

'I was seen as very much a road man, and part of the road programme,' Herety explains, 'whereas the WCPP was all about the track. That was where the most medals had come from in the past, and that was what we were therefore going to concentrate on – which I totally bought into, totally believed in, and still do to this day.'

The problem, explains Herety, was that the then-current crop of top British road pros, who he knew extremely well, such as 1993 Milk Race champion Chris Lillywhite and John Tanner, the British national road-race champion in 1999 and 2000, were not going to get funded. With the UCI doing away with the concept of separate 'pro' and 'amateur' classes for championship events, instead introducing the 'open' classes and the 'under-23 [years old]' in 1996, British Cycling were unwilling to plough money into helping the more established road riders.

'We managed to get funding for the under-23s on the road,' says Herety, who was also managing them, 'but that was tough on the older riders, so it was a difficult time.'

The Lottery-funded under-23 programme was, however, says Herety, 'a disaster', as he continued to simply take his riders to the same races they'd always gone to, with little seen in the way of improvement. The one shining light was Charly Wegelius, whose results in 1999 included finishing second at the European time-trial championships and third in the under-23 Liège–Bastogne–Liège, while he also won the under-23 national road-race championships.

Almost six hours into the 1997 road-race world championships, Matt Stephens was feeling rather hungry. The Englishman was part of an eight-man British team riding the event in San Sebastián, in Spain, and, with two laps to go, Stephens and team leader Max Sciandri were the only two members of the squad left in the race.

'I was in this group of about twenty or twenty-five riders, and Max was in the group in front, so I was there in case he punctured and needed my wheel or anything,' remembers Stephens. 'Although I wasn't exactly comfortable, I was riding OK, and was hoping for a solid finish – maybe top 50.' Few riders are ever comfortable at the Worlds road race: often the longest race day on the calendar, run over 266 kilometres in this instance.

Herety was the manager that day, and laughs about the stress the team went through ahead of the race to ensure that Sciandri's trade-team manager, Marc Madiot, didn't catch him using a pair of ultra-light carbon wheels built by German brand Lightweight rather than his Française des Jeux-team-supplied wheels, which meant swapping them over each time Madiot came to see Sciandri in the British pen. (Even at world championships when representing their national teams, riders are obliged to use the same equipment supplied to them by their usual professional squads, although these days teams are slightly more relaxed about it.)

Stephens, despite being in the mix with the world's top professionals in the new 'open' road-race category, was still officially only an amateur, with a full-time job back in the UK at Marks & Spencer. But here, in the heat of battle, with just a couple of laps to go, it made no difference; he was hungry, and in danger of collapsing completely if he didn't get something to eat soon.

He dropped back to talk to Herety in the team car, but he didn't have any food, either.

'Shit.'

A brief rummage around the car, however, turned up a few cartons of a citrus-flavoured energy drink. 'It was the kind of stuff you could use to clean your car, probably with relative success,' grins Stephens. It wouldn't have been his first choice, but it would have to do in order to keep the wolf from the door. It was down the hatch with a couple of them, with the third stuffed into Stephens's jersey pocket for later.

After a quarter of an hour, the fuel began to take effect.

'I started to get this feeling in the pit of my stomach,' Stephens says. 'The picture in my mind's eye was of a cauldron bubbling . . .'

Another ten minutes passed, and Stephens was feeling increasingly uncomfortable.

'I was having really bad stomach cramps, and it was extremely painful. I couldn't get out of the saddle any more, and, despite there being two climbs on the circuit, I was having to stay in the saddle and clench my arse cheeks.

'Bear in mind that this was a relatively high standard of cycling,' Stephens smiles, with more than a hint of understatement, 'so it was quite a feat to stay in the group while clenching my arse.'

Stephens recalls his distress: the sharp spasms in his gut were suggesting that he should probably stop riding. 'I might as well be quite graphic: my rectum was spasming. I was managing to keep things at bay, but I dropped back to John and said, "John, I need a shit," and he looked at me completely blankly as if I was an absolute idiot, and just shrugged.'

Just finishing the world championships would be an achievement, but attempting to answer such an urgent call of nature so late in the race was never going to help. In addition, the fact that the race was on a circuit meant that there were people lining the entire route.

'I really needed a turd, but there was nowhere to stop, both because of the crowds and the fact that there were advertising hoardings – solid barriers – everywhere.'

Fruitless though he knew it was, Stephens scanned the barriers, desperately searching for somewhere – anywhere – he could stop, having broken into a cold sweat. 'I was clammy, and my stomach was in knots, but I was still managing to hold on to the tail end of that group I was with. It got to the point where I knew that, within a minute, something rather explosive was going to happen if I didn't dismount.

'I thought, "Right, this is it: I've got to have a shit."'

Stephens slammed on his brakes.

'I think I did quite a good skid, actually,' he says, with absolutely zero hint of any pun being intended. The team car pulled to a halt behind him. In the back, the mechanic found a brand-new car sponge, which he handed to Stephens, who by then no longer knew – or cared – where he was.

Stephens got off his bike, and threw off his GB jersey.

'I pulled down my bib shorts – always a bit of a tangle; precious seconds were lost – and then unceremoniously squatted in the middle of the road and did an almighty turd.'

It was, he remembers, incredibly embarrassing, but also a blessed relief.

'I turned to see this immense Mr Whippy on the tarmac, then amazingly managed to wipe my bum in this one deft movement with the car sponge, getting the angle of it just right in the cleft of my arse. I finished by shoving the sponge into the turd – like a Flake sticking out of it. I felt emotionally wrecked by that point, and my legs were like jelly,' Stephens says.

After such excitement, exhaustion crashed down on him like a wave. He managed to pull up his shorts, and picked up his jersey from the road. It was only then that he became aware of a low rumble, a building wall of sound on either side of him: the crowd, who had seen everything, were clapping and laughing, seemingly sharing in the rider's 'triumph'.

'They'd just watched me do this poo on their home roads, and they were cheering and taking photos, so there was nothing else for me to do than to give them a little wave back before riding on my way.'

Unfortunately for Stephens, his ride didn't last much longer. Left behind by the race, he rode to the pits area – where on-the-ground team staff are able to hand food and drink to their riders on each lap – and got off, 'disappointed, but feeling really quite poorly by then, and for a good hour and a half afterwards'.

The British squad that day was made up of Stephens, Sciandri, David Millar, Dan Smith, John Tanner, Julian Winn, Mark Walsham and Jeremy Hunt. None of them would finish, although Chris Boardman picked up Britain's sole medal at those Worlds, taking bronze in the time trial, behind France's Laurent Jalabert and Ukrainian Serhiy Honchar.

In the 1990s, when Team Sky was still just a glint in British Cycling's eye, domestic teams did their best to garner invitations to international events, and to dominate the domestic calendar sufficiently to retain their sponsors for the following season. It was an era often made up of a mishmash of promises, barely-there deals and budgets on the edge.

Matt Stephens was, really, it's not unfair to say, a journeyman pro, despite being one of the best riders in the UK at the time, and indeed officially an amateur for most of his career. Despite that, he's found himself having gone shoulder to shoulder with some of the sport's biggest names. 'I've raced with Roche, Kelly, LeMond, Indurain, Pantani, Armstrong . . . I've raced, competitively, in the eighties, nineties, noughties and the tens – or whatever you call them.'

So Stephens has no real regrets, and neither does he think about how different things might have been if he'd entered into top-level bike racing in the past few years, rather than in 1988.

'People often ask me that, but then I look at what I'm doing now,' he says, having left his job in the police force to work in the cycling media as a commentator and presenter. 'I had a great career with the police, and I'm also doing something I love now. I can ride my bike, and talk about bike riding and racing for a living. Plus, from having been in the sport for a long time, having had a degree of success . . . It's evolved and snowballed, and here I am.'

Here he is, one afternoon in September at Birmingham's NEC at The Cycle Show: the exhibition organized by Tour of Britain race director Mick Bennett.

Stephens talks with the kind of arresting authority that only a former policeman can have. Later in his cycling career, he turned to the police force to make a living, following stints at M&S and Morrisons. But in the early days of his racing career, working a full-time job was the furthest thing from his mind. He wanted to become a professional cyclist, and to get paid for riding his bike, and he knew exactly the way he needed to do it.

'In 1989, John Herety asked me to join the Percy Bilton team, which he was running at the time. I turned them down – turned down what was back then a pretty lucrative deal, well above a living wage. Instead, I opted to go to France for £100 a month with the ACBB – to plough my own furrow.'

'Graduates' of the Athletic Club de Boulogne-Billancourt included Herety, Sean Yates, Graham Jones, Robert Millar, Irishman Stephen Roche and Australians Phil Anderson and Allan Peiper. Stephens snagged the tail end of the ACBB's glory years, and the paltry wage that went with it, in the hope of following in the footsteps of Millar, Yates et al. to a European pro-team con-tract. His ticket there came via Paul Sherwen – of 'Phil and Paul' fame; television commentators Phil Liggett and Paul Sherwen are, despite the achievements of Froome, Wiggo and Cav, arguably still British cycling's best-known exports.

'Paul helped me get the slot at the ACBB through some contacts he had there. It was the route I chose; it wasn't out of disrespect for the British scene,' Stephens says. 'There was a lot of criterium racing back then, whereas I was more of a whippet than I am now, and city-centre racing like that wasn't really my thing, and I wanted to be a pro. I did three years over there, did some good rides, won several big races in France, although I wasn't a prolific winner. A pro contract never came.' Hope had come from the plan that the ACBB was going to develop into a pro team for the 1993 season.

'I had a deal with them, as did Dave Cook. I believe that the sponsors were going to be Basso bikes and Hewlett-Packard. There was apparently a Spanish dairy involved, too.'

Cook, Stephens and Simeon Hempsall had been the British representatives in the men's Olympic road race in Barcelona in 1992, won by the late Fabio Casartelli of Italy. Marie Purvis, Louise Jones and Sally Hodge represented GB in the women's event, but all eyes were on the track that year and Chris Boardman's gold medal in the individual pursuit. Four years later, Olympic cycling would open its doors to professional riders.

But six months after the '92 Games, at the start of the 1993 season, Stephens got a call from the ACBB.

'They rang me that January to tell me that the team had folded – that the ACBB still existed but only at a very low level, and with-out many foreigners, and without a very good racing programme.'

Stephens returned to the UK, got back to racing domestically at amateur level, and got himself a job at M&S in Watford, working in the years that followed in menswear and cream cakes.

'Then, midway through the nineties, I became a regional trainer for fruit and veg,' he explains. It was work – and decent work at that – but a world of iced buns, bananas and non-iron trousers wasn't really where he'd envisaged his career going when he'd packed himself off to Paris a few years earlier.

A useful ride at the 1995 amateur road-race world championships in Duitama, Colombia, garnered the attention of Eddie Borysewicz, a Polish coach working in American cycling, and the *directeur sportif* at the newly formed US Postal team. Britain needed a top-20 finish to qualify a team for the Atlanta Olympics in 1996, and Stephens duly obliged, riding his way to eighth place.

'Borysewicz got in touch with me while I was actually there in Colombia, and things were looking good for me to turn pro with US Postal for the '96 season,' Stephens explains. 'By then, I kind of felt like I deserved it.'

Jeremy Hunt – who would go on to twice become British national road-race champion and be a key member of the squad that helped Mark Cavendish to win the 2011 world championships – was on that same GB team in Colombia, and was subsequently signed by five-time Tour de France winner Miguel Indurain's Banesto team.

But unlike that well-established Spanish squad, US Postal were a new team for 1996, and still a couple of years away from signing Lance Armstrong, who joined in autumn 1998. However, this small American outfit was already hoping to branch out into European racing, and a British rider on their books would have helped their cause.

Stephens returned to the UK, ready and eager to put pen to paper on a pro contract, but the deal fell through. Disappointed, he continued riding for North Wirral Velo – Chris Boardman's last club before he'd turned pro – who were sponsored by Kodak for the 1996 season.

Although he had earned the team its participation, the Olympic selectors overlooked Stephens for Atlanta that summer in favour of John Tanner, Brian Smith, Max Sciandri – who won bronze – and Malcolm Elliott.

'I guess it was a little controversial . . . but there you go. Max medalled there, of course, but if I hadn't finished the Worlds we wouldn't have had a team at the Olympics at all,' Stephens says.

It was an important medal, too – Britain's first in the men's road race since Alan Jackson's bronze in Melbourne in 1956. Held only once every four years, of course, the Olympic road race is similar to the world-championship road race: a long race, and a true war of attrition.

In a period when British riders just finishing races like the world championships or the Olympic road race was considered a success, Sciandri's third place in Atlanta was an important milestone. Sciandri, born in Derby to a British mother and an Italian father, had only 'become' British in 1995, having switched from an Italian to a British racing licence, which made him eligible for selection to the national team – and how needed he was.

At the start of the 1997 season, the domestic road scene wasn't looking in great shape. There was no real television coverage of British racing, and Kodak pulled out as sponsor of Matt Stephens's team.

North Wirral Velo were managed by the late Pete Longbottom, a stage winner at the 1989 Milk Race and a bronze and silver medallist at the Commonwealth Games in 1990 and 1994, respectively, who also represented Great Britain in the team time trial at the 1992 Olympics in Barcelona. In February 1998 Longbottom was killed, aged thirty-eight, after being hit by a car while cycling.

'Pete did the best he could with our team, but we had a budget of £800 for the whole year, so we had to fund ourselves a lot of the time,' says Stephens. 'Kodak said we could keep using the same shorts from the previous season, with their name on them, so we had red shorts and a plain yellow top. It was the worst kit I'd ever seen, but it meant that we didn't have to buy shorts; I mean, that was the kind of level we were at.'

Disillusioned with the sport, Stephens decided to try a new tack: the burgeoning mountain-bike scene.

He contacted former cyclo-cross pro rider, and later GB mountain-bike team manager, Simon Burney, who helped set Stephens up with a place on the Muddy Fox squad.

'And I was shit – shockingly poor!' laughs Stephens. 'I had no real technical ability off-road at all. I lasted about five races, with [three-time MTB national champion] David Baker putting 20 minutes into me on every ride. I realized that mountain-biking maybe wasn't for me after all, so I went back to the road and had some great results on the back end of 1997.'

They included third place at the national road championships, behind Jeremy Hunt and Mark Walsham.

'I remember being really disappointed with that. I think I cried, actually. I was annoyed and upset, and, even though it was close, I felt I should have won it.'

Anyone who followed domestic British bike racing in the 1990s will have experienced a feeling of familiarity while watching on television as the 2012 Olympic road races flashed by a large, green-tinged building on Brompton Road, SW1.

Harrods, a jewel in London's blinged-out crown, is the epitome of Britishness – or perhaps only Englishness, or London-ness, or wealth – attracting 15 million customers each year, desperate for a slice of the high life (including Harrods-branded cups, saucers, cuddly toys and tea towels) at occasionally reasonable prices. Between 1985 and 2010, Harrods was owned by Mohamed Al-Fayed, an Egyptian businessman who, despite having lived in Britain since 1974, was repeatedly denied a British passport throughout his tenure of London's iconic department store. Which was somehow ironic.

In the late 1990s, the British cycling scene was about as far away from Knightsbridge living as you could get. Still a gritty, working-class sport, full of blood, sweat and tears, bike racing had precious little in common with Harrods' glittering jewellery display cases.

In the winter of 1997, Matt Stephens received a call from a man named Tony Foote. He ran the 'bike shop' in Harrods: the corner of the fifth floor devoted to all things cycling, next to ski wear and horse paraphernalia.

Stephens was still working full time at M&S, by now at their Chester branch, using the daily commute from his home in Crewe as training – a 50-mile round trip – with a longer 'café ride' on Saturdays, and racing on Sundays.

'I was doing around 350 miles a week, and it worked, really,' he says. 'I was racing at the highest level I could domestically, with the odd international race thrown in.'

Jeremy Hunt, David Millar, Harry Lodge and Max Sciandri were the only Europe-based pros at the time. Robert Millar had retired in 1995, and Sean Yates at the end of the 1996 season.

'I was working full-time but riding against the pros at the Worlds each year: I was there when Johan Museeuw won in Switzerland in 1996, and in San Sebastián, in Spain, in 1997 when Laurent Brochard won. They were reasonably big national teams then – seven or eight riders – so the best domestic guys would help make up the team: me, John Tanner, Mark Walsham.'

Stephens, rather patiently, was still waiting for his chance to ride regularly at the highest level, and so the phone call from Harrods came at a welcome time. Foote told Stephens that he was setting up a new Harrods-backed team, and that he already had 1993 Milk Race winner Chris Lillywhite on board.

'Chris was a good mate of mine, and it sounded as though it was going to be a good set-up with a good budget,' remembers Stephens. It wasn't enough for him to give up work, or even to go part-time, but Foote was offering a decent race programme with forays abroad to Belgium and France. The team had Giant bikes, 'logo-ed up in gold and green', and the roster also included decent home riders such as Mark McKay, Joe Bayfield and Julian Ramsbottom.

The team launch for the 1998 season took place in one of the restaurants in Harrods, where, in front of an invitation-only audience, Mohamed Al-Fayed himself introduced each rider, all of them wearing arguably the most iconic team kit the domestic scene has ever seen.

The national road-race championships that year were on a gently undulating circuit around Solihull. Everyone who was any-one in British cycling was there: Hunt, Millar, Roger Hammond, Chris Newton, Rob Hayles.

'The idea was for us to ride for Chris Lillywhite, because we thought it might well come down to a big group at the finish,' explains Stephens.

But with just over 30 miles to go of the 130-mile race, there were only 13 riders left in the mix, including Stephens, Lillywhite, Hammond and Team Brite's Hayles and Newton.

'With about 15 miles to go, I said to Chris, "I'll go now and then you can sit on. I know 'Haylesy' will try to bring me back, but I think I can hold them off for a few miles, and give you a bit of a rest." So I went, and got about 25 seconds, and I remember look-ing back and seeing Hayles on the front.'

Team Brite was essentially a national squad, boasting Newton, Hayles, Jonny Clay, Matt Illingworth, Chris Walker and John Tanner in its ranks. It had also sponsored the podium that day in Solihull.

'It was fair of them to assume that one of their riders would win it, as they really were that strong,' says Stephens.

But they hadn't banked on Stephens staying away on his own to win by 20 seconds from Hammond, with Darren Barclay of the Arctic 2000 team in third. Newton was fourth.

'So Brite turned the podium around so that it was just hollow wood for the photos!' laughs Stephens – the new British national champion. It was a dream come true for him.

For the 1999 season, Stephens was offered a place on the Linda McCartney team who, by then into their second year, were offering a full international programme, but expected him to give up work as a result. Despite being tempted, Stephens chose to stay with Harrods.

'McCartney were offering the same salary as I was getting from Harrods, but then I'd be missing out on the money I was making at M&S, who were a really nice company to work for,' says Stephens. 'They were always really supportive – especially when I was turning up from my commute in a Harrods jersey every day! They even had me cut the ribbon for them at the opening of the new homeware and menswear store in Chester.'

Stephens decided to stay put, and the Harrods team launch in 1999 took things up another level. 'We had Eddie Irvine from Formula One, and golfer Colin Montgomerie . . . All these sports stars were there, and then there we were, poncing around with our bikes on a catwalk, with Al-Fayed there again, too. A proper big launch.'

For the first half of the season, with Stephens clad in his special white national champion's jersey, with its red-and-blue bands, and the Harrods logo proudly displayed on the chest, things went well. But then the wheels started to come off; the team ran out of money.

'We learned that there had never been any money from Harrods – or not very much, anyway,' says Stephens. 'They let Tony use their image on the jersey, but it was all in the hope of attracting more sponsors to finance the team. But, from what I understand, when they sold a bike through the cycling department, which was owned by Tony and his mate Nigel, that money was going straight through the till and into the team. The company went bankrupt, basically.'

Only the year before, the team had taken part in the PruTour: the then latest iteration of the Tour of Britain. In the style of the top European squads, Harrods had its own team bus.

'But ours was an actual Harrods bus, the one that they normally drive around London. At the time, we thought that Harrods had just given it to us to use for the race, but in fact it had cost seven grand for the week. We were this team with essentially no budget, and they were splashing the cash, unbeknown to us. But no other teams had a bus like that!'

With the Harrods team on its last legs, and with bills to pay, Stephens went back to Linda McCartney, and to *directeur sportif* Sean Yates and manager Julian Clark.

'I had to say, "I know I didn't sign with you last year, and that was probably a bad decision, but how about taking me on straight away?" Luckily, they said yes, and – bang! – I was in a McCartney jersey a week later.'

Stephens rode the rest of the British season for McCartney, but had no promises for the following year. For 2000, Linda McCartney were making wholesale changes, bringing in British Classics specialist Max Sciandri and 1996 Olympic road-race champion Pascal Richard to bolster the team for a proper crack at top-level racing.

At the end of the 1999 season, Linda McCartney took Stephens to the TransCanada stage race, which was to be make or break as to whether they would take him on for the following season.

It was 'break' – at least, Stephens crashed on the second day, when his handlebar stem broke, and he was forced to quit after tearing muscles in his back.

'The other guy I was contending for a place on the team with was Charly Wegelius, who was a brilliant rider, and we were good mates. He was also riding in Canada as a *stagiaire*, like me, but luckily the Italian Mapei team took him on for the following year, and Sean called me once I was back home to say that I was in, and that I should pack in my job with M&S.

'I was thrilled, and asked him what he needed me to do across the winter,' Stephens continues. 'He told me to just double my training miles!'

As of December, Stephens was doing four- or five-day blocks of six to seven hours' training a day. He had made it as a full-time professional; but, again, his joy was to be short-lived.

The Linda McCartney team performed well on the inter-national circuit in 2000, with Stephens finishing in the top 10 overall at both the Tour Down Under and the Tour de Langkawi, before the team garnered a spot on that year's Giro d'Italia, where David McKenzie – one of two Australians on the team – won a stage, and Stephens had his first, and what turned out to be only, experience of riding a Grand Tour.

But in 2001 the team's season was over almost before it had begun. With supposed new sponsors Jacob's Creek and Jaguar plastered across the redesigned team jersey, the new season had the potential to be the biggest and best yet. However, manager Julian Clark, who had founded the team in 1998, had been premature in announcing the two sponsors, in the naïve hope that some good early results might persuade them to officially come on board. At the Tour Down Under in January, McKenzie had already won a stage, but there was no money, the sponsors hadn't given per-mission for their logos to be used, and the team folded immediately.

It was a bitter blow, just when it looked as though a British pro-fessional team had made it into the higher echelons. In truth, it had made it there the year before, but it was no more than a very short-lived glimpse of life among the top squads. First

ANC–Halfords in 1987, now Linda McCartney. What was it going to take for a British team to make it to the top, and then stay there?

Former Linda McCartney team press officer John Deering, who wrote a highly entertaining book about the team's mixed fortunes – *Team on the Run* – helped find Stephens a place on the Sigma Sport squad, racing mainly in the domestic Premier Calendar series of races while also working full-time as a police officer. Stephens then spent the next decade with the team before retiring from both racing and the police to work in the cycling media.

His story is one of a passionate, talented rider who made things work during a racing career that spanned four decades. Looking back, Stephens says that although he does harbour a small twinge of disappointment that he never had the opportunity to ride the Tour de France, getting the chance to take part in the world championships, the Commonwealth Games, the Olympic Games and the Giro d'Italia goes a long way to making up for it.

Herety continued as the national road-race team manager at British Cycling, but handed over the baton for the under-23 squad to coach Rod Ellingworth, whose idea it was to establish the Olympic Academy for the 2004 season, basing the new intake of young riders in Manchester close to the velodrome, and instilling in them a sense of responsibility and discipline in order that they could take full advantage of the now world-class training facilities and coaching at their disposal. Herety's too modest to say so, but it's clear from reading Ellingworth's book, *Project Rainbow* – about how one of his young charges, a certain Mark Cavendish, eventually became the 2011 road-race world champion – that Ellingworth had more than a little help from Herety with setting up the academy.

'The academy was track-oriented, which I still believe is the best route for young riders, but I also managed those riders when they did road races, and fed back to Rod how they were performing, which was the ideal job for me, really, to be quite honest,' says Herety, humbly.

Herety also continued managing the senior road team until 2005, when Wegelius, by then a pro at the Italian team Liquigas, and Tom Southam, who was riding for the South African Barloworld squad, accepted money from a member of the Italian national team to lend them a hand during that year's world-championship road race in Madrid.

Wegelius tells the story in his excellent autobiography, *Domestique*, but Herety is quite happy to expand on it. 'Charly hinted at what he might do the night before,' says Herety, 'but I decided to keep quiet because it was one of those things that might not happen, either; a certain scenario had to happen for them to be called in to do what they did, basically.'

But when the call came, Wegelius and Southam went to the front of the race to help the Italians peg back the breakaway group that was up the road, the Italians' plan being to ensure that the race ended in a bunch sprint, which would favour their rider Alessandro Petacchi.

'I had a journalist with me in the team car at the time, and when Dave Brailsford phoned through to ask what was going on, I couldn't really tell him,' says Herety. 'The bizarre thing was that the British public out on the circuit were loving it!' he adds. 'It was the first time in a while that British riders had contributed to the Worlds road race . . . Plus we had Roger Hammond there as our team leader, and if there was a breakaway, we needed it to come back anyway as Roger's only chance was a group sprint at the end.'

That became Herety's story anyway, which he admits wasn't perfect, as they might have been able to save Southam and Wegelius to be at the team's disposal later on in the race.

'But Charly's argument,' he says, 'and it's probably the strongest one, actually, was that he didn't think he was going to be of any use to Roger much beyond about 150 kilometres anyway.'

Herety was 'absolutely hounded' by the British cycling press afterwards.

'And I told Brailsford that I'd resign if it was going to save everybody's job, which is what I did. Dave and I never fell out over it at all, and resigning killed it stone dead; what else could they do? It was done, and I just moved on.'

As for Wegelius, after 'betraying' the British team, he never rode for his country again, and wasn't even considered for the road race at the Beijing Olympics, which was run over a hilly course that would have suited him down to the ground.

Nicole Cooke won gold for GB after a rain-lashed women's road race in China, but even after such a momentous achievement, much of the focus fell on the GB track team and their haul of seven gold medals on the boards, won by Victoria Pendleton, Rebecca Romero, Bradley Wiggins in both the individual and team pursuit, and the three medals won by Chris Hoy in the team sprint, the individual sprint and the Keirin.

So it became at British Cycling: take the Lottery funding, spend it on the 'controllable' – i.e. track cycling, and the best clothing, coaching and equipment – and keep as many of your riders as possible living in Manchester and training at the Manchester Velodrome.

Those ploughing their own, more old-school, furrow, attempting to assimilate into the European road game, with its necessary adoption of new cultures, new languages and a new way of life, were pretty much left to their own devices.

David Millar, it seemed, fell somewhere in the middle, adored by Dave Brailsford and trotted out in front of the press ahead of the 2004 Athens Olympics, alongside Cooke, as a medal hope on the road, only for Millar to topple himself with his decision to dope while on the French Cofidis team, where the British set-up was unable to reach him.

Millar and Wegelius (the latter retired in 2011 and became a *directeur sportif* at Millar's Garmin team) are by no means the last of what's become a very long string of British riders who have sought their fortune abroad: a lonely, bounty-hunting existence that could only ever appeal to riders who *really* wanted it. Plenty would try but could never hack it, and would return home to domestic racing.

But today's crop of riders who head to France and Belgium, helped out by organizations such as the Dave Rayner Fund and the Braveheart Fund, now often do so in the hope of attracting British Cycling's stretched attention and a Lottery-funded berth on the academy programme, or indeed a place beneath the same umbrella at Team Sky.

11

THE SECRET SQUIRREL CLUB

When Chris Boardman won gold in the individual pursuit at the 1992 Olympic Games in Barcelona, he reignited a passion for cycling in Britain that had not been seen since the post-war years, and which has steadily increased ever since.

He didn't even have to go the full 4,000-metre distance; when Boardman caught his German opponent, Jens Lehmann, with a lap to go, he ended the duel by default, and pumped the air with his fist in celebration.

Boardman was the perfect British cereal-box hero: all outward confidence and German-beating, aboard his futuristic-looking carbon-fibre Lotus super-bike. He turned professional with three-time Tour de France winner Greg LeMond's Gan team the following year, then won the prologue time trial at the 1994 Tour to take the leader's yellow jersey – only the second Briton to do so, after Tom Simpson in 1962.

When he subsequently appeared with annoying puppets Zig and Zag on *The Big Breakfast* on Channel 4, his yellow jersey from winning the prologue at the Dauphiné Libéré standing in as a

Tour yellow jersey (to my annoyance at the time) well, then he'd really made it.

Prior to the '92 Olympics, Boardman was already well known within the British cycling fraternity as a member of the all-conquering Manchester Wheelers cycling club: a four-time winner of the national hill-climb championships, a three-time national pursuit champion and, by 1993, a five-time 25-mile championships winner.

Riding for England at the Commonwealth Games, his results included bronze in the team pursuit in Edinburgh in 1986, and another bronze four years later, in Auckland, again in the team pursuit, as well as in the team time trial on the road.

The rider who became his greatest rival – the Blur to his Oasis – was Scotland's Graeme Obree, who was just as well known on the national time-trial circuit. The pair soon battled on the international stage, too, while representing Great Britain, alternating victories at the individual pursuit world championships: Obree winning in 1993 and 1995, Boardman in 1994 and 1996. But it was their Hour record attempts that really captured the imagination of the press and public, although there were few of either at Obree's quiet 1993 attempt to beat Italian Francesco Moser's 1984 figure of 51.151 kilometres at the velodrome in Hamar, Norway.

That first attempt, with Obree in his trademark arms-tucked-beneath-his-chest 'praying mantis' position, was on a bike that had been built out of carbon-fibre by Mike Burrows: the man behind Boardman's 1992 Olympic Lotus bike. But, having failed to take the record by 461 metres, Obree went for it again the next day, this time on his own bike, which he'd built himself and which had appropriately been christened Old Faithful. This time, he recorded 51.596 kilometres, beating Moser's record by 445 metres.

Less than a week later, Boardman took to the track in Bordeaux, ready to better Obree's record time. Cleverly planned to take place on the day that stage 18 of the 1993 Tour de France finished in the city – with its resulting media coverage – Boardman did it, recording 52.270 kilometres.

But Obree wasn't finished yet: the following April, at the same Bordeaux velodrome where Boardman had taken the record, Obree upped it to 52.713 kilometres, before it was again swept away later that year by Spanish Tour de France star Miguel Indurain and then Switzerland's Tony Rominger.

The British duo had rekindled international interest in the Hour record, and when, in September 1996, Boardman bested Rominger by over a kilometre to record 56.375 kilometres in the Manchester Velodrome, he did so using the radical new Obree-developed 'Superman position', knitting the two riders' achievements together rather nicely.

Both Obree and Boardman's full racing stories are wonderfully told in the excellent 2013 book by Edward Pickering, *The Race Against Time*, but how did Boardman's racing success directly affect British Cycling's Olympic 'Class of 2008'? Although there's little doubt that it was while racing – under former coach Peter Keen's tutelage – that Boardman put in the groundwork, it's off the bike that Boardman has arguably been at his most effective, and has had a huge impact on the success of today's riders.

Those riders have been helped in no small part by Boardman's 'Secret Squirrel Club': the nickname for British Cycling's research and development team, which came into being in 2004 after Dave Brailsford had taken over from Keen at the helm of the federation as performance director.

Boardman, perhaps just as much as Brailsford and Keen, and arguably more so through his work leading the 'Secret Squirrels', has played a major role in Britain's Olympic and international cycling successes both on the track and on the road, and therefore in the subsequent adoption by the British of cycling as a sport, pastime and mode of transport.

*

I meet Chris Boardman MBE in a café in Covent Garden in late November, the morning after the Champions of CycleSport Dinner in west London: an annual event that raises money for the charity Action Medical Research. Luckily, there's not even a sniff of a hangover, and, almost immediately, Graeme Obree becomes the topic of conversation after I ask Boardman to recount his story of the setting up of the Secret Squirrel Club.

'Graeme, in his own way, was really the first person to look at the aggregation of marginal gains,' says Boardman, using the phrase later made famous by British Cycling's performance director and general manager of Team Sky, Dave Brailsford.

'Graeme was the first to put aside the history of an event and look at the demands of it instead. He said, "Well, these 'tubes' in air are awful, so what if I get rid of them?" and so he tucked his arms under his chest, rather than having them exposed in front of him. And when that new position was banned, he said, "OK, I'll do this," and put his arms straight out in front of him, in the "Superman position", and he was pilloried for it – not least by me. Peter Keen and I were supposed to have this scientific approach, but we didn't even realize we were just pouring scorn because it was different. But he had the courage to go out and do it, despite people giggling and laughing.'

He's not proud of it, but Boardman's prepared to admit that he wasn't as welcoming to Obree's different approach to making himself faster on a bike as he should have been.

'Looking back, Peter and I were nowhere near as rigorous, scientifically, as we thought we were being at the time. But Graeme's approach was just annoying. We'd look at things, we'd measure things, and then we'd have an idea to make things better, and then measure how that worked. We were fascinated by the process of getting better. But Graeme came from left field – that is, he powered himself with marmalade sandwiches, and made his bike out of old bits himself, and it seemed to just be taking the piss a bit when we'd fought and worked so hard to get to the point we were at, and so it rankled.'

However, Boardman and Keen were just about curious enough to take a closer look at Obree's radical positions.

'We looked at the "Superman position" in particular, just as a nod to being open-minded,' explains Boardman. 'We didn't even do any measurements, like we normally would, but it took only a couple of laps of the track in that position before I went, "Oh shit. We're going to have to do this, aren't we?" The improvement was just enormous – absolutely enormous.'

While Keen and Boardman were the 'science nerds', Obree, Boardman says, simply had a very instinctive way of looking at things. Not that his ideas were always perfect.

'I mean, he did some other things that were perhaps a bit too left field, like deciding that he wasn't going to shave his legs because he thought the hairs were good for heat dissipation. So Pete asked him, "How do you know that?" and Graeme said, "Well, camels are hairy." But then Pete reminded him that it gets to about $-5°C$ at night in the desert, and Graeme replied, "Oh yeah, you're right."

'Pete was all about performance – holistic performance – while Graeme did things in a more rudimentary way. But he really deserves the mention here, because he was the first ground-thinker; just in a really instinctive way, Graeme looked at the demands of the event rather than the history.'

It's a theme that comes up time and again in our conversation. Obree may have first got Boardman thinking in a different way, but it became almost Boardman's *raison d'être* to try to get Britain's elite cyclists, and the management at British Cycling, to take the history of top-level bicycle racing out of the equation and 'simply' look at the ways in which they could get faster.

'Yet the theory and the logic and the emotional side of it all just don't mesh,' says Boardman. 'You know that 80–90 per cent of your energy is used just pushing air out of the way, so that tells you, logically, that aerodynamics is everything. But because of the history of the sport, people then go, "Yeah, it's absolutely every-thing . . . But anyway, let's now measure power, and all these other things that are so much less important."

'The logic's just not there,' he all but fumes, exasperated by the memory of what he's been preaching over the last ten-plus years. 'And then there's fashion, too. You wouldn't think it would come into it, but if I said to somebody, "Right, go and use 150mm cranks," they wouldn't even consider why I was suggesting it. They'd just think, "You don't do that," and then they'd try to find rational reasons why it wasn't a good idea, without actually know-ing whether it was or not.'

But, he patiently explains, if you could get a rider to move from their current crank length of 175mm or 170mm to 167mm, then to 165mm the following year, then 160, and so on over a few years to 150mm, then you could get them on board. It's a fascinat-ing insight into the methods he's been forced to employ to get others to even try new ideas. It also seems extraordinary, then, to look back at the boneshaker used by James Moore – remember him; the British winner of the first-ever bike race? – and note that it had cranks that were adjustable for length.

Out of interest, I ask Boardman, he's not really suggesting 150mm cranks are the way to go, is he?

'It's definitely something to be looked at,' he shoots back. 'The physiologist – or "sports biomechanist" – at British Cycling, Paul Barratt, is one of the smartest guys on the whole programme. One of the reasons he's so good – and he was in the Secret Squirrel Club as well – is because he gives the coaches information but he doesn't make himself responsible for whether they take it. So he's done some very high-rev testing, and, for reasons I don't know, they use very short cranks, which may even be shorter than 150mm. They use a fully instrumented ergometer in the lab, and he's logged that, even at peak power, torque doesn't go down. You can nearly halve the length of the crank, and it's just not going down. Yet, aerodynamically, you've reduced the amount of everything, and increased the frequency you can do something, and you may be able to get a lower position because your legs aren't coming up as far, so there are many potential advantages. So that piece of information is there, but it just sits there, and no one's really recognizing it, even though the coaches are aware of it.'

For Boardman the rider, working with a scientific mind like that of Peter Keen brought him the one key thing that he was lacking: confidence. Keen's fascination with finding out how things work, and how best to approach training as a result, and then on top of that rigorously pulling it all apart afterwards to help better understand it, drew Boardman in.

'Peter brought process,' Boardman says, 'and that was invaluable to me. It took the emotion out of winning and losing – elation and despair, all of that got taken away. It was just all about being better. The result itself wasn't important; it was what it was, and understanding it was the passion, and how to make it better – how to be better. And for a young kid back then, low in self-confidence and self-esteem, that was a hell of a good tool to be able to cope with failure. So Peter made it about the performance, not about the result, and he introduced process, to squeeze every last drop out of every experience you had, and that was huge. And that legacy, I think, set up British Cycling.'

Dave Brailsford originally worked for Keen at the British federation; Brailsford bringing an invaluable 'can do' attitude to the table that made him, as Boardman puts it, 'the person to manage to get stuff done'.

'I've often wondered whether it would have been even better if it had been the other way around – if Dave had been in charge and

Pete had worked for Dave,' Boardman reflects. 'But I don't think that it would have worked then.'

Then, in 2003, GlaxoSmithKline came a-knocking, and Keen took up a position with them as performance director of the new Lucozade Sports Science Academy – leaving Brailsford holding the reins, with the 2004 Athens Olympics just around the corner.

'They were going to do Athens together, but Pete got the job offer, and off he went. Dave was absolutely crapping himself,' laughs Boardman, albeit sympathetically. 'He was really quite daunted by it, but he very quickly grew in confidence. Well, not very quickly, actually, but he quickly gathered people around him that made him feel secure and confident: your Shane Suttons, me, Steve Peters. From there, he just grew as a manager and leader of people.'

Four years before, the 2000 Olympic Games in Sydney had given British Cycling their first track medals since Boardman's gold medal in Barcelona in 1992. Jason Queally won the 1-kilometre time trial, and there was silver for Queally, Craig MacLean and a 24-year-old Chris Hoy in the team sprint. Yvonne McGregor – who would go on to become pursuit world champion later in the year at the age of thirty-nine – took bronze in the women's individual pursuit, and there was bronze again in the men's team pursuit through a cleverly used combination of Jonny Clay, Bradley Wiggins, Rob Hayles, Paul Manning, Bryan Steel and Chris Newton.

In 2004, in Athens, with Brailsford a little nervously at the head of affairs, British track cycling went one better again, producing two Olympic gold medals, one silver and one bronze. The two golden boys were Hoy and Wiggins, winning the 1-kilometre time trial and the individual pursuit, respectively, while Wiggins, Manning, Hayles and Steve Cummings were well beaten by a strong Australian quartet in the final of the team pursuit, and had to settle for silver. And it was Hayles and Wiggins again who took bronze in the Madison, won by Australia's Stuart O'Grady and Graeme Brown, with Swiss duo Franco Marvulli and Bruno Risi taking home silver.

There, in Athens, the British riders were using new carbon-fibre bicycles developed for British Cycling by a former member of the Greek track team. In 2001, commissioned by Keen, rider-turned-composites-engineer Dimitris Katsanis set to work building the fastest, most efficient machines the sport had yet seen – which, as Boardman is at pains to point out, are still very much in use by the squad today. Hoy had used the new bike to great effect at the 2002 track world championships in Copenhagen, winning his first world title in the 1-kilometre time trial, albeit by just 0.001 seconds from France's Arnaud Tournant.

But it was only under Brailsford that the Secret Squirrel Club proper came into being, after British Cycling had gratefully taken receipt of a new investment of National Lottery funding ahead of London's successful 2005 bid for the 2012 Olympics.

'We sort of looked at everything and said, "Well, it's a very technical sport, and we're quite good at the physical side of it, but what about all the other 'stuff'?"' remembers Boardman. 'So I was tasked with going and being head of "stuff". It was later massaged to become "the aggregation of marginal gains", but to start with I was just head of "stuff" and had to put a team together to go and look at that.'

UK Sport's Scott Drawer was the man holding the purse strings, and it was Drawer who went out to talk to people from the sports industry, academia, the military, Formula One – basically anyone who might just be useful for bringing in new experiences, insights or ideas that could be moulded into useful 'stuff' for British Cycling.

'I soon realized that we needed people that didn't think like us – people that you might not even necessarily get along with – because you need difference. You all want to be looking at this one thing from different perspectives. If you all get on, you're just all looking at this, but missing all of this,' Boardman smiles, his arms moving from a foot apart to wide apart, followed by a not overly sincere apology that my tape recorder wouldn't really pick that up.

Boardman recalls the early days of getting the band together, and a day in 2004 in Sheffield, in particular.

'We had a kind of boffins' day – a kind of unofficial interview for all these people we'd gathered together – and we said, "Right, here's an event; what would you do?" And they'd ask, "Can we do this?" And we'd say whether they could or couldn't, depending on the rules, but without telling them the rules.'

It was an effort to see how people worked, and how they worked together, in particular, and there was one person who really caught Boardman's eye. 'There was this guy called Pete Bentley who worked in sailing; the sport had the budget for one person, and Pete Bentley was it. He had quite a few ideas, and was quite a forceful character, and when we said, "No, you can't do that," he'd say, "Well, what about doing it this way, then?" He really championed his own cause, and I looked at him, and thought, "If I only had the budget for one person, you'd be it. But if I'm going to have a team, there's no way you're going to be in it, because your idea is going to be more important than the best idea," because I could tell he wanted to win.'

It's by no means a criticism of Bentley; in fact, it's rather complimentary. But it's an insight into the vetting process Boardman used to ensure he brought together just the right combination of people for his project. Soon, what he kindly calls 'an eclectic group of individuals, very different characters' began to take shape.

'And they fought and squabbled their way forwards for the next eight years,' Boardman grins. 'But they got on, because everyone always referenced back: "Is this the most efficient, best way to get the most gold medals?" It was the only thing that everything was measured against, and that became the glue that kept such differ-ent characters working in the same direction.'

Some 'Secret Squirrels' came and went, but the core, consistent group was made up of seven people from different backgrounds and areas of expertise who gelled to become one of sport's most exclusive and successful clubs: a fellowship to give even Frodo and friends a run for their money when it came to diversity banding together for the common good.

The VII were:

Paul Barrett – 'who was physiology'
Jason Queally – 'who was the athlete early on, and who sat in the wind tunnel and gave an athlete's perspective'
Scott Drawer – 'from UK Sport; the agent'
Dimitris Katsanis – 'the engineer, and the guy who had built the UK Sport bikes a few years before'
Rob Lewis – 'the aerodynamicist, and his company, TotalSim'
Sally Cowan – 'a materials specialist from the world of fashion, and underwear specifically'
Chris Boardman – 'head of stuff'

The secrecy was all the more cemented by the fact that they didn't have a base, but simply met up wherever they needed to be: sometimes at Rob Lewis's TotalSim in Brackley, between Oxford and Northampton; often at wind tunnels, and at Southampton University's facility, in Hampshire, in particular.

Those days in the wind tunnel, remembers Boardman, were always intense.

'You'd be in this windowless building all day, and then come out in the dark and go to the pub, and carry on going at the bar,' he says, meaning continuing to discuss things at the bar, although no one would begrudge them a drink.

Presumably 'Jason's brother' was left behind in the tunnel; it became the nickname for the life-sized dummy-replica made of Jason Queally that the 'squirrels' used to get more accurate readings.

'A wind tunnel is a bit like a set of bathroom scales,' explains Boardman. 'While you're weighing heavy things, it's absolutely fine. But when you've weighed all the heavy things and are then trying to weigh peas, it gives you a different result each time, and it starts to get really difficult. One of the ways for us to get accuracy in the wind tunnel was to stop everything moving – so we made the mannequin. That made things a lot more accurate, but then you have this "war" between accuracy and what's happening in the real world, and that fight's still going on.'

Sally Cowan, the materials specialist, who has also worked with Team Sky and, most recently, with Team GB's Olympians ahead of the Sochi Winter Games, has so far made somewhere in the region of 10,000 garments, swatches and tubes of material to test in the wind tunnel. She also now proudly displays Queally's bottom half in her studio in Belper, near Derby, after his legs snapped off, according to the *Derby Telegraph*. Someone, somewhere, must own the rest of poor Jason.

Clearly, Boardman was never going to divulge all those findings the Secret Squirrel Club uncovered – other than what's in full view at each track world championship, Olympics or World Cup – for risk of handing other nations the key to the castle. 'But I'll tell you one, which is quite a good one,' Boardman reneges, rather generously. The fact that less than half of the group were cyclists was, he says, a massive advantage: they didn't know what you 'couldn't' do.

'Someone like Rob Lewis therefore only looked at the demands of the event, which was exactly what we wanted. He was never blinkered by tradition because he didn't have a history in cycling, and he was very imaginative as a result. He'd say, "Right, OK, you just tell me "yes" or "no". "Can I do this?" and start sketching on a piece of paper.'

One day, he drew 'Rob's dangler' . . . 'It was a tennis ball hanging off the helmet in front of the rider,' Boardman explains, his face a contorted mixture of mirth and sincerity.

'Can you do that?' Lewis asked him, and proceeded to explain how a ship's wake isn't straight; that it splays outwards, like an arrowhead.

'He was very good at translating things into layman's terms,' remembers Boardman. 'By placing something in front of the rider, everything behind it rides in the hole that that thing's made.'

But short of Boardman's riders lapping the track with tennis balls hanging off the front of their helmets, like thoroughbred donkeys chasing a carrot on a stick, Lewis was forced to look harder at the real world. 'So he'd say, "What about that bike computer? Does it have to be there?" and he'd tilt the computer up 90 degrees, so that it was actually more exposed, and, thinking like that, we'd look at placing things – a bluff body – to make drag on purpose.

'There was lots of thinking along those lines. Rob would bring a concept like his "dangler" to the table and it would help us develop a way of thinking to first of all work out what we wanted to do, and then to find a way to make it legal, rather than start by immediately constraining ourselves by the rules.'

The group's momentum kept building between 2004 and 2008, with the big stamp of approval coming at the 2007 track world championships in Majorca where Great Britain won seven golds. 'I remember standing in the middle of the track with Dave,' Boardman continues, 'and saying, "Make the most of this, Dave, because we're probably never going to see the likes of this again."'

Perhaps understandably, Boardman thought that such a large medal haul was as good as it was going to get, but fast-forward 12 months to the next track world championships – this time in Manchester – and Brailsford's boys and girls took an astounding nine golds.

But it was only five months later again, at the 2008 Beijing Olympics, that the mainstream press, and therefore public attention, really focused on the British athletes and their phenomenal performances. The British camp took seven golds out of a possible 10, plus three silvers and two bronzes, having reaped the full benefits of Boardman's Secret Squirrel Club.

And then, after a short rest for all involved, the Olympic cycle – and the Secret Squirrel Club's efforts – began again.

'A four-year programme of "explore, experiment, prototype, manufacture" has served us well,' says Boardman, with typical modesty. 'There'd be a few months of recovery after the Games, and the rest of that year would be a case of "explore". The second year would then be "experiment": looking to see if any of those theories we'd come up with held true. Then the third year would be prototyping: let's take those experiments and see if we can make them into a really functional thing. And then the last six months was just hell-for-leather production.'

That hell-for-leather production yielded new, improved clothing and components for the 2012 London Olympics, including some hollow carbon-fibre cranks.

'They were delivered at 11 p.m. the night before Ed Clancy used them in the omnium, which is pretty scary to watch on television. And when Philip Hindes "fell off" in the team sprint,' says Boardman, twitching two fingers of each hand in the air to create quote marks around 'fell off', referring to the moment when Hindes took advantage of a race rule allowing the team to get a better start, 'I was actually doing live television commentary and thinking, "Oh no, no, no!" as I thought he'd snapped his cranks. But we'd hung the equivalent of a lift full of people off them – nearly 700kg off one crank – before we got one to crack, and even then it didn't completely fail. They really were amazing pieces of engineering.'

*

Commentary stints for the BBC during the Olympics, and regular punditry for ITV's coverage of the Tour de France – not to mention Boardman Bikes, the eponymous bicycle company at which Boardman acts as director of research and development – have all kept him incredibly busy in recent years.

Boardman decided to call it a day as the head of British Cycling's secret society, following the repeat track success at the London Olympics in 2012, where Team GB again won seven out of a possible 10 gold medals, plus a silver and a bronze. On the road, too, there was Bradley Wiggins's gold and Chris Froome's silver in the time trial, and Lizzie Armitstead's silver in the road race, all using Secret Squirrel Club-developed skinsuits and helmets, and, in Wiggins's case, a UK Sport bike.

'I sat down with Dave for a cup of coffee, and I said that it'd been great, but that I was done. It was quite emotional, really – a ten-year chunk of my life ended,' Boardman admits.

That was at the start of 2013, and Boardman promised Brailsford that he'd help in the process of finding his successor. With further help from UK Sport's Scott Drawer, that man was Tony Purnell, an aerodynamics expert who's a visiting professor at Cambridge, and who used to own the Jaguar Formula One team, before selling it to Red Bull.

'Tony's got a hell of a history and understanding of aerodynamics, but a good philosophy as well – very open-minded. I'm not sure he realized what he was getting into, but I tricked him into it,' Boardman laughs. 'He's now in charge, but I said that I'd consult with him regularly, although he hasn't used me much at all. That's not a criticism; he hasn't needed to, which is brilliant for me, so I'm actually only doing about ten days a year now.'

Boardman's involvement with the Secret Squirrel Club may now be minimal, but he's kept his connection with British Cycling as their policy adviser, helping to promote cycling as a means of transport.

'I think the further away I get from bike racing, the more I realize just how much of my life I've spent trying to go round in circles faster than other people,' he laughs. 'Talking about using bikes for transport feels like a meaningful thing to be doing: bikes as a form of transport, but also for leisure, and maybe competition. But first and foremost getting people cycling to solve most of the problems we've got in this country, because it does surprisingly link into all of them.'

Think for a moment, and it dawns on you just how right he is: obesity and health issues, the environment, traffic congestion. The humble bicycle has the potential to help resolve so many issues. Yet although Boardman is adamant that cycling itself is an extremely safe pursuit, cyclists need to be able to ride safely in an environment in which other, heavier, faster road users – motor vehicles – also exist.

'It's a bit like the short cranks. People can see the logic of it [measures for cycle safety], but then they say, "Yeah, but we can't do that because it will slow the cars down." It just beggars belief.'

Boardman says that he thinks it could be about two years before cycling as a 'fashion' starts to fade; before it becomes 'normalized' and the passion that exists right now diminishes.

'So we've got two years to get traction – to get a foothold for it to become a genuine mode of transport in the UK,' he says. 'It has the potential to be a real election issue. You'd think it wasn't big enough for that, but Labour have just produced their cycling manifesto, which isn't detailed enough yet, and that could start a "bidding war" with the other parties; it could prove to be the catalyst for something quite big, so watch this space.'

As for bike design, going forward, Boardman is as passionate as ever, and enjoys his role on the research and development side of Boardman Bikes: 'I've got a good idea of what bikes are going to look like in five years' time, but if I produced it tomorrow, people would go, "Oh yeah that looks great; I'm not buying it, though!"

So you have to fit in with what people can cope with now.'

It's the trickle-down effect from the sport's top-level equipment that we're going to see in the bikes of the future, says Boardman.

'In the same way as the aerospace industry brought us Teflon pans and Velcro, you get spin-offs, so that programme – that little Secret Squirrel Club – has actually shaped all forms of cycle sport: clothing, covered helmets . . . That's where it came from.'

Take, for example, those really rather ugly white helmets that Mark Cavendish and Bradley Wiggins wore for the Madison track event at the 2008 Olympics in Beijing: the result of the Secret Squirrels' meticulous attention to detail after hours in the wind tunnel. Unfortunately, their effectiveness was somewhat dampened by the fact that Wiggins simply didn't have the legs on the day, having already defended his Olympic title in the individual pursuit and won gold, too, in the team pursuit, as well as having come into the Games ill already. Cavendish and Wiggins could only finish ninth.

Although those helmets were built from the bottom up, 'aero-ifying' normal road helmets was something that Boardman was already an expert in, having done exactly that for his attempt at the 'Athlete's Hour' in 2000. This was Boardman's final race as a pro, and an attempt to better Eddy Merckx's 1972 Hour record using a 'normal' – i.e. not aero – bike, handlebars and wheels, and a non-aero helmet (Merckx had used a leather 'hairnet' helmet).

The Boardman camp bought into the concept entirely, keen that their man should take on Merckx's record on an equal footing, while ensuring that future attempts would be able to stick within the new rules, too.

'We didn't want to use a helmet at all, because that would be the same now or a million years into the future, as the shape of the human head is going to be the same,' says Boardman. The UCI rules, however, stated that a helmet had to be worn, and it couldn't be an aerodynamic time-trial helmet, either.

'With a helmet on, it was losing us a kilometre, and we weren't even wind-tunnel testing back then – just measuring effects – so that was massive. So it just seemed instinctive that if we could smooth the helmet over, covering the vents, we could get some time back.'

Over an hour, that equated to 500 metres; Boardman beat Merckx's old record by just 10 metres, recording 49.441km.

This was knowledge that Boardman already had up his sleeve, and so he brought it into the future for use by the Secret Squirrel Club, having asked himself, 'Why aren't we using this piece of information for all these other cycling events?' So the GB squad did exactly that, and now all the major helmet manufacturers make the so-called aero road helmets, which are used for an aerodynamic advantage both on the track and in road racing.

But in what's an almost criminally underrated series of mini episodes that appeared on ITV's Tour de France website in 2013 – entitled, rather wonderfully, *The Last Airbenders*, and put together by production company Vsquared – Boardman and TV presenter Ned Boulting took a closer look at the effect of aerodynamics in cycling, and revealed exactly where the advantages were to be had. Positioning on the bike, skinsuits and helmets were all discussed, all presented from the familiar environs – for Boardman – of Southampton University's wind tunnel.

With Boulting acting his socks off in the role of comic relief – the guinea pig in the tunnel, having the telltale smoke blown over him as he tries out different equipment and positions – Boardman is the straight man, explaining what needs to be explained, such as pointing out in one of the episodes that full aerodynamic 'time trial'-style helmets are perfectly legal for massed-start road racing. Cue Boulting's mock (or perhaps real) shock that no one uses one.

'I'm wondering who's going to be the first team to lead their sprinter on to the Champs-Elysées all wearing these,' says Boardman. 'I think it'll be Saur-Sojasun,' Boulting guesses, a little hopefully, suggesting the small and very traditional – and now defunct – French team.

'People just think full aero helmets look stupid,' Boardman tells me. '*I* think they look stupid, but at least I'm now aware of the fact that that's what would be stopping me from wearing one. But people just continue to come up with reasons why they wouldn't do it; they can't just go with the fact that it looks horrible. They're always trying to find that logical reason: "Oh, it's too hot, or . . ."'

Rudely, I interrupt, trying – only a little – to catch him out. What about the 1996 Olympic time trial in Atlanta, I ask, recalling a picture of him with a bare head on his way to a bronze medal. He didn't even wear an aero time-trial helmet then.

'I did, actually,' he corrects me, 'but I took it off after a while as it was so hot there – 90 per cent humidity. Heat was a major issue – or trying to dissipate heat was. I felt really hot, and I had a piece of clothing on [the helmet] that I could remove, so I removed it. But it was really only covering the part of my head covered with hair anyway, so taking it off probably didn't make any difference at all.'

But blocking up vents on a road helmet has to make you hotter, I start arguing. Probably around half of the pro peloton now frequently wear aero helmets, and most track riders use them now, too. But what about the heat effect during, say, July's Tour de France?

I quickly realize that I sound exactly like the people who try to come up with a logical reason for not doing something that annoy Boardman. He barely flinches; he must have been asked this hundreds of times.

'Well, that's what you have to weigh up,' he says, patiently. 'You make emotive decisions when you don't have information – like I did in Atlanta in the time trial. But nowadays you can measure the aerodynamic effect of something, so you can see what something's worth. If I've got to slow down by X amount because of heat, am I left with a net gain or a net loss? Aerodynamics is weighing stuff up. You may have a position that isn't the most efficient, for example, in which you lose some power production, but you might still have a net gain because you've got reduced drag.

'You might find that a skinsuit is the most aerodynamic thing to use, but that it gives you other disadvantages – and I can't think of any offhand, apart from going to the toilet! You can make an informed choice. But people are still making decisions based on tradition and history, and what something looks like. I'm amazed that more cyclists aren't routinely in wind tunnels, because that's the biggest force you're trying to overcome. That's the biggest piece of knowledge that you need, and yet we're still using pulse monitors and power meters.'

It's an eloquent summary of Boardman's frustrations, and yet he's clearly influenced the choices made by today's pro peloton to use aero road helmets, bikes and skinsuits. Riders had experimented with skinsuits in road races in the past – Stephen Roche, David Zabriskie, and Boardman himself – but it's only really been the British national team and Team Sky who have used them on a regular basis.

Aero road helmets are a very recent phenomenon, only catching on after Cavendish used a clear plastic cover over his helmet to help him win the 2011 road world championships in Copenhagen. The entire British team used skinsuits that day, too.

Rob Hayles – the 2005 team pursuit and Madison world champion, who won the latter in partnership with a then 19-year-old Cavendish – was a regular Secret Squirrel Club guinea pig, often sharing wind-tunnel-testing duties with Jason Queally. It was Hayles's idea to cover up the vents on Cavendish's helmet in an effort to make him even more aerodynamic.

'Cavendish came to the wind tunnel and went through a full day's experimentation,' reveals Boardman. 'The reason he went to the Worlds dressed as he did was because he'd come to the tunnel and we'd given him different helmets and clothing to try and he'd seen the difference it made.'

An aero road helmet, versus a normal road helmet, could reduce drag by 5 per cent, but getting the athletes into the wind tunnel to see the effects for themselves was absolutely key, says Boardman. 'Free-form time, we called it. We gave them live data, which was in a format that they'd chosen, so it could be time-saved in their event, power, newtons of force – whatever they wanted to see. We'd hand them pieces of clothing and helmets, and then they'd experiment, and see what happened. Sure enough, they'd come to the same conclusions as us, and that information belonged to them, so that was the best way to influence behaviour. You had to have them as part of the process; it had to belong to them.

'Chris Hoy was in the wind tunnel a fair bit, looking at his position, and the difference it made,' continues Boardman. 'He worked a lot on it, and put up with the discomfort to try new things. We'd get someone like him to try out some 28-centimetre-wide handlebars, and people would laugh, but if you gave them a suite of handlebars, and they went through them and saw the difference it made, then they'd buy into it.'

That the British national team benefits from the Lottery funding that British Cycling receives is all well and good, and has helped bring it up to the lofty heights of success that it enjoys today. But how much of it filters down to Team Sky – Brailsford's other project?

'Loads,' comes the honest reply from Boardman, who himself has no connection to Sky. 'You can't unknow things, and we found that out very early on. It's the knowledge itself that has the value – you can't unknow it. So Dave was always in a totally com-promised position in that he was trying to do two things with conflicting interests: he's got lots of different nationalities at Sky, and, for them to go faster, he wanted to give them the information that Lottery funding paid for over here, which was an uncomfortable position for me because I ended up being the police a lot of the time – even down to Bradley using skinsuits, which we'd designed for the British team, at the Tour de France in 2012.

'The only way I dealt with it was to say, "Right, I'm going to tell you what I think, and then you are the boss, and you can make the choice, whether I agree with it or not." It came down to that a lot,' continues Boardman. 'But that's Dave, really – he's all about performance. He had people around him like [British Cycling chief executive] Ian Drake and UK Sport who saw that passion and supported him in it.

'But, unlike me, Dave's comfortable being uncomfortable – which I think is another catchphrase he rolled out at some point, and which means he was always much better suited to being in charge than me.'

In 2010, UK Sport commissioned an independent audit by Deloitte to review the relationship between the then-new Sky team and British Cycling. Brailsford might have been slightly annoyed by the investigation, but had nothing to worry about; the two entities could continue to work side by side.

However, in April 2014, Brailsford reconsidered his dual role, and made the difficult decision to step down as British Cycling's performance director in order to devote all of his time to Team Sky, with Shane Sutton moving sideways and up a bit to fill the void in his new role as BC's technical director.

So, where next, research-and-development-wise, for British Cycling on the road and track?

Boardman may have himself sidestepped into a less 'competitive' role, but it's difficult to imagine that he won't continue to be called upon for his input for some time to come.

'It's a horrible cliché, but we've certainly had all the low-hanging fruit,' Boardman says, then pauses, further considering a question that's very difficult to answer. He comes up with a story.

'Two years ago, I stood in the gallery at McLaren's place,' he says, explaining that he used to consult for the engineering group behind the famous Formula One team. 'I was with a guy called Paddy Lowe, the chief engineer [who moved to Mercedes in 2013], and we were leaning on the gantry looking down on the cars, which are racked up together from each year. All very sexy. And I asked him exactly that: "How the hell do you keep coming up with new things?"

'Paddy turned to me and said, "Well, you see that one down there? When that one rolled off the production line, I thought that was it – that it was the best we could do." He then pointed to the car from the following year, and said, "That one was one-and-a-half per cent better, and that one, the year after, was three per cent better."

'He said he just came to the point where he had to have faith: that if you look, you'll find. And if you don't look, you definitely won't find, so I suppose it's that, really. Conceptually, you do think, "Yeah, that's got to be nearly it," but you keep looking and you keep finding something else, and something else. It's certainly getting harder, and it gets more expensive. F1 has put numbers on it – a "how much it costs per tenth of a per cent" kind of thing. There's a huge rise in costs to find every extra gain, so we've had the most efficient bit, yeah.'

Through all the bikes, clothing, helmets and materials at the British national team's disposal, and through everything he's put out there, both physically and through explanation – those ITV aerodynamics episodes, for example – only a relative few in the cycling world have picked up and run with Boardman's wealth of knowledge and expertise. It's almost the equivalent of someone having left their car door unlocked, with the key in the ignition, or perhaps even left it running and stuck a sign on the windscreen that reads, 'Feel free to take my car'. It's that key.

Boardman has been that key, arguably, for modern British cycling's success. That's to take nothing away from Dave Brailsford, his staff or the now scores of athletes who have won world and Olympic titles, and beaten the best at the sport's biggest and greatest events. But, since his 1992 Olympic success, and even well before that, Boardman has been a constant presence.

12

RACING FOR (A HOPELESS CHANCE OF) GLORY

You always look straight ahead – even better, straight down – when using the urinals in a public toilet. Them's the rules.

So it was probably only while washing my hands that I realized that my brother and I had been having a wee next to none other than Chris Boardman.

As Alan-Partridge-esque tales go, the incident at an unmemorable services on the M6 somewhere between Manchester and Birmingham shouldn't really be the highlight of anyone's 'dealings' with celebrity. The 'having a wee' bit, I mean, not the fact that it was Chris Boardman.

But aged eighteen, and a massive fan of professional cycling, meeting Boardman was, for me, easily as good as it could possibly get.

'A'right Chris?' we chirruped; or perhaps only my older brother was brave enough to speak.

Boardman probably answered something mildly encouraging back in his Wirral accent.

Was it a complete coincidence that we ran into Boardman while we were on the way back from my having ridden at the newly opened Manchester Velodrome in 1995, where I was to discover that my future career was almost certainly unlikely to be as a professional cyclist? Actually, yes. There, at the splinter-new (but splinter-free) indoor track, I'd been beaten, hands down and squarely, by a crop of junior riders with whom I spent two days on the smooth, fast pine boards.

My dad, brother and I stayed in a vacated-for-the-summer Manchester University hall of residence, and the two of them watched from the stands as I took part in a weekend of sprinting and Madison hand-slings.

After the two days were up, my only victory had come in a 'track stand' competition: in the centre of the velodrome, rather than on the track itself. A ring of water bottles had created a rudimentary arena, where a dozen or so of us had to try to stand stock-still on our bikes for as long as possible, whilst allowed to nudge our opponents with a shoulder in the hope that they'd have to put a foot down, in which case they were 'out'.

When we first hit the track, I was pleased not to be among the handful of riders who suffered the ignominy of sliding seven metres down the 42.5-degree banking by not riding fast enough at the top and losing traction. The coaches there, no doubt looking for a positive from a negative, having seen my track-stand prowess and lack of falling-off, informed my dad that I was a very good bike handler. In other words, I was nowhere near as talented as the rest of them when it came to out-and-out speed, but they probably thought that I'd be exceptionally deft at keeping out of other riders' way when being lapped.

I know now that I was on the cusp of British Cycling's golden era, when Lottery funding was about to help them nurture young riders and produce future champions. I wasn't to be one of them, but, through track-racing sessions like that one, the national federation was able to identify raw talent and begin the process of crafting such riders into world-beaters.

Back then, we had all been selected from the various track leagues around the country: the 'best' junior riders from each one. Tony Yorke – then the British Cycling Federation's national coaching development officer – had suggested that I take part, explaining that the BCF would be hosting us at the new Manchester Velodrome, and I jumped at the chance to ride on an indoor track. That I was chosen due to the fact that I was the only junior at the Wednesday-night track sessions at the Preston Park track in Brighton showed the lack of any real interest from youngsters at the time, compared to the thriving track leagues of today.

I'd begun racing at Preston Park that summer; it's one of Britain's oldest cycling tracks, constructed in 1877. It's an outdoor tarmac track, with a little bit of banking on the final corner, so it bears little resemblance to the 'wooden bowls' of 'real' track racing. Still, it does the job just fine.

During my first evening of racing there, a rider's handlebars hooked on the railings, and my dad arrived to watch me just as the ambulance turned up to take the unfortunate cyclist away. It was a reminder – not that it was needed – of bike racing's inherent danger, but really there are few safer places to race than at the various track leagues across the country, which provide a controlled, traffic-free environment in which to let loose.

And track racing's infinitely safer than pedalling up and down a dual carriageway on a midweek summer's evening. Time trialling, so long a staple of British racing, continues to draw a crowd – at least in terms of participants; most events would be pleased to welcome more than about a dozen spectators. Unlike track racing, time trialling is far from spectator-friendly. The only friendly aspects of it, really, are the post-race chats and the cup of tea and slice of home-made cake at the finish (normally included in the entry fee), which, when you've often only paid a quid or two to take part anyway, is such good value that it's enough to put the likes of Greggs to shame.

The appeal lies in trying to beat your own best time, and perhaps in the fact that you ride alone. Up and down the country each summer, the weekly 'evening-10' series organized by most cycling clubs are a perfect introduction to competitive riding, and often the only form of racing many British cyclists ever try. We've always tended to be rather good at it, too.

However, the thrill of the race only just outweighs the danger of huge lorries passing by about an inch to your right, and throughout the well over a hundred years that the discipline has been practised in the UK, it has become more and more dangerous, in parallel with the increasing amount of traffic on British roads.

I find it hard to believe now that my parents were ever actually happy to let my 12-year-old self loose on the A24 between Findon and Washington in West Sussex. They probably weren't, but my brother, who was two years older than me, was already taking part, and I was clearly champing at the bit, waiting until I reached the minimum age permitted by the national time-trial governing body, which was then called the Road Time Trials Council (RTTC) and is now Cycling Time Trials (CTT).

The way to do it – then, and still now – was to join an RTTC/CTT-affiliated cycling club, which would often be, but didn't necessarily have to be, affiliated to British Cycling. The national cycling federation and the national governing body for time trials remain entirely separate organizations.

Having joined, it couldn't really be simpler to enter your first race: fill in a form, get your possibly reluctant parents to sign it if you're under eighteen, pay your money and turn up on a Thursday evening – as it was at the Worthing Excelsior Cycling Club – at 7 p.m. ready to ride.

Worthing Excelsior is one of the UK's oldest clubs, formed in 1887 as the Worthing Working Men's Excelsior Cycling Club. Members have always enjoyed both the social and the competitive sides of cycling: from road racing, to touring, to track racing. But most racing members tended to favour time trialling: 'the race of truth'.

The summer evening-10 series – held, as the name suggests, over 10 miles – were where I cut my racing teeth. The danger barely registered with me. I was sensible, serious and an experienced rider, even at that age, and so what's riding 10 miles as fast as you possibly can when you're an enthusiastic 12-year-old?

I did something over 30 minutes in my first outing; perhaps more like 32, but I soon got down to well below the half-hour-mark. I think I eventually got down to 25 minutes, dead-on, which remained my best until some years later, and even then – at my supposed 'racing peak' of late-twenties/early thirties – I didn't better it by much.

What, I once asked my dad, would I have to do to try to become a professional cyclist? Rather than warn me off it, he explained, quite rightly, that for a start I'd need to be winning these evening 10s. Aged twelve, that wasn't going to happen any time soon, but did I have the commitment, drive and, most importantly, talent to achieve that in the coming years? Not even close; I didn't train – I had other things to do, like playing computer games, doing a paper round, playing football with my friends . . . Clearly, I didn't want it enough, and was happy to just keep racing once a week, trying to better my time against the clock while watching the Tour de France on Channel 4 for inspiration.

My brother and I took part in those time trials for years, with our dad enabling us to get there by giving us a lift after a mad dash home from work for him on a Thursday night. In time-honoured tradition, he was the one who had got us into cycling in the first place, riding the 12 miles to and from work each day on the various Peugeot and Dawes bikes he owned over the years.

At the evening 10s, he often took on the role of 'pusher-off': holding up each rider, so that they could be clipped into their pedals and ready to go as the timekeeper counted them down to their start. Still unsure to this day whether to give the riders an extra shove on their way or to just let go and let them move forward under their own steam, my dad always plumped for the former, to all the riders' advantage.

I didn't really make any friends out of cycling back then. The members of Worthing Excelsior were certainly friendly enough, but most were considerably older than me, and so I kept my school friends as my friends – friends who at that point couldn't have cared less about cycling, other than as a means of transport to get to school.

The few other youngsters at the club tended to focus more on road racing, and on the 'Goodwood Gallops' in particular, which took place at the Goodwood motor circuit near Chichester (which also hosted the road world championships in 1982). These boys certainly seemed a different breed to the older riders taking part in the time trials: they had all the latest gear, and showed it off with their glistening, warm-up-oiled and shaven legs.

At that age, my legs weren't hairy enough for me to even consider shaving. But I had my Reynolds-500-tubed Geoffrey Butler frame, built up with the cheapest Campagnolo groupset I could buy, all paid for by the sale of my Star Wars toys and a little help from my parents. For time trialling, I'd saved up for a pair of matching fluorescent yellow Profile Aero II clip-on 'tri bars' – similar to those used by Greg LeMond to help him win the 1989 Tour de France – and taking them off would have left me with a perfectly good road-racing machine. Making that step to road racing to join the oily boys, however, seemed a leap too big, and I stuck with time trialling before, aged eighteen, I headed off to university and left the evening 10s behind me.

I'd used that same Geoffrey Butler frame for my first season of track racing around the same time – adapted to make it into a fixed-wheel bike. The chain-line, however, was just a tiny bit off, which meant that my chain popped off at high speed a couple of times, which wasn't going to do anyone any favours. I'll be eternally grateful, then, that the organizers at Preston Park helped put together an old steel-framed track bike for me to use instead, ensuring that the league retained at least one junior rider.

I still have that bike – and still use it – but it's a constant reminder, nagging at me, that I, too, need to give more back to the sport in terms of giving stuff away and volunteering. I was able to give a few bits and pieces to my old club a couple of years ago: some clothing, helmets and shoes that I'd acquired over the years. But it's an incredibly expensive sport, and those of us sitting on our old kit probably underestimate the good it can do to people – and especially to youngsters just starting out, who would be more than happy to use it, and perhaps then upgrade later.

It might have been all about time trialling for me for many years, but, at Southampton University, eventually, in my final year, I took the plunge and started my first road race.

After a couple of years of duathlon-ing and triathlon-ing, some of us started a specific university cycling club, taking part in some local time trials in the New Forest, and using one of the university minibuses to get to the Thruxton motor circuit, near Andover, in Hampshire.

In my first road race there, I managed to crash, having been forced up on to one of the red-and-white-striped kerbs thanks to a lack of elbow-use on my part. Remounting, I finished the race alone before climbing into the back of a St John's ambulance to be bandaged up.

It didn't put me off, luckily, and I returned to Thruxton a few weeks later to finish comfortably mid-pack in my next race, before heading to the British Universities road race championships at the end of my final academic year, which I didn't finish (the race – not my degree).

Even at the lower end, this isn't pub football. Just finishing a bike race requires at least a good base level of fitness, confidence and concentration. Starting with the fourth-category ('4th cat'), the levels of difficulty increase through 3rd, 2nd, 1st and Elite ('E'). And then you can think about turning professional. Starting out as a 4th cat is tough, and you'll only progress to the next level by scoring points – i.e. by placing highly in a race. Luckily, these days British Cycling has also introduced the Go-Race category for complete beginners, which can be found at some events, although you may often be put together with the 4th cats in those, too. Scoring enough points to make the jump from 4th to 3rd means you'll never go back to being a 4th, however.

You'll also need a racing licence, which you buy after becoming a member of British Cycling, although for those wanting to give racing a try without committing to a full licence, it's usually possible to pay for a 'day licence' at the event.

There are various combinations of categories lumped together, often dependent on demand: you may find a 4th-cat-only event, or 4th and 3rd cats together ('3/4'), or Elites, 1st, 2nd and 3rd cats in one race ('E/1/2/3'). Particularly in the lower categories, women's races have often also been thrown in with the men's, but the increased interest in bike racing has meant an increase in women-only events.

Youth races are run on the basis of age up until the age of sixteen, when riders become 'juniors', who are sometimes put alongside the men in 3/4 races. In 2010, British Cycling intro-duced Go-Ride Racing for under-16s looking to get their foot on the racing ladder: events organized by Go-Ride affiliated clubs in all cycling disciplines, with prizes supplied by British Cycling, allowing youngsters to race against other riders of a similar age and ability in local races, with no need for a racing licence, before perhaps stepping up to regional junior competitions.

No matter your age or sex, starting out in road racing is not for the faint-hearted, and other racers occasionally seem to forget that they, too, started out somewhere. There's already the difficulty of the racing itself, but when you add in the pre-race fears about crashing or being worried that you won't be able to keep up, the last thing anyone needs is an unfriendly attitude from someone on a flash bike who thinks they're too talented to be nice.

But, once you're in, you're normally in for life; there's always next week, and the pull of competition usually proves too much.

In the years that followed university, and having moved to London, I often took part in races at Eastway. The iconic and much-loved road-race circuit near Stratford, and part of the Lee Valley Regional Park, was razed in 2006 to make way for the Olympic Park and, ironically, the Olympic Velodrome and 'replacement' road-race circuit, which wouldn't be available until well after the Games. In the meantime, the Hog Hill circuit in Redbridge opened, in 2008, and riders – including me – were able to take up where Eastway left off with a packed programme of racing and training days. I've never moved up from being a 4th cat, though.

In 2008, I peaked. At least, I had a good year. I ran my fastest-ever marathon, did well in some duathlons and returned to my old Worthing Excelsior evening-10 course, where I recorded my best-ever time.

Living in south London, I really should have been racing at the Herne Hill track, but one evening that year I returned to Preston Park, where I had the strength, just, to attack off the front of a scratch race that contained former pro Sean Yates – a local, of sorts, hailing from nearby Forest Row – and his brother. I was reeled in less than a lap later.

But a sustained period of serious training, which was probably really only a few weeks, yielded real results, and I realized how work and real life normally get, and still do get, in the way of any kind of sustained period of training for most of us. Perhaps I'd reached my peak in my early thirties, as pro cyclists supposedly do – but I don't really believe that. I truly believe that anyone, at any age, can still get to a reasonable level of fitness and competition with a little focused training.

After too long away from regular competition, I hope to start racing again soon: at the track in Welwyn Garden City, at Herne Hill, at Hog Hill and hopefully at the new Lee Valley VeloPark, too. With thriving cycling clubs, track leagues and closed-road circuits all over the country, the opportunity to take up bike racing has never been easier – even if the racing itself will be as tough as it's ever been.

13

TIME TRIALLING WITH DOCTOR HUTCH

My enjoyment of time trialling has always been tempered slightly by a complete and utter lack of success. Contrast that to Michael Hutchinson, who's enjoyed such success that the number of national titles he's won against the clock puts him behind only the great Beryl Burton.

While Burton's 96 national titles across Cycling Time Trials (CTT) events seem like an untouchable figure – and it surely is – Hutchinson hobbles home with 56 national titles. Or thereabouts. Even he isn't entirely sure how many it is, exactly.

'I just tend to trust my Wikipedia page, which says it's 56, and which seems about right,' he laughs.

Give it a few more years, I suggest, and Burton's record might hove into sight.

'I'm not catching Beryl Burton!' he laughs again. 'I'm really not. I'm barely halfway there! She won the National 25 [mile time trial] twenty-seven times, or something ludicrous!

'Plus she started when she was eighteen and was still plugging away in her forties,' he adds, by way of an 'excuse', as if any were needed. 'I'd already started ten years too late!'

It doesn't seem appropriate to remind Hutchinson that he's now crept into his forties himself, although perhaps that's his point.

Not that he's showing any signs of slowing down. In 2013, he won the CTT National 10 title for the ninth time (a distance for which he held the British record – 17 minutes and 45 seconds – until 2014, when three-time British time-trial national champion Alex Dowsett lowered it by another 25 seconds to 17–20).

In a display of Burton-esque dominance, Hutchinson also won the 50-mile title thirteen times in a row between 2000 and 2012, but missed out on the opportunity of defending his title in 2013 due to illness, when Matt Bottrill took on the mantle of CTT 50-mile champion. Bottrill fits his training in around family life and working as a postman; Hutchinson is an author and journalist, but did ride the national time-trial circuit as a professional for five years from 2001.

'Everyone thinks that I still am a pro, but I gave that up in 2006,' Hutchinson explains. 'I wanted to do other things. I published *The Hour* [his first book, about his attempt to follow in the footsteps of Chris Boardman and Graeme Obree to break the Hour record] that year, and had started doing work for Radio 4 as a reporter for the *Today* programme at one point. I'd started doing my column for *Cycling Weekly*, then, too; I'd decided it was time I grew up and moved on to other things.'

Hutchinson's columns for *Cycling Weekly* provided, and continue to provide, some comic relief in a sport that often takes itself rather seriously, although, whether he'd admit to it or not, his has always been a voice of reason. He's been there and done it when it comes to racing in Britain, and, as 'Doctor Hutch', he tends to tell it like it is.

Hutchinson also explains that one of the other reasons not to continue as a professional beyond 2006 was that it was the year when *Cycling Weekly* shifted its traditional focus from time-trial reports and results to the more general health and fitness benefits of cycling, and to the burgeoning discipline of cyclosportives – or sportives, as they're more simply, and increasingly, called: mass-participation rides in the UK and Europe under race-like conditions, that aren't actually races; the most well known being the Etape du Tour, during which amateur riders tackle a stage of the Tour de France. Soon, British pros' track and road exploits also took precedence over time trialling.

'When you started to get people like Bradley Wiggins going to the Tour to try to get a result, and riders such as Geraint Thomas winning the junior Paris–Roubaix [in 2004; Andy Fenn also won it in 2008], I can see why, from a commercial point of view, the idea of giving over half the magazine to domestic bike racing didn't work any more.

'My job as a pro was, essentially, to get my name and my picture in the magazine as often as I could, because it produced awareness of a brand. I rode for Giant for several years, and it did amazing things for them in terms of selling their bikes to time triallists. But when *Cycling Weekly* stopped reporting on time trialling as much, and you just got a picture on an eighth of a page . . . I mean, before, if you won the Nationals, you'd get on the cover and they'd issue bloody posters of you! A pull-out poster of "Hutch", and all that stuff! So when they stopped doing that it got harder to justify someone giving you a living wage for a year to ride time trials.'

Hutchinson may no longer be a full-time rider, but he continues to be supported by sponsors in his quest for more titles and faster times.

'I get help to cover my costs; if people are willing to help, then it's nice that the sport doesn't cost me a fortune,' he says. 'But I still don't make a profit on time trialling because I still have to buy lots of equipment; I'm not coming out in front by any stretch. There have only ever been a handful of people who've ever made a living out of time trialling in Britain. I was one, and Stuart Dangerfield was another.'

Not that giving up racing as a full-time pro meant slowing down. On the contrary: Hutchinson sees the last few years of the 2000s as his best years, 'although I'd have won an awful lot more before that if I hadn't come up against the likes of Dangerfield'.

Dangerfield is a four-time British time-trial national champion, and, like Hutchinson, a six-time winner of the CTT's 25-mile title.

'I was lucky in that later period in that I seemed to be on top of most of the people I was racing with,' adds Hutchinson, 'and for several years I also felt that I was one jump ahead on the technology side of things as well, which helped. I was one of the first to go into a wind tunnel and take that side of things seriously.'

There appear to be two extremes when it comes to how people view time trialling in the UK. There are those that treat it almost like a poor man's Formula One, with all the carbon-fibre kit that comes with it, and for whom failing to beat their previous best time is viewed as abject failure. And then there are those who see it as a semi-friendly, once-a–week summer meet-up next to a dual carriageway where they have a bit of a ride and then a slice of cake and a cup of tea afterwards.

And then there's every combination of the extremes in between, as people realize that they're improving, and so perhaps invest in better equipment, or find they're slowing down with their advancing years, or are getting a bit faster thanks to improving fitness. Hutchinson concurs – to a point.

'I think that the first thing to say about time trialling is that it's an historical anachronism. It really only exists in the UK, because of the history of racing in Britain and how it developed. And I think that one of the reasons why it seems to mean something different to almost everybody is that it *is* genuinely something different to almost everybody.

'You go to a "club 10" and see it all,' he continues. 'At one end, all modesty set aside, there's me: the reigning [2013 10-mile] national champion. I'm not as good as I once was, but I'm not a bad bike rider; I can go to a world championships and hold my own. At the other end, there are riders in their fifties and sixties who've just taken up cycling recently and who have just turned up on their road bikes to ride round.

'I'm not doing the same thing they're doing, yet we're doing what we're doing at the same place and at the same time. We're all doing the same sport, and there's almost nothing else I can think of that's quite like that.

'Except perhaps sailing,' he adds, having thought for a moment. Hutchinson had been a keen dinghy racer as a teenager, and recounts rediscovering his love for sailing in his second book, which was initially published as *Hello Sailor* – a title Hutchinson describes as 'a mistake' – and later reissued as *Missing the Boat*.

'*Hello Sailor* had just been a working title, which then turned up on the contract, and which I couldn't dislodge,' Hutchinson laughs. 'The publishers thought it was a hilarious title, but if I'd been able to come up with *Missing the Boat*, which is much better, a bit earlier, I reckon I could have swung it.'

His point about sailing and cycling is that they're quite similar in terms of the breadth of people who take part in it. 'At one end you'd get people in carbon-fibre boats who'd spent an enormous amount of money, and at the other end you'd get people who were just out to sail around a bit.

'Similarly, you can even go to the National 10, and at one end you could find Alex Dowsett, and at the other end someone in their early sixties, who has a full-time job and fits training in when they can, and who's there looking for the age-group championships, but who's going to be four or five minutes slower.'

Time trialling, in other words, says Hutchinson, offers everyone the opportunity to achieve goals on their own terms. Unlike road racing. 'If you do a road race and get dropped on the second lap of an eight-lap race – if you're a middle-aged guy of no particularly extraordinary talent with no particularly extraordinary amount of time during which to train – then you'll spend an awful lot of time driving to road races, getting dropped early and then driving home again,' says Hutchinson. 'But in time trialling, if you want to actually go and race, anyone can do it, and anyone can get a result. That's the attraction, I think. It's a bit like playing amateur football: no matter how bad you are, you're often still getting ninety minutes.'

Indeed, time trialling has to be one of the few sports where the less ability you have, the longer it takes you, and so the better value for money it is.

They call time trialling 'the race of truth'. A few people do, anyway. Something to do with there being nowhere to hide: just you against the clock. For some, it's this loneliness – this lack of relying on anyone else – that appeals. But do you have to be a certain type of person to enjoy racing on your own? Is it cycling's 'lonely' discipline?

'"Lonely" isn't really the word I'd use; it's no different from running,' Hutchinson points out. Running on your own, he means, which for some reason isn't viewed as being 'lonely' in quite the same way as cycling on your own seems to be.

Besides, he says, there isn't exactly a lot of social life going on in the middle of a marathon, either; everybody's running in the same direction at the same time, but there's nothing particularly social about it. 'There are plenty of road races like that, too. Not a lot of yak goes on in a criterium.'

He certainly doesn't think that people choose time trialling over road racing because they just want to be on their own.

'The thing I like about it is that in order to win a time trial you just have to be the fastest person there. I've always liked that purity to it,' he explains. 'I definitely don't consider myself to be anti-social or a loner or anything like that!'

Followers of the faster end of British time trialling may or may not be aware that, since 2011, Hutchinson has held an Irish racing licence. That makes no difference to his continuing quest for, and probable taking of, further CTT records or titles; a person of any nationality can become a British CTT national champion, providing that they've resided in the UK for two years, while anyone – including Switzerland's four-time time-trial world champion Fabian Cancellara or three-time world champion Tony Martin of Germany – is free to come and set the British record at any of the CTT distances. Which would be interesting to see.

But what having an Irish racing licence does mean is that Hutchinson is no longer eligible for the separate, British-Cycling-run time-trial national championships, which he won three times, in 2002, 2004 and 2008. He's now won the Irish time-trial championships three times in a row – in 2012, 2013 and 2014.

Hutchinson is from Northern Ireland, which means that he holds dual citizenship – he can hold both an Ireland and UK passport – which in turn means that, in the sporting world, he can hold either an Irish or British licence.

'The first race I ever did was in England, and so I had a British racing licence simply because I'd taken up racing in the UK,' he says. 'But at that point I didn't think, "I shall take up cycling and I shall become an international cyclist!"'

That thought came soon enough, however, once he realized how good he was.

'When I became interested in potentially representing Ireland, in about 1999 or 2000, I was told that if you had dual nationality you could only ever race for the nation where you'd done your first race, although I was never completely convinced about that.

'But I just stuck with the GB licence I had, and not long after that the Great Britain national squad came and asked me if I wanted to go and train with them, so I did. This was 2000 or 2001 – when I wasn't quite on and wasn't quite off the GB track squad.'

Despite going on to win the British national pursuit championships in 2002, Hutchinson was never funded by the British programme as he didn't meet the standard time to qualify for funding. 'The frustration was that it was perfectly obvious to both me and the coaching staff that I had the physical ability to make the standard time, but I never quite seemed to do it,' he explains. 'I was within a couple of tenths of a second of getting it on several occasions, but these things just don't click sometimes.'

If he'd moved to Manchester in order to be able to train on the track every day, then he thinks he might have been able to make the standard time he needed to qualify for funding.

'I definitely thought about moving, but at that point I owned a flat in the south of England, and was also making a living riding time trials, which I would have had to have stopped doing to do the GB track thing properly. They don't go well together, despite Chris Boardman's success in both. At the time, it just felt like quite a big risk to me – to give up my job and to move house.

'I look back at it now and think I should have done that: obviously I should have,' he admits. 'But you've also got to bear in mind that I could have made the standard, and got on to the squad, and got the funding, and then could have spent two years barely riding an event because at every individual pursuit, at every Olympics or world championships, Brad Wiggins was going to get the first squad place and Rob Hayles was probably going to get the second, as you were looking at two guys there who were cracking out 4–18s [four minutes and 18 seconds for 4,000 metres] and 4–19s fairly regularly, while my all-time best 4km PB was only ever about 4–24.'

In the Commonwealth Games, British athletes compete for their constituent country: England, Scotland, Northern Ireland or Wales. Hutchinson rides for Northern Ireland.

The Northern Ireland coach at the 2010 Commonwealth Games in Delhi – where Hutchinson finished fourth in the time trial, just as he had at the Melbourne Games in 2006 – was also the coach for the Irish elite squad, and told Hutchinson that he'd certainly never come across the supposed policy of not being able to represent a nation that you were eligible for just because you'd taken part in your first race in a different country. 'Certainly, it wasn't enforced any more, I was told, and so they asked me if I was still interested in racing for Ireland,' says Hutchinson. 'Remember, I'd always originally wanted to represent Ireland internationally, so I said yes.'

He wasn't ever agonizing over whether to give up his British licence to take out an Irish racing licence, then?

'Not at all. Cycling Ireland had said that they were happy to have me, I had the nationality, and I clearly wasn't about to be representing GB internationally any time soon, so why wouldn't I do it?' No one from the British or Irish cycling establishments has ever raised an eyebrow, he says, and neither would he expect them to. 'None of it's really an issue,' Hutchinson continues. 'I think that in any of the home nations at the Commonwealth Games there's quite a bit of fluidity: you find people from England with a Northern Irish background who represent Northern Ireland, or people living in Ireland with a Northern Irish background repre-senting Northern Ireland.

'And I'll always remember at the 2006 Commonwealth Games watching Shane Sutton [an Australian] wearing a Scottish jacket to hold up Chris Hoy at the start of the kilo [1-kilometre time trial], and then the next rider up would be Jason Queally, and Shane would put an English jacket on to hold him up! Yet at the time he was actually the Welsh coach, so I think he'd grasped the fluidity of it all . . .'

On the theme of international competition, 'Doctor Hutch' is perhaps less well known as the three-time winner of the Brompton

World Championships. The annual race, duked out between competitors on bikes built by the British folding-bike brand, is raced on the Goodwood motor circuit in West Sussex, and involves riders – dressed in business attire – running to their Bromptons and unfolding them before starting on their four laps of the circuit. Like time trialling, it's a peculiarly British form of racing, although the 2008 edition did attract Lance Armstrong's former US Postal teammate Roberto Heras from Spain, who was so disappointed to finish second (to Britain's Alastair Kay) that he returned in 2009 to make sure he won it, which he did.

Hutchinson was second to Heras that year, then won it in 2011, and Hutchinson has dominated the competition ever since. There was no suggestion that it was going to be any different in 2014, provided he actually made it to the start line; he was just awaiting a phone call to find out whether he was going to be heading to Glasgow instead.

'The Brompton world champs clash with the Commonwealth Games in 2014,' he explains, glumly, and I'm left seriously contemplating which event he'd rather ride.

14

MILLAR TIME

It was probably the fact that David Millar was only a month older than me that grated. If I'd not played so much Sensible Soccer on my mate's (also called David) Atari ST and had done some proper training instead, then maybe I, too, would have been capable of winning the prologue time trial at the 2000 Tour de France, and with it the yellow jersey.

Having accepted that football-themed computer games had scuppered my Tour dream, I even bought one of those 'It's Millar Time' T-shirts the following year, printed and sold via *Procycling* magazine by his sister, Fran – now at Team Sky where she has the improbable job title of Head of Winning Behaviours – and, with my dad, I went to the prologue of the 2001 Tour in Dunkirk in the hope of witnessing Millar do it again. But he crashed, and could only limp home, 110th.

I was a fan, although there was something quite odd about being a fan of someone my own age, as opposed to the Greg LeMonds, Sean Kellys and Sean Yateses who'd occupied my bedroom-wall space in the years before. Turns out I was just getting older, and the possibility of ever riding the Tour de France – ha! – had irrevocably passed me by.

I first met Millar in Copenhagen, where I was then living, at the 2001 Tour of Denmark, which he won. I asked him for a photo with me, and when I went to have the film developed I found that I'd forgotten to put one in the camera. It makes me laugh now when cycling magazines print that photo of a young Mark Cavendish with Millar at the Isle of Man Cycling Week in 1999. Cavendish looks such a fan – just like I would have done in that non-existent photograph.

Years later, when I'd become a journalist, I remember thinking what a lonely figure Millar seemed to cut at the start villages of the 2006 Tour – the first after his doping ban – rarely, it seemed, in the company of his new Saunier Duval teammates. He appeared only too aware that doping was still rife, and he was right: the Puerto doping affair had blown up at the start of that Tour, and in 2007 his Saunier Duval teammate Iban Mayo tested positive for EPO.

In 2008, Millar's saviour – not to over-blow it – came in the form of a fellow former doper called Jonathan Vaughters, who was a former teammate of Lance Armstrong. Vaughters' Garmin team – the rest of us discovered later – was a safe haven for reformed characters, and an environment in which they and young, clean pros, could coexist without pressure or recourse to banned substances, which was exactly what Millar needed. And he thrived, winning stages of all three Grand Tours and gold in the 2010 Commonwealth Games time trial – riding for Scotland – during his time with Vaughters. And it's with the Garmin team that Millar will bring the curtain down on his career at the end of the 2014 season – now married, and with two children, he's older, wiser, happier.

Until 2004 – when Millar would admit to having used EPO to help him win the 2003 time-trial world championships – British cycling had been ticking along, as it always had, with just flashes of brilliance and success. An overall victory at the Tour de France seemed about as likely as a French one – or rather the first French one since 1985, when Bernard Hinault had won his fifth and final Tour. And while, ahead of the 2014 Tour, Great Britain has now won two, the French *attendent toujours*.

In 1984, it had been 'Millar Time' part one, when Scotland's Robert Millar (no relation) finished fourth overall at the Tour, and won the King of the Mountains jersey in the process. In the years that followed, starting with Chris Boardman's Lotus-bike exploits at the 1992 Barcelona Olympics, British cycling success had pretty much revolved around, and been measured by, Boardman and Obree's battle of the bikes on the track and then, in Boardman's case, his time-trial exploits on the road.

When the wins came, they were usually in time trials: 'the race of truth' that was the staple diet of British racing cyclists. Sean Yates won the stage-six time trial at the 1988 Tour, Boardman the prologue at the Tour in '94, '97 and '98, and then David Millar took the opening-stage time trial at the 2000 Tour in Futuroscope, and was time-trial world champion by the end of 2003.

The French sniffed and shrugged: so the Brits were good against the clock. There were few signs that British riders were ever going to amount to much more than that.

But Millar shrugged off that stereotype, embracing French culture and the life of a European-based professional bike rider. He lived the life he believed a pro was meant to lead, and when the French police searched his apartment in Biarritz and uncovered empty EPO syringes in 2004, he lost everything, including his self-respect for a while. His journey – and it is a journey – is documented in marvellous detail in his 2011 autobiography, *Racing Through the Dark: The Fall and Rise of David Millar*. Unlike many of his caught colleagues, Millar came across as genuinely repentant in the aftermath of his confession. He joined the World Anti-Doping Agency's (WADA) Athletes Committee –

a position of responsibility that he very much enjoyed – and he also became very much the go-to guy in the wake of any subsequent doping bust in the pro peloton. Still is.

When he made his return to competition, Millar demonstrated that he had the potential, and the actual ability, to feature in Brailsford's grand track plans by winning the 2006 British individual pursuit championships. If only British Olympic Association (BOA) rules of the time hadn't prevented him from ever competing in the Olympics again.

But his heart was in European road racing, and he returned to the 2006 Tour riding for the Spanish Saunier Duval outfit, before moving to Garmin in 2008.

In April 2010, I sat down for an interview with Millar at the Château Hôtel Mont Royal in Chantilly, where the Garmin team were staying, the evening before Paris–Roubaix.

At that time, I was just on the brink of leaving *Procycling* magazine to join *Cycle Sport* and *Cycling Weekly*, and the piece eventually ran in the *Weekly* as part of a preview for that year's Tour de France, in which eight Britons were taking part; this was the most since the 1968 Tour, when a ten-man squad had included Barry Hoban, Arthur Metcalfe, Hugh Porter and Colin Lewis.

Millar was already having an excellent season in 2010: he won the time trial at the Critérium International in March, and then the overall classification in the Three Days of De Panne through a planned, methodical execution, just ten days before our interview. He admitted that he was racing more aggressively than ever, taking more chances as he felt he had little to lose because his Garmin bosses didn't have the same expectations of him. Ironically, he was going better as the result of a lack of pressure.

'It's [now about] passion – trying things,' he told me. 'I'm not scared to try racing the way I have lately any more.'

You could almost hear the mindset-switch on stage six of the 2009 Tour de France, between Girona and Barcelona, when a lone

Millar gave it everything to hold off a speeding, hungry peloton, only to be gobbled up with just over a kilometre left to go.

As we chatted in the hotel bar, Millar was as candid as ever about his return to the sport more generally, too, calling himself 'lucky' to have gone through – or come through – everything he did. 'That's why I work very much in the anti-doping world; I want to do that because I feel very strongly that it's a horrific practice and affects you in very deep ways,' he admitted. 'And it's cheating, and it's wrong, and it shouldn't happen. But I did it, and it's made me the person I am. It's actually made me a better person than I was before. It took that much for me to sort my shit out. For me it's ended up working a treat, but it's been a horrible way to do it.'

He explained that, looking back, he found it difficult to even recognize his 23- or 24-year-old self, and that now, at 32, he felt like a very different person.

'How you handle things is how you become. But we're not taught how. You have to make your own mistakes. Mine was big enough to force me to actually look at myself. But, for many people, their mistakes are not big enough, and it turns them into a ****,' he said, really enunciating the last word, which I couldn't help thinking he'd used entirely legitimately, such was the passion and purpose behind it.

'That's what happens to most people: they turn into ****s,' I heard Millar say again. I hadn't really expected the word to be used a second time, although French appeared to be the language of choice surrounding us, and our fellow patrons would have understood only if they'd heard the word *chatte*, used in its very worst form . . .

Then he said it again: 'And I was well on the way to being a ****, so I'm kind of glad I'm out of that.'

A not insignificant number of his compatriots – both members of the cycling press and the public – had made up their minds that

Above: A rather retro winner's jersey for the Austrian Richard Durlacher, inaugural champion of the 'Milk-for-Stamina Cycle Tour of Britain 1958'.

Right: Bill Bradley was the first British winner of the Milk Race, in both 1959 and here in 1960.

Below: On the day that she received the MBE in 1964, Beryl Burton joins stage seven winner Mike Cowley in the traditional milk-drinking.

Above: The Milk Race did not always enjoy bumper crowds and also had its fair share of teething problems, for instance (**left**) in 1968, when two lorries blocked the road during the stage from Bournemouth to Paignton.

Below: Stage one of the 1976 Milk Race in Brighton, always one of Britain's most popular cycling towns.

Above: Malcolm Elliott celebrates winning the Kellogg's Tour of Britain in 1988 after a city-centre finish in London.

Right: Robert Millar in the distinctive Kellogg's 'K polka-dot' King of the Mountains jersey in 1990. Channel 4's television coverage gave cycling a new audience.

Below: Bradley Wiggins joined the great pantheon of Tour of Britain winners in 2013, and the race continues to go from strength to strength.

Above: Barry Hoban takes the plaudits after one of his eight Tour de France stage wins, in Montpellier in 1974. That would be a record for a British rider until Mark Cavendish came along.

Left: Robert Millar with a stage victory at the Tour in 1983. He would break new ground by winning the mountains classification the following year.

Below: Support for Sean Yates, another of the great British Tour riders and select group of yellow jersey wearers.

Right: Cavendish is congratulated by his road team captain, David Millar, after becoming world champion in Copenhagen in 2011.

Below: Bradley Wiggins greets the hordes of British fans after winning the Tour de France in 2012. With Chris Froome's victory the following year, the colours of red, white and blue were by now firmly established at the top of the cycling world.

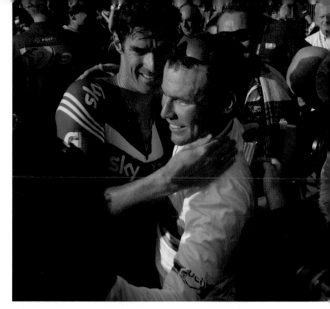

Left: The Tour de France first landed on British shores in 1974, but it was under the cover of Devon darkness.

Below: The solitary 1974 stage speeds along the Plympton by-pass, not that many people are looking at Barry Hoban leading the race.

Bottom: There was a far better reception for the Tour in 1994, especially after Chris Boardman had been in yellow. Here he shares a joke with Tony Rominger and Greg LeMond on stage four from Dover to Brighton.

Above: When Christian Prudhomme announced the return of the Tour de France to Britain in 2014, paying due homage to Tommy Simpson, it was in the full knowledge of the massive success of its visit seven years previously (**below**), when Bradley Wiggins narrowly failed to make the podium in the prologue on a wonderful day in London.

Above: Emma and Laura Trott chat before the start of stage four of the Women's Tour in 2014 – it was an historic week in cycling history met with a rapturous reception – while few people could have foreseen the sheer quantity of fans (**below**) who turned out to watch the Tour de France in Yorkshire. Just brilliant.

he already was a **** once they discovered Millar had been doping, and he was forced to face the backlash when he left his home in France to live in Manchester, closer to those involved with British Cycling, who perhaps knew him best.

'The ironic thing was that I was most hated by the British press, villainized by the UK, and yet I went back there and realized that it was my home,' he said. 'It was much easier where I lived in France, in Biarritz. The French have been the most forgiving, and most empathetic, through it all. That was one of the most wonderful things about it: how supportive everyone in Biarritz was. Random people – people I'd never spoken to – came up to me and asked me if I was OK. So it was odd that I ended up leaving Biarritz and the people who had supported me. I came back to the UK, where I was the Antichrist.'

Having been born to Scottish parents in Malta, and having grown up both in England, with his mother, and in Hong Kong, where his father lived after his parents divorced, Millar had previously described himself as being 'international' – or perhaps 'nation-less' would have been the better adjective. 'Wherever I lay my hat . . .' and all that. 'I do feel more Scottish now,' Millar said. 'But when all the chips were down, I really realized who my friends and family are, and what my nationality is. And that's British, too, but my roots are in Scotland. It's easy when you're young and cocky and brash to think that you don't have any roots, that you don't owe anything to anybody, whereas now I'm very aware of my background and very proud of my roots. And that's why the Commonwealth Games means a huge amount to me, and why I'm aiming at it this year.'

There was no ban on him riding in the Commonwealth Games, which allowed Millar to win time-trial gold for Scotland that October in Delhi, where he beat England's Alex Dowsett, who's now a pro with the Spanish Movistar squad. As for Team Sky, the new British team had started that season, but Millar, *persona non grata* as he was, could never be a part of it, such was – and still is – their policy of not signing former dopers.

'I'd love to be eighteen now, coming through the new system that is in place now,' Millar said, referring to British Cycling's then-new academy programme, and young riders' opportunities to stay with the same core of managers and coaches by potentially turning pro with Sky. 'I wouldn't want anyone to go through what I went through, the way I did it.'

After our interview, on my way out of the bar, I bumped into journalist and writer Jeremy Whittle, who'd been my editor at *Procycling* a few years before. He was there at the hotel to talk to Millar about *Racing Through the Dark*, which Millar genuinely wrote himself, but with a guiding hand from Whittle, with whom he'd been friends for some years.

On 27 July 2004, in *Procycling*'s London office, Jeremy Whittle answered a call from his friend, David Millar, to say that he was ready – ready to do an interview with Whittle about having doped. When? Immediately, if Whittle was able to. Millar was in town, and could meet as soon as Whittle could get to Leicester Square.

As he was both editor of the magazine and the cycling correspondent for *The Times*, this was an ideal opportunity for Whittle to kill two birds with one stone – if he could find a photographer at such short notice. Pete Goding, now an established, and extremely talented, sports and travel photographer, went on his first 'proper' shoot that day. Day-to-day, he was the picture editor on both *Procycling* and *Real Homes*, and would set up various shoots for them. But as this Millar interview was also for *The Times*, the pressure was on.

'I remember Jez grabbing me and asking if I could do it. It was going to be my first national newspaper job, and a picture editor at *The Times* told me beforehand that they were after a nice portrait of Millar, but there actually wasn't much of a brief other than that,' says Goding. It was a Tuesday, he remembers – or, at least, the metadata from his camera reminds him – 'and there was this beautiful light over Leicester Square'.

Photographers notice such things; this one was set to go far. Goding and Whittle pitched up in a taxi and found Millar in the foyer of one of the hotels overlooking the square. Whittle did his interview, and Goding then had just five or ten minutes to come up with some decent shots. 'I sat him outside, on the square, in the shade,' says Goding. 'I didn't know him like Jez did, but I think I had met him briefly once before somewhere, although it can't have been at a race because at that point I hadn't actually been to one before.

'And he was pretty affable. He clearly wasn't happy at the time, and had just been going through everything with Jez, so I was aware of not wanting to be too obtrusive; it wasn't exactly a "smile to camera!" kind of moment. But we got some good pictures, and I sent them across to *The Times*. Originally, they were going to put the piece on the back page, but then it got bumped to just inside, which was a bit gutting, but then when I saw how huge the picture they used actually was, I was over the moon.'

Almost a decade on, Goding jogs our memories with the set of photos he took that day. Millar's in a light green T-shirt, which says 'Fullerton BMX Squad' on it, and the silhouette of a BMXer pulling a radical jump underneath. Below that it says 'Your ass is grass!' – a little inappropriately somehow, given the gravity of the situation.

He's in blue jeans and his hair's cropped short. He's wearing a yellow Livestrong bracelet, too. They'd been friends, Armstrong and Millar – brothers-in-arms, two among many, in a culture that all but embraced doping – but they wouldn't be friends for much longer. A tourist-friendly red phone box in the background serves to complete the set of primary colours in the photo.

'And it was beautiful light: this beautiful light on an almost empty Leicester Square,' Goding reminds me. 'It really was quite atmospheric.'

Whittle, meanwhile, had got close to Millar in the previous years since he'd turned pro in 1997. The atmosphere in the hotel foyer, though, was strained. Millar's sister, Fran, was there, too.

'We sat there talking for about an hour, but it was all very depressing, and he looked very rough; exhausted, as though he'd been clubbing for a week,' remembers Whittle, which may not have been overly far from the truth. 'He was staying in London with Fran, who was really looking after him and defending him, as he was very vulnerable and frail, and she looked as though she'd rip my head off if I said the wrong thing. I was really worried about him.'

Whittle had first seen Millar earlier that season at the Paris–Nice stage race, in March.

'He had a goatee, and this was around the time that he called [former Cofidis teammate] Philippe Gaumont a "nutter",' recalls Whittle, after the Frenchman, who had admitted to doping himself, had named Millar as one of the riders who was calling the shots when questioned during a police investigation into suspected drug taking at the Cofidis team. Gaumont died, aged forty, from a heart attack in May 2013.

Millar had denied everything back then, but Whittle admits that he wasn't so convinced.

'I distinctly remember standing outside this café, having a coffee, and having this really awful feeling that he was lying to me; knowing that I really liked him, but that he was lying to me, and that he was definitely doping. And I was thinking, "That's why he's grown a beard, because a beard's about guilt, and he's hiding his face" – all this metaphysical stuff!'

Whittle saw Millar again a couple of months later at the Football Association's headquarters on Soho Square in London (the FA has since moved to Wembley Stadium), where he and

Welsh star Nicole Cooke – the then reigning Commonwealth Games road race champion and winner of the 2003 UCI World Cup – were being presented at a press conference as the two great hopes of Great Britain's 2004 Athens Olympic road-cycling teams.

'As he describes in his book, he thought it was all behind him then, that nothing was going to happen and that the French had lost interest,' says Whittle. 'And then the drugs squad arrived in Biarritz in June – what was it, a week before the Tour?'

It was the evening of 24 June, a date that must be seared in Millar's mind. It was just nine days before the start of the Tour in Liège, in Belgium, and there were only seven weeks to go until the start of the Athens Olympics, where Millar was set to be one of Team GB's stars.

There was an ironic connection to the massive success that was to visit British cycling in the years to come in that it was British Cycling supremo Dave Brailsford that Millar was dining with at a Biarritz restaurant when the French police swooped. Yet there was a happy ending for British Cycling in that a repentant Millar would eventually return to the national squad and help pilot the young lad he'd posed with for a photo on the Isle of Man in 1999 to the rainbow jersey of world champion. When Mark Cavendish won the men's road-race world championships in Copenhagen in 2011, it was a dream come true not just for him, but for a number of people on the team and behind the scenes at British Cycling, as well as legions of fans of British cycling – small 'c' – who'd had to wait forty-six years for a British rider to repeat Tom Simpson's feat of 1965.

But in 2004, cycling simply carried on without Millar, who was nevertheless a great embarrassment to British Cycling at the time. As per the UCI's rules, they were the ones who had to dish out the ban – two years, post-dated from the day he was caught, which put him in the running for riding the 2006 Tour. It also took him out of the running for the Olympics – the 2004 Games, of course, but also 2008, 2012, 2016 . . . Under a British Olympic Association bylaw, introduced in 1992, as a convicted doper banned for over six months, Millar was prohibited from ever representing Great Britain at the Games again.

However, in April 2012, the BOA life-ban was judged by the Court of Arbitration for Sport to contravene WADA's World Anti-Doping Code, reopening the door for Millar and 100-metre sprinter Dwain Chambers – handed a two-year doping ban in 2003 after testing positive for the anabolic steroid THG – to return to the Olympic fold for London 2012.

Both athletes subsequently took part, but was it right that the likes of Chambers and Millar could 'use up' highly sought after Olympic spots that could otherwise have been filled by athletes who had never turned to drugs? Certainly, until then, Millar had never expected to be able to.

'The question as to whether he should ever have been allowed to take part again is really difficult to answer,' admits Whittle, and then relates a story, the crux of which turns out to be that we're all human and that the reality of human relationships doesn't necessarily tally with faceless rules and bureaucracy.

'After David's book was nominated for the 2011 William Hill Sports Book of the Year, I was with him for the awards evening, and we had high hopes,' Whittle says. 'I still think it was the best book that year – and I know I'm bound to say that, but I do.'

Millar's book didn't win – the prize went to the football book *A Life Too Short: The Tragedy of Robert Enke*, by Ronald Reng – but Whittle believes that Millar's BOA ban, heading into an Olympic year, could not have done the book any favours in the judges' eyes.

'What was funny was that that same evening, after the awards, we went to this do in Knightsbridge, which we probably weren't supposed to go to, at the Royal Thames Yacht Club. We walked in, and Gary Lineker was there, and Seb Coe – the then chairman of the London Organizing Committee for the Olympic Games – and [BOA chairman] Lord Moynihan.

'As soon as David walked in, there was this kind of draw of breath; it was like a saloon in an old western when the music stops playing,' Whittle recalls. 'David was the family's black sheep, his arrival heralded with a bum note on the piano.'

At one point, Millar went and introduced himself to Lord Moynihan.

'It was funny to watch, as David's something like six foot three, while Lord Moynihan used to be a cox,' Whittle points out, but says that within fifteen minutes the two of them were as thick as thieves.

Chambers, although he apologized for having used steroids, was, says Whittle, 'ostracized and alienated and cast out – never really accepted again'.

'But should David have been allowed to ride at the Olympics again? I don't know, but at that moment when he went over to Lord Moynihan, it had been to the sound of another drawn breath, and I remember Lord Moynihan saying, "Lovely to meet you," and they proceeded to get along famously. That would have been in November 2011, and the ban was lifted in spring the following year.

'But it's easy just to string people up and hang them, rather than talk to them,' Whittle says. 'I remember in 2006, before David started racing again, that he went to do this talk for UK Anti-Doping in Russell Square. I arrived just as it ended, and was waiting to meet him at the bar. And he was shaking; I thought he'd burst into tears. Then a few delegates came up, to tell him that they'd learned more in his fifteen-minute talk than in their seven years, or whatever it was, of working in anti-doping.

'David's experience is valid in the history of British sport, and in the understanding of doping, and will be seen as a lightning rod for change,' says Whittle. 'He's been effective, and provoked debate.'

The 2014 season will be Millar's last as a professional bike rider. For better and for worse, he leaves a lasting legacy in British cycling's history: yes, he was a doper, but he was also one of the people key to helping clean up the sport.

And what's next for him? For now, only he knows the answer to that, but the clock hands will likely come around to 'Millar time' again.

15

BRAVEHEART

In 1995, David Millar became the first recipient of funding from the Dave Rayner Fund, which helped finance him in moving towards his goal of living and racing in France as a young amateur, and culminated in his turning professional with the Cofidis team in 1997.

The now-retired Charly Wegelius, who these days works as a *directeur sportif* on Millar's Garmin team, also benefited from the fund back in 1996 and 1997 as an amateur, while more recently it's helped now-big-name riders such as Wegelius's charge at Garmin, Dan Martin – winner of the 2013 one-day Classic Liège–Bastogne–Liège – and former BMC rider Adam Blythe, who in 2014 is riding for the British NFTO squad.

The fund very quickly became one of the principal routes for British riders who weren't following the Lottery-funded British Cycling path, hoping to give things a crack with amateur European teams instead. There to provide a little extra financial aid to help fund their seasons, the fund was looking after twenty-five riders in 2014. They included Hannah Barnes, who also received funding in 2011, and who dominated women's domestic road racing during the 2013 season, culminating in her being rewarded with a contract to ride in the USA with the UnitedHealthcare team in 2014.

Prior to such funding, young riders relied on decent European contacts – perhaps via older club-mates – to help place them with a French or Belgian amateur team, living hand to mouth on meagre prize money, if they were lucky. The really lucky ones might get spotted and picked up by the ACBB club in Paris, which was a feeder team to the Peugeot professional squad; a relationship maintained throughout the 1960s, '70s and '80s. British ACBB graduates include Sean Yates, John Herety, Paul Sherwen and Graham Jones.

Dave Rayner was a gifted pro from Bradford who made a name for himself on the domestic scene, winning the Milk Race's best young rider prize in 1987 and 1989, and in 1990 winning the Scottish Provident League city-centre series – a later iteration of the hugely popular Kellogg's-sponsored city-centre series of the early-to-mid-1980s.

Those results helped the Yorkshireman secure a contract for the 1991 and 1992 seasons with top Dutch team Buckler, managed by legendary former pro Jan Raas, winner of Paris–Roubaix, the Tour of Flanders and Milan–San Remo during his career.

I can remember watching the Scottish Provident League races on Channel 4 and wanting handlebars like the ones Rayner and his Banana-Falcon teammates, like Shane Sutton and Chris Walker, used: track-style bars, curved at the top to give you more space for your forearms when down on the drops, yet when boldly used on their road bikes only serving to heighten the impression that these riders were giving it everything. I loved the Scottish Provident League; it seemed to be such a different world to the Tour de France, and not in a bad way.

But it was nothing short of an utterly tragic waste of a gifted young rider's life when in 1994 Rayner was involved in an altercation with a nightclub bouncer on a night out in Bradford, and as a result of whatever exactly ensued – the bouncer was sentenced to community service after a charge of manslaughter wasn't upheld due to lack of evidence – Rayner died from severe head injuries, aged twenty-seven.

He's remembered through the fund, which holds the Dave Rayner Fund dinner each year, where most of the money is raised to be able to help some of the stars of tomorrow for the following season.

On the racing front, the 1994 season was Brian Smith's best ever. The Scot spent the year riding for Andy Hampsten and Lance Armstrong at the American Motorola team that year, scoring the second of his two road-race national championships, riding – and finishing – the Tour of Italy in the service of Hampsten, and winning the Danish one-day race, the GP Herning. But his good friend Dave Rayner's death at the end of the season was devastating.

Today, as well as being a regular commentator for Eurosport's bike-racing coverage, Smith oversees the Braveheart Fund, helping young Scottish riders to live and race abroad, following in the tyre tracks of Scottish greats like Ian Steel, Billy Bilsland, Robert Millar, Smith himself and, to a lesser extent – not that he isn't equally great – Graeme Obree, who has always tended to forge his own path.

As it heads into its twelfth year of existence, the fund has helped well over 50 riders, and Smith hopes that it can yet help many more. Unwittingly, he got the ball rolling just as his own racing career neared its end, when he realized that no Scottish team had been entered in the 2002 Girvan Three-Day stage race.

'And the answer as to why there hadn't been, was that maybe it was a wee bit too hard because all the top British riders went there!' Smith says, with mock-bordering-on-real outrage.

'Away you go!' was his response. 'I'd ridden the race at the age of eighteen. You need to learn, and if there's a big race on your doorstep, then it's the perfect opportunity to learn. The Girvan was the only major event in Scotland, and there had always been a Scottish team in it as far as I knew.'

Smith contacted his friend Alan Miller – son of former Girvan race organizer George Miller – and asked him what was going on, and whether they should do something about it. They suggested to Scottish Cycling that, if no one else was going to do it, they'd enter and manage a team themselves.

'We were able to get some subsidized accommodation for a team, and that was kind of the start of things,' says Smith. At that point, however, Smith didn't really know what they'd started, but, after the race, he asked the riders what was next for them.

'They turned around and said, "Oh, we'd love to do the Lincoln Grand Prix," and this event and that event' – in other words, Britain's top Premier Calendar series of races – 'so I realized that there was a real situation here to look at if these riders were feeling so limited.'

The problem? Money, even more so than the perceived toughness of races outside of their own backyard.

'After the Girvan, we also received an invitation to go to the Shay Elliott [Memorial Race] in Ireland, and Alan and I said, "Right. Let's do it," and I contacted the organizer and asked whether they'd be able to help by paying some of our expenses – if you don't ask, you don't get – and they agreed,' says Smith.

Next on the race wish-list was the Lincoln Grand Prix, organized by former BCF president Ian Emmerson, who agreed to make room for a Scottish team at the race.

'But where could we get more money from?' comes the rhetorical question from Smith. Then someone hit on the idea of auctioning a place in the team car at the Lincoln race, which raised another £150, and 'helped towards the petrol'.

'We'd raised our first bit of money, which is when it really got into my head that we needed to keep raising more,' Smith says.

Miller put together a website, another friend offered to put on a fund-raising dinner at the North Beach Hotel in Prestwick, and, just like that, the Braveheart Cycling Fund was born. 'This was in 2003, and we had ten tables of ten, made up of family and friends, and we got a few jerseys together to auction off, and raised about £3,000,' recalls Smith.

'I'd been great friends with Dave Rayner, and his fund was run by his former team manager, Keith Lambert, and teammates and friends like Chris Walker and Jonny Clay, and I thought that see-ing as they were all also my friends, I'd contact them to check that they didn't mind if we set up something similar in Scotland.

'And they didn't mind at all,' continues Smith. 'In fact, they said that if it meant we could look after the Scots, then they wouldn't have to, and would be able to support other riders.'

In the nicest possible way, of course.

So, is it fair to call the Braveheart Fund the Scottish equivalent of the Dave Rayner Fund?

'I think so, yes,' says Smith. 'Dave was, as I say, a great friend of mine, so it was a big shock when he died in 1994, and I still keep in touch with his mum and dad, John and Barbara. So when it came to the Braveheart, when the Dave Rayner Fund already existed, it was a case of, "Why try to reinvent the wheel?" and it meant that we could work in unison and effectively give away more money as a nation.'

Next, it was time to bring out the big guns, and Smith asked Chris Hoy – the 2002 world champion in the 1-kilometre time trial and team sprint – if he'd like to attend the dinner and help out.

'I must have asked just before he went to the Athens Olympics, as he then brought the gold medal he won in the 1-kilometre time trial at the 2004 Games along with him,' recalls Smith. 'And he really was helping out, too. He asked what he could do, and we said, "Right, we need someone tearing the raffle tickets off," so that's what he did. I think we had just over a hundred people for the dinner that year, and raised about £7,000.'

The fund has been very lucky to have Chris on board from early on, says Smith. 'When he first came in 2004, I asked him whether he'd consider being patron of the fund, and he was genuinely taken aback. He said yes, and what a privilege it would be for him, but said he didn't know how he could really be of any help.'

But apart from tearing off raffle tickets, Hoy's regular presence at the dinner most years – along with a whole host of other big names from the cycling world – has helped keep people, and therefore the money, coming in. 'In fact, he's thanked us ever since,' laughs Smith, 'because there were times when his Scottishness was being questioned by some who were saying he was turning his back on Scotland by living in Manchester to train with the British Cycling team. He wasn't, of course, but he was able to show his heart was still with Scotland through the fund, and he's been an absolute inspiration to Scottish riders.'

Hoy knows that when he attends the dinners, he'll be able to relax and enjoy himself; the evening is great fun, and always attracts big-name riders from all over Britain, and from further afield, happy and eager to join in and let their hair down a bit at the end of the season, and also help raise a bit more money.

'That's why you get so many people, like [2012 road-race world champion] Philippe Gilbert saying they want to come back. The fund's special guest in 2013' – arguably the best female cyclist in the world currently, Marianne Vos – 'told us that there was nothing like this in the Netherlands, and was really interested in what we were doing.'

By 2006, after three years in Prestwick, the fund had outgrown its dinner venue, and moved ten miles up the road to Kilmarnock, and the Park Hotel, where it's been ever since, hosting around 400–500 dinner guests.

When it comes to deciding where the money raised can be best used, the Braveheart Fund liaises with Scottish Cycling, although riders can apply directly to the fund for consideration. In 2013, Smith received such an application from a young track rider called Katie Archibald.

'I was looking at the kinds of times she was doing, and thought, "There's some real potential here," and so we funded her,' says Smith. 'No one knew what she was going to do, but I think we've been quite lucky at spotting the talent and helping them to come through.'

You can say that again. Already in 2013, Archibald had begun muscling her way into the British endurance squad, and in 2014, at the track world championships in Cali, Colombia, she became world champion, at the age of nineteen, in the team pursuit. Her next goal has to be nothing short of Olympic gold in Rio de Janeiro in 2016, with the question now being just how many world and Olympic titles she'll be able to achieve in her career; she has huge potential.

She also happens to be the author of arguably the most eloquent and humorous rider-diary/blog around, which can be found on the Braveheart Cycling Fund's website.

It's not huge money that the fund has to give away, though.

'Even when I was young, I was getting some local grants of £300 and £500 to help me,' says Smith, 'which meant a lot. But the biggest thing that someone can give you is belief and trust. That's the biggest compliment.'

He gives the example of Charline Joiner, who broke her back in a training crash at the start of 2014. The fund stuck by her, continuing to support her as she battled to recover in time to represent Scotland on the track at the Commonwealth Games, where she hoped to go one better than the silver medal she won in the team sprint in Delhi in 2010. 'As soon as we'd released the new funding, she got in contact to say thank you for our continued belief in her. It means a lot to these youngsters.'

The fact that the 2014 Commonwealth Games were awarded to Glasgow made it even more important for the likes of Joiner to make sure they were ready to go. For cycling, 2014 became a huge year in the UK, with the Games in Glasgow in August, the start of the Giro d'Italia in Belfast in May, the new Women's Tour stage race and, of course, the *Grand Départ* of the Tour de France in Yorkshire in July. Such visibility of cycling – both on the ground for spectators and with ever-increasing television coverage – continues to push the sport forward in the UK, as do grants from funds like the Braveheart for home-grown initiatives.

The largest amount the fund has given away so far, says Smith, is £5,000 to the group WoSCA – the West of Scotland Cycling Association. 'What they've done with that money is incredible,' Smith says. 'That's where the next champions will come from. It's a big thing – a big expense – even getting out of Scotland, and what we wanted to do was not just look at placing individuals on teams in Europe, but also to try to help some of the youth teams to ride in youth tours on the Isle of Man, and places like that.'

Although it works closely with Scottish Cycling, the fund also has the ability to assign money to recipients other than riders under the age of twenty-five, although Smith admits that's where they try to keep most of the funding.

Belgium-based Louise Thomas, for example, received money from the fund to help her try to achieve her goal of riding in the Commonwealth Games, and the Braveheart Fund was also supporting multiple Scottish and British time-trial champion Jason MacIntyre, trying to help him get to the Beijing Olympics, when MacIntyre was tragically killed after colliding with a van while training in January 2008.

'Jason's disabled daughter had lost not only her dad but her carer as well, so we were able to raise about £45,000 for the Jason MacIntyre Memorial Fund, which helped the family out a bit in such terrible circumstances,' says Smith. His point is that there's some flexibility in what they can do with the money – a flexibility you don't get when it comes to public funding.

The long-term aim, though, isn't to have a Braveheart team that dominates racing in Scotland. Instead, Smith wants to fund riders to help them get out of Scotland, to go further afield and have their eyes opened.

'When I raced as a schoolboy, you'd get twenty to twenty-five riders in a race, and I was able to win,' remembers Smith. 'Then I'd go down for the British championships, and there'd be sixty riders on the start line, and you'd get a hard time. Then you could go to Belgium and be racing against 150 riders.

'My philosophy is to help get these small fish into a bigger pond,' he explains. 'As a youngster, I wanted to ride the bigger races, but people would ask, "Why do you want to do that? You'll get battered." But it was sink or swim, and I was prepared to give it a go. And yeah – I got a kicking at a lot of the races, but I swam. I wanted to educate myself, and I did that by opening the door. I went on to ride for Scotland at the Commonwealth Games in my first year as a senior, and from there I went on to win a lot of races. I could win in Scotland, but I wanted to do it in Britain, and I want to expose a lot of these riders to what else is out there.'

When he was starting out, Smith knew nothing about the Tour de France, and still less about a rider called Robert Millar, who would come to Scotland and ride with Smith's training group in the winter. ' "Who's that?" I used to ask, "and how does he make his money?" Those were the questions I was asking as a young teenager, so I really want these youngsters to have the opportunity to see the bigger picture.'

Robert Millar, of course, was Scottish cycling's greatest export, fervently followed by Scottish – and Welsh, Irish and English – cycling fans throughout the 1980s and early '90s.

From Glasgow, Millar followed the same tried-and-tested route taken by Brits like Graham Jones and Paul Sherwen, joining the

French amateur club ACBB before stepping up to a pro squad – in Millar's case the same Peugeot team as Jones, in 1980.

His breakthrough season came in 1983 when, riding his first Tour de France, Millar crashed on the third stage, losing almost 20 minutes. It was an inauspicious start to an event for which he appeared to be well suited, but he rallied to out-climb rising Spanish star Pedro Delgado for the stage victory at Bagnères-de-Luchon on stage 10 in the Pyrenees, ending an eight-year drought since the last British stage win, by Barry Hoban in Bordeaux in 1975.

For six seasons in a row, between 1984 and 1989, Millar finished in the top 10 overall of the Tour de France, the Tour of Italy or the Tour of Spain.

Think of Robert Millar, and more often than not you'll think of him toiling up a climb in the white jersey with the red polka dots. Winning that King of the Mountains jersey at the 1984 Tour de France, and finishing fourth overall, instantly made him Britain's most successful Tour rider, which would remain the case for almost two decades.

He finished second at the Tour of Spain in both 1985 and 1986, then won the climber's competition – and finished second overall, behind Ireland's Stephen Roche – at the 1987 Giro d'Italia. He's the only British rider to have won the Tour's polka-dot jersey and the climber's jersey at the Giro.

At the 1991 Tour, Millar won himself legions of new fans for a whole different reason. Having crashed in the closing kilometres of stage six between Arras and Le Havre, Millar limped home almost six minutes behind. 'I can't turn my head to the left,' he calmly told Paul Sherwen – who by then was working as a commentator for Channel 4 – at the finish, and turned up at the start the next day in a full neck brace and swathes of bandages on the rest of his body.

Millar looked almost cartoonish, and certainly like someone

who shouldn't have been riding a bike, let alone racing in the Tour de France. But he gamely battled his way through the rest of the race, finishing 72nd in Paris, although he'd been unable to help his Z team leader and three-time Tour winner Greg LeMond defend his title; Spain's Miguel Indurain instead began his five-Tour-winning reign.

Millar retired a little ahead of plan when, midway through the 1995 season, his new Le Groupement team folded. But during a fifteen-year pro career, Millar had flown the flag for Scotland in Europe, in what was then still a pretty hostile environment for English-speakers, with aplomb.

Indeed, despite Millar's success abroad, there were still very few Scottish riders prepared to fly the nest to try racing anywhere else when he was younger, Brian Smith says. 'Before me there was Millar, and before Millar there was Billy Bilsland, and before him Ian Steel . . . But there are really very few riders to have come out of Scotland. But Ian used to look after Billy, Billy used to look after Robert, and Robert used to look after me, so you kind of pass it down, and I've tried to bring the next generation through with our fund.'

One of the new generation of Scottish riders following in Millar's footsteps, and taking full advantage of his Braveheart funding, is Craig Wallace, who rides for the under-23 Zirauna-Infisport team in the Basque Country, and who, Smith says proudly, finished fourth in his first race with them in 2014.

'The opportunities for young riders today are huge,' says Smith. 'It's like night and day compared to when I was riding. To anyone hoping to turn pro today, I'd say, "Get your act together, as you'll never have a better opportunity."

'What Peter Keen did, and what Dave Brailsford's done, has been huge for British cycling,' he continues. 'It's a much cleaner sport, and you've got inspirational figures like Chris Hoy and Victoria Pendleton. But to get on the national track team now, you need to be super. Ten years ago, to get on the track as a youngster, you had a good chance, but now you have to be head and shoulders above everyone else.'

What Smith would like to see now is the emergence of another top-level road team, and there could be room for more funding models like the Dave Rayner and Braveheart, too. 'A lot of the money has been going to Manchester, to the Olympic Development and Academy programmes,' says Smith, 'so it's been a case of, "How do we even get people to those programmes?" With the Braveheart Fund, we've tried to fill the hole.

'We've even thought of perhaps launching a Dragonheart Fund, in Wales; I've talked to Nicole Cooke about it,' reveals Smith. 'Then you go down the road of thinking about a Lionheart in England, and a Celticheart in Ireland. But we can't do it all. You need people who live there to set it all up. But the blueprint is there: if you want to give away £30–35,000 for the local area, you can, but it does take a lot of effort.'

Smith says he and Miller, and others, have worked hard over the past eleven years to get the Braveheart Fund to where it is now. 'It's not been easy, but we've got to the point where we now have to think about how we can move it on, and whether we actually want to make it bigger.'

In 2013, the presence of Dutch star Vos helped swell the numbers taking part in the sportive that the fund also organizes on the same day as the dinner to 700, but this means increasing the number of people needed to run such an event.

'To have around 500 people for the ride in the morning and the same amount for the dinner in the evening is about right, I think. It's still a lot of work – about three months a year for me and Alan – but we started it and we're going to finish it,' Smith says, figuratively speaking. Funds like the Braveheart and the Dave Rayner remain essential for bringing on young British riders.

16

THE ROAD TO BEIJING

'What a year!' the cover of the 2002 end-of-year, 120-page special of *Cycling Weekly* screams.

'Britain's best-ever season,' it adds, in a slightly smaller font. Its 'all-star interviews' are exactly that: the magazine is packed with a veritable Who's Who of 'noughties' British riders, from Chris Newton to Nicole Cooke, to Bradley Wiggins, to Jamie Staff, to David Millar, to Chris Hoy . . .

Cooke is arguably the most impressive of them all: at just nineteen years old, in 2002 Cooke had won the road-race national championships for the third time and become the Commonwealth Games road-race champion. Her 2001 season was always going to take some beating: as well as having become national road champion for a second time, she also took the national cyclo-cross title, and was junior national champion in, staggeringly, the time trial, road race and mountain biking, demonstrating her diversity – and domination – across all disciplines, although she ultimately chose the road. Having left the junior ranks behind her in 2002, Cooke described her Commonwealth Games victory in Manchester as her finest senior victory to date.

In most of the other interviews, the riders gush about the influx of money to their sport as a result of Peter Keen's World Class Performance Plan (WCPP).

'The whole way it works, with top-end equipment, helpers and advisers, is brilliant,' says Chris Newton, who became the points-race world champion in Copenhagen that year.

I was working at those world championships as a press assistant, gathering and translating quotes from the riders as they finished their events, and, having been a little out of the loop regarding how British cycling had developed in the few years I'd been living in Denmark, I was astounded by just how great the leap forward had been. I witnessed Newton race to gold, and Chris Hoy do the same – twice – in the 1-kilometre time trial and then the team sprint, alongside Craig MacLean and Jamie Staff. I also watched Tony Gibb's silver-medal ride in the scratch race, and saw Wiggins, Newton, Paul Manning and Bryan Steel take bronze in the team pursuit. Not such a bad haul at all.

'Winning the Commonwealth Games in Manchester has been great for my confidence; I'm extremely pleased with my per-formance tonight,' Hoy told me after winning the 1-kilometre time trial, where he beat Frenchman Arnaud Tournant by just one thousandth of a second to earn the first rainbow jersey of his career. 'Comparing it with Manchester, the track here in Copenhagen is a little technical with its longer straights and tighter bends, but otherwise it's very similar.

'I hope people will take notice of my win here,' he added, referring to the British press and public. 'I'm sure I'll get a couple of inches in the newspapers anyway . . .'

Hoy's final, throwaway line demonstrated the vast indifference to British cycling that still existed then. Real public attention was still six years away, but what more did British riders have to do if becoming world champions wasn't enough? Turns out that what the British public *really* appreciates is Olympic golds . . .

The mastermind behind those future golds, Dave Brailsford, was still British Cycling's programmes director in 2002, only taking over from Keen as performance director in 2004. It had already been a massive leap forward from the Dave Brailsford who was 'washing bottles' at the road-race world championships in 1993, when John Herety was looking after the pro riders who were representing the GB team.

'Brailsford was our masseur in Oslo,' explains Herety. 'A former rider of mine at the Percy Bilton team, Rob Holden, knew him. He was straight out of university and looking for a job, so he came over to Norway to wash bottles for me.

'Then I went to work for Muddy Fox [mountain bikes] for a brief period, and they were looking for an area sales manager, so I helped him get an interview – and he walked out with the marketing manager's job!'

Herety then joined Peter Keen as part of the new WCPP as road manager, and when they needed new bikes and clothing, quickly, they called on Brailsford and his relationships with all the European suppliers and distributors through his job at Muddy Fox, and ended up with Concorde bikes and Ultima clothing.

'It was Dave who placed those orders, and then he met Peter, had an interview, and they then forged a relationship in which Dave started doing all the financial side of things and Peter did the sporting aspect of it,' says Herety.

Shane Sutton, Nicole Cooke's coach at Welsh Cycling, also made the jump to British Cycling in 2002, becoming an immediate hit with the athletes, and another heavy-duty weapon in Keen's, and subsequently Brailsford's, armoury.

From washing bottles in Oslo in 1993 to overseeing the sporting side of British Cycling's success, by 2005 Brailsford had settled into his new role as BC's performance director. Herety had been his boss back during those world championships in Oslo in the 1990s; now, twelve years later, Herety was having to go to

Brailsford to hand in his resignation following the actions of Charly Wegelius and Tom Southam at the world championships in Madrid, where the pair had colluded with the Italian team in the road race.

David Millar, too – one of Brailsford's hopes for success on the road at the Athens Games the year before – was halfway through a two-year doping ban, having missed the Olympics completely.

Things weren't looking overly rosy on the road side of things, although Hammond and Nicole Cooke had held the British end up with seventh place and fifth place, respectively, in the 2004 Olympic road races.

The ever-brightening shining light, however, was the Lottery-funded track team, and on the track in Athens things had looked considerably more promising as Bradley Wiggins took gold in the individual pursuit, while Chris Hoy won the 1-kilometre time trial. There was silver for the men's team-pursuit team, well beaten by Australia in the final, and a bronze medal for Rob Hayles and Wiggins in the Madison.

The British team was still waiting for the women's squad to perform at Olympic level, however, and track sprinter Victoria Pendleton had returned from Athens empty-handed and frustrated. But, in 2005, she was able to turn her domination at national level into a world title, winning the individual sprint in Los Angeles, while Mark Cavendish won his first world title, in the Madison, partnering Hayles. There was success, too, for the men's team sprint and team pursuit. Track was where it was at.

Bradley Wiggins had officially turned professional with the Linda McCartney team in 2001, but, when the team folded early that season, Wiggins returned to the GB set-up, continuing to race both on the road and track. He turned pro with French team Française des Jeux (FDJ) for 2002, and remained with French squads for the next six years, while being released for international track duty for the world championships and Olympics. He joined Crédit Agricole in 2004 after two years with FDJ, then joined Cofidis in 2006, with whom he rode his first Tour that year, finishing 121st, having ridden his first Grand Tour – the Giro d'Italia – in 2005, where he was 123rd.

In Mallorca in 2007 – at the same track world championships that had prompted Chris Boardman to suggest to Dave Brailsford that this was quite likely as good as it was ever going to get, where the GB team won seven gold medals, two silvers and two bronzes – Wiggins won the individual-pursuit title and was part of the victorious team-pursuit squad.

Wiggins's fourth place at the London prologue of the 2007 Tour was a continuation of the winning road time-trial rides he was now capable of turning out; he'd won the time-trial stage at the Four Days of Dunkirk earlier that year, and the prologue of the Critérium du Dauphiné just weeks before the Tour. And on stage six, between Semur-en-Auxois and Bourg-en-Bresse, Wiggins went on the attack, slipping away just two kilometres into the 199.5-kilometre stage and settling in to the longest 'time trial' of his life, alone in front for 190 kilometres, only eventually caught by the peloton with around seven kilometres to go. It was a valiant effort, deemed all the more appropriate, a savvy press had written, in that Wiggins had gone on such a spectacular break on the 40th anniversary of Tom Simpson's death.

It turned out that Wiggins had absolutely no idea of the significance of the date; it had been pure coincidence.

But what should have been a memorable year became memorable for all the wrong reasons later at that 2007 Tour when, at the conclusion of stage 16, Wiggins's Cofidis teammate Cristian Moreni was arrested after the news was revealed that the Italian had tested positive for elevated levels of testosterone after stage 11. Wiggins and the rest of his teammates were questioned by the police, and left the race. Wiggins was furious with Moreni, and later admitted that he had already felt like quitting the sport altogether after Kazakh rider Alexander Vinokourov had been caught for blood doping the day before Moreni's arrest.

Yet at that same Tour – in fact, the very evening after Wiggins's attack on stage six – Brailsford outlined the details of what would become Team Sky to a handful of journalists, and effectively laid the plans for Wiggins's extremely bright future. Conversations between Brailsford and GB coach Shane Sutton over the past year and a half about setting up a top-level British road team had resulted in them deciding to go for it, and the success of the *Grand Départ* in London, Brailsford said, 'showed there could be an appetite for the sport in Britain'. And how right he was; the British public was very hungry indeed, and was on the eve of having it all.

Perhaps it was a slightly dodgy way of doing it, but having been invited to spend the duration of the 2008 Beijing Olympics in the presence of Oakley eyewear, with exclusive access to their athletes, and the opportunity to fill virtually a whole issue of *Procycling* magazine with said exclusive material, it became a no-brainer, and I gratefully accepted.

And it was good that I did. More than one journalist got in touch to say that I could become a very rich man by passing on quotes to a British press pack starved of access and stories, while I had first – and pretty much only – dibs on cycling's biggest names. Or those sponsored by Oakley, anyway.

They'd mooch around in that inimitable way that professional cyclists do in Oakley's 'safe house' in central Beijing, where food, drink and build-your-own-eyewear were abundant, and they were all more than happy to chat. The pro-road-team trail had gone a little cold while the British team focused on the Games, but Bradley Wiggins was only too pleased to bring it up as he lounged on one of the sofas.

'British Cycling have got the infrastructure from having done it on the track. Obviously it will be a bit different on the road, but people are interested; there are potential backers, like Sky, who are sponsoring the track programme now,' Wiggins said, all but giving the game away, well ahead of the following year's official announcement.

Sky had signed a five-year deal as British Cycling's 'principal partner' just ahead of the Olympics, which meant supporting all facets of the federation, and not only the track – from schools pro-grammes to para-cycling to the talent-development programme; and Sky's logo was soon ubiquitous on almost everything British-Cycling-related.

In Beijing, though, Wiggins evaded the question of whether he might be involved in the road squad himself. It turned out that he would be the team leader from the very beginning, although that role perhaps only came about on the back of his fourth place at the '09 Tour – or third, as it later became, after Lance Armstrong's third place was taken away from him.

But in 2008 Wiggins had intentionally missed the Tour in order to concentrate fully on the Games, where he'd ride the individual pursuit (and win gold) and the team pursuit (and take gold) and the Madison, where he and Mark Cavendish would come away empty-handed, and Cavendish extremely disappointed.

Cavendish was in an exquisite mood when he turned up for a chat a day or so before the Madison, and to get himself some new glasses. He was fresh from winning his first four stages of the Tour de France the month before, and already that made him a British cycling superstar, but few could have imagined at that point how far he'd go. Cavendish had turned pro in 2005 with the German Sparkasse squad – a feeder team to the T-Mobile team. In 2006, he won gold in the scratch race on the track at the Commonwealth Games in Melbourne.

He signed with T-Mobile for the 2007 season, and his real road breakthrough came that April, when he won the one-day Scheldeprijs in Belgium, beating established sprinters Robbie McEwen and Gert Steegmans.

It helped earn him a place in T-Mobile's nine-man squad for the Tour de France, which started in London. And while many fans quite rightly remember the 25 stage wins that the Manxman racked up between the 2008 and 2013 Tours de France, people often forget that he in fact cut his teeth at that 2007 edition, and came away with nothing; save, perhaps, for a determination and understanding of just what it was going to take to be on the level of the world's very best sprinters.

It would be a school of hard knocks, and with 25 kilometres left to go of the first stage from London to Canterbury, Cavendish was left on the tarmac in tears after a crash. To rub salt into the wound, someone in the crowd nicked his special pink, T-Mobile-kit-matching Oakley sunglasses while he was down.

Those tears aside, Cavendish's confidence – which increased immeasurably once he'd got the measure of the Tour in 2008 and screamed to victory on stages five, eight, 12 and 13 – was often perceived as cockiness, or even arrogance. He soon worked out his response to that.

'I never come out saying, "I'm the best,"' he explained to me in Beijing. 'Journalists ask me, "Do you think you're the best?" and I say, "Yeah." The fact is, you look at the replays of my wins at the Tour, and I'm the fastest sprinter. I'm stating a fact. It's not me just saying, "I'm the fastest sprinter" without backing it up – I'm stating a fact, you know?'

Cavendish was at the Beijing Olympics for just one event: the Madison, with Wiggins. The two of them had partnered up to win the same event at the world championships earlier in the year, and Cavendish was brimming with confidence as a result.

'I've never not been confident,' he said, with typical honesty. 'When Brad and I won the Madison in March, I wasn't even in my best form. But now . . . Well, it should be good. Hopefully Brad will still be going well after all his pursuiting. It should work out.'

But it didn't work out: it didn't work out at all. Wiggins, who'd even gone into the Games having been unwell, performed at the highest level to win gold in both the individual and team pursuit. But by the time the Madison came around, he had nothing left, and a frustrated Cavendish could do nothing but watch a medal slip away.

He was the only member of the track squad who went home without a medal, and perhaps he already knew that was going to be the case when, immediately after the race, he said nothing to anyone, picked up and put on his rucksack, got on to his road bike and rolled down the ramp in the middle of the track in the direction of the changing rooms.

I saw Wiggins again at the airport on the way back from Beijing, and he said the two of them still hadn't spoken. They wouldn't again for some time.

Just a couple of days before their competition, the men's team sprint squad sauntered into Oakley's building: Chris Hoy, Jamie Staff and . . . perhaps a team helper in tow.

I'd misidentified Jason Kenny. I thought Hoy and Staff's bespectacled mate was a *soigneur*, or a Team GB member of staff. He didn't look like the world-beater he was about to become back then, and certainly didn't resemble the butcher's dog silhouettes of his two teammates. Not that I'd say that to him now, of course; he's matured in every way now – a beefy sprinter in the mould of the others. He would have been nervous back then in Beijing, too, but it would turn out that there was no need to be. Both Hoy and Staff had experienced the Games before – Hoy twice and Staff once – and Kenny was soon up to speed.

The three of them were happy to sit and shoot the breeze – and rest their legs . . .

Hoy had muttered something, quite coyly, about having taken the bus there, and we'd all laughed, and I hadn't thought much more about it. Until six years later, when I find myself asking Staff if they'd really taken the bus that day.

For a second, he acts a little coy himself down the phone line from the Olympic Training Center in Chula Vista, California, where Staff now works for USA Cycling – British Cycling's American counterpart – as director of BMX, having recently switched from being their sprint coach. But then he laughs.

'Well, we'd taken a taxi, but the driver didn't know where he was, so he dropped us off,' Staff explains, 'and we were walking around Beijing for, like, an hour, panicking, before we found a bus. We said to each other, "No one must know about this! How much walking have we just done?" So it was something kept quiet about until after our event, yeah!'

The long walk didn't appear to do them any harm; the trio stormed to the gold medal, beating France in the final, and recording a new world record in the qualifying rounds.

I'll always remember a furious, but passionate and brutally honest, Ross Edgar in Beijing telling me of his frustration at having been overlooked for the team sprint, his place taken by the then young and relatively inexperienced Kenny. But it's exactly how the 'new' British Cycling has always operated: that, as an athlete, you know that there's always going to be someone snapping at your heels.

Plus there was a silver lining for Edgar in that he headed home from Beijing with a silver medal in his pocket, having been beaten to the top spot in the Keirin only by his teammate Hoy.

Staff was a little atypical compared to most of the members of the GB cycling squad in that he came in from the world of top-end BMX racing in the US, joining the British set-up in 2002.

'There were three sprinters – Craig MacLean, Jason Queally and Chris Hoy – when I first came into the programme,' explains

Staff. 'They were all relatively comfortable in their positions; they were already part of the team sprint squad. I was the fourth man in, so instantly I put pressure on everyone, which would mean that, in theory, they could be thinking, "Shit – whose position is he going to take?" So you need to get a handle on that from a performance perspective; you need to handle that pressure. It's not always nice being the athlete, not knowing if you're going to ride or not, but, from a management standpoint, it's the best thing that can happen. You never want people getting into a comfort zone, and that's how I like it to be with the athletes I coach. If, as an athlete, you get told four months out from the Olympics that you're definitely in the team, believe me when I say that you go into cruise control, which is the last thing you want going into a competition.

'So it's a hard one, but the more mature the athlete, the more they're able to deal with that pressure. It still sucks for the person who doesn't get to ride, but unfortunately that's the name of the game at this level.'

Staff appears to be more at ease about the pressure athletes face of potentially losing their place than any other athlete I've ever spoken to about it. His philosophy seems to be that the best athlete makes the grade, and to make the grade, you have to make sure you're the best athlete.

British Cycling's psychiatrist Steve Peters has played a massive role in teaching the techniques needed to handle such pressure.

'I wasn't ever focusing on what my challengers for my position were doing; I was focusing on myself, and doing just what I could do in my daily routine to maximize my potential going forward,' says Staff. 'And, yes, that was something that Steve taught me.'

Peters was, says Staff, hugely instrumental in the success of the British team in Beijing, and so it's no great surprise that he was brought in to help the England football team ahead of their (ultimately unsuccessful) World Cup campaign, having already worked with Steven Gerrard and his Liverpool teammates during the team's impressive 2013/14 Premier League campaign, in which they eventually finished second, two points behind Manchester City. Peters also worked with Ronnie O'Sullivan, helping to turn around the snooker player's flagging career.

'The guy's my hero,' says Staff. 'I'd put him right up there, maybe even ahead of Dave [Brailsford], in terms of the impact that he had on the team, and on me personally. I'd seen a few psychologists in my time, but Steve wasn't like all the others. He simply explained to us how the brain works: that the brain is a mechanism, and this is what it does, so, when you're in a competition, these are the thoughts you have, whereas these are the thoughts you need to be having and this is how you can get to be having those thoughts, and not negative ones.'

Once Peters had taught the athletes how their brains worked, they could then set about controlling them. 'I still use the techniques he taught us today, passing that knowledge on to the athletes I now coach. I mean, it was life changing, it really was,' Staff continues. 'And yet, it's not rocket science – it's the kind of stuff they should be teaching to kids. I mean, we all think we're crazy when we're young, and we have these thoughts going through our heads, asking ourselves whether there's something wrong with us, and yet there's not – the brain is just a complex bit of kit.'

The riders he describes as 'more emotional' – himself and Victoria Pendleton – perhaps benefited most from having Peters around, 'whereas those who were a little less emotional, like Chris Hoy and Jason Kenny, perhaps didn't benefit as much as me, although Steve still had a big impact on those guys too'.

Staff says he thinks that he might not have been in a position to win gold if he hadn't had Peters around, who chose to leave British Cycling in order to concentrate on his other work in April 2014, at the same time that Brailsford stepped down from his position as performance director.

'I put a big part of our success down to Dave, too,' Staff says. 'He did such a great job of putting people, as he says, in the right seat for the job – of finding the right people for all the different roles. He was always just such a good team leader, and it was always nice to have him around, popping into a training session. He was like the rock.'

Staff remembers Brailsford getting some sort of job offer after Beijing. 'And he said that unless he could bring all his staff with him, then he wasn't interested.'

Success at British Cycling bred success, Staff says. 'Going into competitions knowing that you were part of a winning team instilled so much more confidence in you as an athlete. There was the physical aspect – knowing you'd been doing the right training – but we also had the luxury of knowing that we had some of the best equipment in the world, too.

'It was really a magical time,' says Staff of his time with British Cycling. 'It was amazing to be part of it.'

On the road in Beijing, Nicole Cooke led the charge with a superbly taken gold medal in the road race, in the foulest of weather. Three days later, Emma Pooley won an excellent silver in the time trial.

For all that Cooke was a big part of the 'magical time' described by Jamie Staff, her achievements may never get the recognition they deserve; if women's cycling in Britain today is about to boom, and begin to get more coverage, then Cooke, who retired in 2013, might unjustly end up having been just a few years ahead of her time.

Pooley, meanwhile, was part of the new Women's Tour in 2014, having returned full time to racing after a scaled-back 2013 season while she finished her PhD in geotechnical engineering. She's also joined the UCI's Women's Commission to help promote women's cycling, principally through improved media coverage, and was involved in the setting up of a petition to have a women's Tour de France that would run concurrently with the men's, which was put in front of Tour boss Christian Prudhomme with more than 80,000 signatures.

Alas, Prudhomme and organizers ASO deemed it impossible, logistically, to effectively run two events at the same time across three weeks, but compromised with the introduction in 2014 of the one-day La Course: an elite women's road race held on the traditional Champs-Elysées circuit in Paris on the final Sunday of the men's Tour, ahead of the final stage.

While Cooke and Pooley had successfully flown the flag on the road in Beijing, the men's team fared considerably less well. In the road race, they faced a stinking hot and humid day, and although young Jonny Bellis – another Manxman, like Cavendish – bravely made it into the day's 25-man break, the heat became too much and he climbed off before the finish, along with the rest of the GB team: Roger Hammond, Steve Cummings and Ben Swift.

'We'd been hoping to get more out of it,' Hammond told me afterwards. 'Steve and I looked at each other on the climb, and we couldn't do anything more – our heart rates were through the roof. It was good experience for the younger guys on the squad, though.'

Indeed, Swift would go on to join Team Sky in 2010, and Cummings – who was GB's sole representative in the time trial in Beijing, finishing 11th – would join Sky, too.

Bellis, however, would end the 2009 season fighting for his life after a horrific motor-scooter accident in Italy, where he was living and training with the British Olympic academy programme. He recovered to make a return to professional cycling, and was riding for the modest Danish squad Christina Watches-KUMA in 2014.

Back down on the track in Beijing, Chris Hoy, Rebecca Romero, Victoria Pendleton and the men's team pursuit and team sprint squads were hoovering up the gold medals on offer.

Like Cooke in the road race, Pendleton shone in the individual sprint, meeting the athlete who would become her fiercest rival – Australia's Anna Meares – in the final, with Pendleton beating her in 'straight sets' to come out on top on this occasion. Romero's win in the individual pursuit was all the more spectacular for the fact that she'd also won silver four years earlier, in Athens: as a rower in the quadruple sculls.

Team GB went home with a gold and a silver medal from four road events, and clutching seven golds out of a possible ten on the track. And the British press and public loved it.

Cavendish would put the disappointment of the Beijing Olympics behind him and redouble his efforts on the road, which paid off handsomely in the spring of 2009 when he won the one-day Classic Milan–San Remo – one of the five 'Monuments' – by what was said to be no more than an inch from Heinrich Haussler.

A couple of months later, in May, Cavendish added three Giro d'Italia stage wins to the two he'd won the year before, and by July and the Tour de France he was on fire, bagging six stages, which took his total tally of Tour stage wins to 10 at the tender age of just twenty-five, surpassing previous 'record holder' Barry Hoban's eight Tour stage wins.

For the 2009 Tour, Cavendish and his Columbia-HTC squad had perfected their 'lead-out train': the line of riders who take their sprinter into the maelstrom that is the final sprint for the line by allowing him to shelter behind them from the wind before unleashing him in the last couple of hundred metres of the stage. American George Hincapie, German Tony Martin and Australian Mark Renshaw – an excellent sprinter in his own right – were among those who sacrificed themselves in the final kilometres of the flatter stages to ensure that their man hit the front of the race at top speed, Renshaw normally acting as 'last man'. Using his low, almost crouched, aerodynamic style to great effect, all Cavendish had to do was hold his speed to the line, and he'd win. Easy; at least, they certainly made it look that way. Cavendish's sixth win that year was on the Champs-Elysées, beginning what would be a four-year run of winning the final stage in Paris.

Wiggins, meanwhile, decided that he'd had enough of track racing after Beijing, having achieved pretty much everything there was to achieve at both Olympic and world–championship level. He therefore went into the 2009 season, having joined Jonathan Vaughters's Garmin team, with the aim of being more competitive on the road, and of making the Tour squad that would be led by American Christian Vande Velde.

A new, even-more-slimline-than-usual Wiggins climbed well at the Giro d'Italia that May, riding well to the fore in the mountains, and then finished second in the final time trial after three weeks of hard racing. By the start of the Tour in July, he weighed just 71 kilos – down from 78 kilos at the 2007 Tour (he didn't ride it in 2008, in order to concentrate on the Olympic track events). When you're 6' 3", 71 kilos is featherweight, and puts you only just on the right side of being in good health.

But his climbing went up another level, and he was keeping pace in the Alps and the Pyrenees with the overall contenders such as eventual winner Alberto Contador, Andreas Klöden, Frank and Andy Schleck, plus a newly un-retired Lance Armstrong.

It seemed extraordinary that Armstrong – seven-time winner of the Tour de France – should have ended up being the only thing between Wiggins and a podium place. Wiggins finished fourth in Paris, equalling Robert Millar's fourth place overall in 1984. Coupled with Cavendish firing on all cylinders in the sprints, Wiggins showed just how far British cycling had come, and on the back of the track success in Beijing, it was a huge surprise that suddenly a British rider was now in the mix for a podium place at the world's greatest race.

And Wiggins got it, too – eventually, three and a half years later, when in January 2013 Armstrong admitted to Oprah Winfrey that he'd doped, and had his results annulled, although he still insists he never doped after his comeback. Wiggins could have been bitter about never having got to stand on the podium, albeit a step below Contador and Schleck, but by 2012 it mattered less: Wiggins would be on that top step himself.

In 2009, it was clear that something good was afoot in British cycling, and it was about to get even bigger. First the nation had begun to dominate track racing, and then – almost as suddenly – Britain seemed to be going somewhere on the road, too, thanks to Cavendish and Wiggins. The two riders who had failed to fire during their Madison track event in Beijing were on the brink of becoming two of Britain's most celebrated road cyclists.

17

BLUE-SKY THINKING

Dave Brailsford and Shane Sutton had first chatted non-chalantly about setting up a British pro team at the Melbourne Park Velodrome during the 2006 Commonwealth Games track events. The idea would be that they'd use everything they'd learned from establishing what had become a world-beating track team and apply it to the road.

But if 2006 had been the year the seed was sown in terms of building a top-level, potentially world-beating road squad, 2007 was the year when the seed was watered, and grew; it was not yet flowering – patience was required – but it had begun pushing upwards towards the sky. Or should that be Sky?

It was at the track World Cup in January, nearly a year after the initial idea, that Sutton and Brailsford decided to go for it. Brailsford was the one who then went out pressing the flesh and sounding out potential sponsors for the nascent road team; Sutton was left holding the British Cycling babies, who were to come of age at the most successful Olympic Games a British cycling squad had ever enjoyed.

Fast-forward to 2010, and Team Sky were launched at the

Millbank Tower, near Westminster – a fancy do with special blue lighting and Sky News presenter Dermot Murnaghan as the host. Bradley Wiggins was the star of the show, and Chris Froome was there, too, of course, but as he was still then a bit of an unknown quantity, he was largely ignored by the press. Sky perhaps knew his potential, though, and Brailsford's stated goal was for the team to have a British winner within five years, which seemed extremely ambitious.

The team got off to the perfect start, winning its very first race when Kiwi sprinter Greg Henderson powered to victory at the Cancer Council Helpline Classic in Adelaide – the 'warm-up' race to the Tour Down Under stage race, which started two days later – with Sky's Chris Sutton taking second. Their positions were reversed on the final stage of the Tour Down Under when Sutton Shane Sutton's nephew – won ahead of Henderson. And in March, Russell Downing scored Sky's first victory by a British rider when he won the second stage of the Critérium International.

But general teething problems, staff issues, and the fact that it wasn't possible to simply run a pro road team in the same way as British Cycling had always been run, made for a difficult first year on the whole.

'I really didn't enjoy Team Sky's first season in cycling. I wouldn't ever want to have to go through the stress of 2010 again,' Rod Ellingworth – the team's 'race coach' as he was then, and their 'performance manager' today – writes in his excellent book *Project Rainbow*.

At time trials, black screens set up beside the big, black team bus, soon nicknamed the Death Star (a *Star Wars* reference) shielded the riders from the public's gaze. The idea was that they'd help the riders concentrate while they warmed up, but one of the main appeals of bike racing – versus football, or, in fact, most sports – had always been that the barrier between the riders and fans was virtually non-existent. Sky tried to change the way things were done in that first year, but trying to professionalize what had in the past often been a charmingly unprofessional professional sport didn't always work.

Things didn't go well for the new leader of the team, either. Having joined Sky from Garmin, where he'd enjoyed a relatively pressure-free role that had seen him finish fourth at the 2009 Tour, much more was expected of Wiggins at the new team, and he quickly discovered that he wasn't a natural leader.

Joining the team in the first place had appeared to be a canny move; Wiggins had been a part of the British Cycling programme since he was eighteen, which meant that he and Brailsford knew each other well, while Shane Sutton, who had known Wiggins's dad, was like a father to him. The process of getting Wiggins out of his two-year contract with Garmin, however, was long and drawn out. Only in December of 2009 did it finally get sorted – the last thing Garmin wanted to do was lose a potential Tour contender – and Wiggins could finally be announced as Team Sky's new leader.

The contract negotiations, however, had come at a time when he should already have been well into his pre-season training; Wiggins felt he was only really getting going that December – a good couple of months behind where he should have been.

Quite reasonably, Wiggins and the Sky management team tried to replicate his 2009 season by following a similar race programme, which included riding the Giro in May. He won the opening time trial to take the leader's pink jersey – and from the outside, it looked as if this could be his year – but he had won on natural time trialling ability alone. It was all downhill from there, and he was never in contention, finishing 40th overall in Verona.

The pre-Tour training camp didn't go much better; Wiggins was getting dropped by the teammates who were supposed to be riding for him. At the prologue time trial in Rotterdam, in the

Netherlands, which was hosting the 2010 Tour's *Grand Départ*, Team Sky's well-intentioned plan to set Wiggins off earlier in the day – as opposed to being one of the last riders to start, as is traditional for the favourites – backfired spectacularly when the rain they were trying to outwit fell squarely on Wiggins, who finished 77th on the stage, 30 seconds down from the outset on rivals like Alberto Contador and Lance Armstrong.

Just like in the Giro, an unfit Wiggins failed to fire on all cylinders during the race, and he finished in Paris a lowly 24th, almost 40 minutes off the pace. As he recalls in his autobiography, *My Time*, he couldn't help letting out his frustration when a journalist asked him what the difference was between 2010 and 2009 after Wiggins had finished almost five minutes behind stage winner Christophe Riblon on stage 14 between Revel and the summit finish at Ax 3 Domaines.

'I'm fucked. I've got nothing,' he told the media back at the team bus. 'I don't have the form, it's as simple as that. I just haven't got it as I did last year. I just feel consistently mediocre. Not brilliant, not shit, just mediocre. I just haven't got it right this year.' Wiggins's 2010 season ended up with him alone and drunk, in a Milan airport hotel, trying to get home after failing to finish the Tour of Lombardy. Things could only get better.

It had been a steep learning curve in their first season, but Sky soon learned.

The 2011 season went considerably better for the team. Problems were ironed out, things began to click for riders and staff members, and, heading into the Tour de France, Bradley Wiggins was looking in good shape to be in contention for the yellow jersey.

Already he'd finished third overall at the Paris–Nice stage race in March, and then won the Critérium du Dauphiné in June, having taken the race lead after the time trial on stage three and riding consistently on the climbs to defend his lead for the rest of the race.

Once at the Tour, resplendent in his white jersey with the red-and-blue bands denoting him as the British road-race champion – the title he'd taken just a week before the start of the Tour – everything was going to plan for Wiggins. But then – suddenly – on stage seven, from Le Mans to Châteauroux, with 40 kilometres to go, he crashed.

While Mark Cavendish – that year riding for the HTC-Highroad outfit – screamed across the finish line to take the 17th Tour stage win of his career, and the second of what would be five stage victories at that Tour, his former Madison partner was on his way to hospital. Wiggins had broken his collarbone, and was out of the race.

Were Sky really going to be able to achieve their aim of having a British Tour winner within five years? They only had three more 'tries' left.

In the Wiggins documentary film *A Year in Yellow*, filmed across the build-up to, and immediate aftermath of, Wiggins's 2012 Tour win, Shane Sutton tells the camera: 'I actually think he's missed his chance,' which is typical of his propensity to tell it the way he sees it. 'If Brad was ever going to win the Tour, it was last year [2011].

'Last year, Brad Wiggins should have been drinking champagne approaching the Champs-Elysées. But unfortunately . . .' Sutton shrugs, and tails off.

He would have been mightily pleased that he was wrong.

Indeed, as Brailsford pointed out after Chris Froome's win in 2013, Sky ended up winning the Tour twice in four years. Besides, before they'd even won it once, by September 2011, things were already looking up when Froome won a stage and finished second at the Vuelta a España, just 13 seconds behind winner Juan José Cobo, and a recovered Wiggins took third, another minute and a half back, both Sky riders having worn the red leader's jersey along the way. It ended up having been a mistake making Froome work for Wiggins; the team admits today that Froome could have won had they put faith in his ability.

But, at the time, Froome was still somewhat of an unknown quantity over a three-week race. Indeed, until that stand-out performance so late in the season, he had yet to renew his contract. Suddenly, Froome had become a bona fide grand-tour contender – just like Wiggins.

Less than two weeks later, Froome and Wiggins would be key members of the British national team that helped Cavendish to his road-race world champion's title. And in October, Sky announced that they'd secured Cavendish's signature for the 2012 season. He'd become, by then, arguably the biggest name in professional cycling.

That summer, on assignment for *Cycle Sport* magazine, I'd spent an afternoon pedalling around a couple of laps of the Copenhagen world-championship road-race course with Brian Holm, stopping every now and again for photographer Mike King to get some nice pictures.

Holm was Cavendish's *directeur sportif* at HTC, and knew both the course and Cavendish well. The world championships in Copenhagen had been earmarked by Cavendish's coach, Rod Ellingworth, three years before, as winnable for Cavendish. 'Project Rainbow', they'd called it – a painstaking plan to bring everything and everyone together for that one day in September 2011 in the hope of winning Britain's first rainbow jersey in the elite men's event since Tom Simpson had won the Worlds road race in 1965.

Ellingworth recalls one of the meetings they had in June 2009, which brought together the riders who were on the shortlist to feature in the Worlds team, including Jeremy Hunt, Roger Hammond, David Millar, Ian Stannard, Ben Swift, Froome, Geraint Thomas and Cavendish.

Wiggins was a notable absence. 'He wasn't at the meeting because he didn't turn up,' Ellingworth writes.

Ellingworth showed them old film footage of Simpson's 1965 Worlds win, and when he turned the lights back on, he had one of Simpson's rainbow jerseys there with him, in a picture frame. Millar and Cavendish in particular, Ellingworth recalls, cooed over it.

Now the goal was that much more tangible.

'Seventeen laps of this will grind you down,' Holm had told me on our recce of the Copenhagen Worlds course for my magazine race preview. 'Although that happens no matter what the course is like. If it's flat, then the race just goes faster.'

The climb up to the start/finish line – Geels Bakke – was one of two slopes that Cavendish was going to have to get over, seventeen times, if he wanted to be in with a shot of becoming champion of the world.

'It doesn't feel too bad riding up,' Holm said of the final climb, having made short work of it. He stopped, and took a glance behind him. 'But then you look back and realize that it actually is pretty steep, so it will be important that you don't start your sprint too early.

'But a good Cav could win this by 20 metres,' Holm added. 'If he's got the legs, he can win, but he also needs a very strong team around him.'

It was nigh on prophetic – apart from the '20 metres' part.

I was sworn to secrecy, but Holm had also told me then that he was going to be in the British team car, alongside Ellingworth, on the day. He was Cavendish's long-time *directeur sportif*, at T-Mobile, Columbia and HTC, and, being from Copenhagen, even used to train on parts of the course as a youngster. Ellingworth would drive the car, and Holm – a voice of reason and experience, and, like Ellingworth, one of Cavendish's trusted confidants – would make the calls tactics-wise.

The 'strong team' that Holm had said Cavendish needed had been whittled down and carefully put together by Ellingworth: Cavendish, of course, and then Steve Cummings, Froome, Hunt, Stannard, Thomas, Wiggins, and Millar as 'road captain', who could make the calls on the road if things started to go awry.

It was a veritable who's who of British road-race talent, with three former national road-race champions in their ranks – Hunt (1997 and 2001), Millar (2007), Thomas (2010) – as well as the reigning one in Wiggins, plus two in waiting, with Stannard taking the title in 2012 and Cavendish himself in 2013.

At the Worlds, getting Cavendish repeatedly over the main climb – the one in the middle of the course – without exhausting him too much would be the experienced Hunt's responsibility, starting with Cavendish as close to the front as possible on each lap and then letting themselves drift slowly backwards through the bunch over the course of the climb, saving energy, before slowly moving up again once back on the flat.

It worked a treat.

We all filed into the press conference to listen to Cavendish at his most eloquent and grateful, still stunned, just a little perhaps, at having written the newest chapter in British cycling history. For anyone else, it might have taken a while for it to sink in that they'd become world champion, but Cavendish seemed to know exactly what he had on his shoulders – the same-coloured shirt as Tom Simpson had first worn forty-six years ago.

This wasn't a dream realized; this was a goal achieved. Now Cavendish could get on with achieving others while wearing this most iconic of jerseys.

But he had a few people to thank first.

Ellingworth was singled out, and Cavendish was also grateful to all the riders who weren't there as part of the squad but had been involved all along, and who had helped qualify an eight-man team by virtue of the UCI points they'd scored in other events.

As for his teammates on the day: 'The guys rode out of their skins today, and I won on behalf of them. I'll wear this jersey next year, but there's always going to be seven guys in my heart when it comes to this jersey. It's a shame that they can't wear it as well, because I just did the last part today.'

It was typical Cavendish: always grateful, always aware that he was just a cog – albeit a bloody fast spinning one – in a much bigger wheel. Even early on in his career, he'd taken to buying thank-you gifts for his teammates.

The team had turned themselves inside out to ensure that the race ended in the bunch sprint that they required.

'No one else was really willing to help,' Cavendish said. 'We were attacked every which way by the other nations, but we've got the best riders in the world riding for Great Britain.'

And here, he singled out his old friend. If there had been any lasting effects of Cavendish's frustration when they'd been unable to win gold in the Madison at the 2008 Beijing Olympics, they had definitely all been washed away now: 'Bradley Wiggins pretty much rode the last lap at the front on his own. He did an incredible job. All I had to do was sit there.'

Wiggins had played a major role in helping Cavendish win his 2011 rainbow jersey, but it's hard to imagine that any rider will ever be shone upon quite so brightly as Wiggins was in the summer of 2012. The British rider's build-up to the Tour – his crash in 2011 just a distant memory – consisted of winnable races that the team would race full bore, each member practising their role in an effort to recreate, or 'pre-create', the roles they'd take on at the Tour.

Wiggins was virtually unstoppable: after third place overall at the Tour of Algarve in February, where he won the final time trial, he won Paris–Nice in March, the Tour de Romandie in April – where he even won the bunch sprint on the opening stage – and the Critérium du Dauphiné in June, defending his title there.

At the Tour – which started in Liège on 30 June, having been brought forward slightly on the calendar to allow the riders sufficient time to recover before the London Olympics – Wiggins and his team appeared to be in complete control. They say you make your own luck, but that's hard to do at the Tour, where a crash can take you out of the running at any moment. Wiggins, however, really did seem to have used up his bad luck the year before; at the 2012 Tour, he didn't puncture even once in 3,500 kilometres – almost 2,200 miles – of racing.

Time-trial specialist Fabian Cancellara won the prologue time trial. Wiggins was second, seven seconds off the pace, which was a blessing in a quite obvious disguise: it meant that Cancellara's RadioShack squad would have to take control of the race to defend the race lead for as long as possible. Had Wiggins taken the race lead that early, it would have put unnecessary pressure on the team.

Stage seven, one of the first true tests of that year's Tour, was when Sky's long-term plan was rolled out in earnest. It was time for the team to put into practice what they'd been learning to do at the multiple training camps that they had taken part in on the mountainous Spanish island of Tenerife, and then in full racing conditions at Paris–Nice, Romandie and the Dauphiné.

The climb up to the top of La Planche des Belles Filles – also used by the 2014 Tour – at the finish of the seventh stage was the first serious climb on the 2012 route, and so the first opportunity to use Sky's 'climbing train', which was reminiscent of the 'sprint trains' used by sprinters like Cavendish to keep out of the wind at the end of a flat stage before being unleashed.

In the mountains, though, it meant that the man on the front would ride at an uncomfortable tempo for as long as possible – kilometres at a time rather than the hundreds of metres at a time in a sprint train – which would serve to both pace Wiggins at a speed that the team knew he could sustain, and shed as many riders as possible who weren't able to follow such a relentless speed. 'Pure' climbers often prefer to ride the mountains at more of a stop–start pace, accelerating when they want to, or when their rivals look weak. Sky's more calculated, more scientific approach, relying on the knowledge of what kinds of effort were possible through training and practice, was far more effective than simply going on 'feel'.

In his book, Wiggins explains how it worked that day on La Planche des Belles Filles.

'Mick [Rogers] would go as hard as he could which would probably be a kilometre and a half, Richie [Porte] would take over and do the same thing, then Froomie. Eventually we would get to the summit and there shouldn't be many other guys left with us.'

It had been a method used by Lance Armstrong and his US Postal teammates like George Hincapie and Tyler Hamilton in their heyday – the 'blue train', as it became known – and while being compared to the American team's dominating display in the mountains would have been a compliment a few short years earlier, in 2012 such comparisons were far from gratefully received as the net tightened around Armstrong.

When it was suggested at the post-stage-eight press conference in Porrentruy, in Switzerland, that the internet was alive with suggestions that Sky's tactics looked very similar to US Postal's, Wiggins's response was succinct. 'It's easy for them to sit under a pseudonym on Twitter and write that sort of shit rather than get off their arses in their own lives and apply themselves and work hard at something and achieve something. And that's ultimately it. ****s,' he said, ending with one of David Millar's favourite words.

On La Planche des Belles Filles, Sky's race tactic had worked like clockwork, and left Wiggins and teammate Froome with only defending Tour champion Cadel Evans and Italian Vincenzo Nibali for company. Evans tried to get the better of the Sky tandem in the final few hundred metres, with Nibali hanging on for grim death at the back of the quartet, but it was Froome who then made an even bigger push for home, winning the stage, while Evans was second, with Wiggins on the Australian's wheel in third.

A week into the race, Wiggins was now in yellow. The fact that Froome had won the stage was the icing on the cake.

For Sky, the 2010 and 2011 Tours had been an anticlimax, for two very different reasons, but in 2012 the race was under their stewardship. The team controlled the race on the climbs, and Nibali proved to be the only rider capable of staying even within ten minutes of Wiggins and Froome by the time the race reached Paris. The only real 'threat' to Wiggins's lead – not that Froome ever even was one – had come from within their own team. It looked like an enviable position to be in.

But demonstrations of Froome's climbing ability, as witnessed on stage seven to La Planche des Belles Filles, would be seen again along the way. On stage 11, with its summit finish on La Toussuire, the pace was too much for Evans; it was effectively the day that his Tour challenge ended. Froome, however, was keen to put Nibali in trouble, too, and attacked with two kilometres to go.

'And that's when Sean said on the radio, "What are you doing?"' Wiggins says of the incident in *My Time*. Sean was Sean Yates, Sky's sports director at the time, who could speak to his charges from the team car, his messages relayed to earpieces that each rider wore.

'I was thinking, "What on earth's he [Froome] doing? I'm leading this race by two minutes,"' Wiggins writes. 'So he stopped, we got back to him and then we rode the tempo that we'd planned to ride all day, up to the finish.'

It was played down by the team, but at the time there was clear tension on Twitter (where else?) where things got a little tetchy between Wiggins's wife, Cath, and Froome's girlfriend Michelle.

'See Mick Rogers and Richie Porte for examples of genuine, selfless effort and true professionalism,' Mrs Wiggins tweeted.

'Typical!' Michelle added to a retweet of Cath's tweet.

The episode on La Toussuire had rattled Wiggins, he admitted in his book. 'After La Toussuire I wanted to come home. I thought, "Fuck this, I'm not doing another two weeks of this, not knowing what to expect." '

With unequivocal support for Wiggins from Brailsford and Yates, it should have been the end of it. But on the final mountain stage – stage 17 between Bagnères-de-Luchon and Peyragudes – Froome again gave a clear demonstration of who the better climber was. Three kilometres from the finish, on the final climb, Froome pushed on ahead of the group of riders containing Nibali and Wiggins, but then seemed to check himself, and instead began chivvying his team leader along as they began to leave their rivals behind.

With two kilometres to go, the gap between them widened again, and again Froome was forced to slow down and wait for Wiggins. Both of them could be seen talking to each other, too.

In the final kilometre, the road flattened out, and Wiggins stuck to Froome's back wheel like a limpet as they sped towards the finish. They crossed the line together, 20 seconds behind stage winner Alejandro Valverde, a clear smile on Wiggins's lips, relieved that the mountains were now behind them. Or was it a grimace? Quite possibly both.

'Putting more time into our main opposition was just what we needed going into the final time trial,' Froome told ITV4 at the finish when asked about the late push by the Sky pair. But what was it that he'd been saying to Wiggins? 'Just that we'd got rid of Nibali and that it was about to flatten out and just stay on my wheel,' he explained.

And asked whether when he distanced Wiggins it was because his team leader was encouraging him to go on ahead and win the stage, he replied: 'No. We were just . . . The plan was to stay together and . . . yeah, we did that, so . . . so that's all good.'

Wiggins, safely still in yellow, could now almost see the Eiffel Tower. Getting through the final mountain stage in one piece, with just three stages to go, including the time trial on stage 19, allowed him to relax a little.

'I think Chris will have his day, for sure, 100 per cent,' Wiggins told the TV cameras, 'and I'll be there to support him every inch of the way when he does at the Tour.'

Two days later, Wiggins won that 53.5-kilometre time trial by one minute and 16 seconds from Froome. Their Tour one-two was in the bag.

The two riders were never required to be best friends for Sky to succeed. And succeed it had: Froome's second place overall would have alone been Britain's highest-ever finish at the Tour; winning it and taking second place was far beyond what anyone had ever imagined. And it meant that Sky had two very real Tour de France contenders in the same ranks.

For Wiggins, being the first British winner of the Tour de France was huge, but to then 'back it up' with a gold medal in the time trial at the Olympic Games in his home country, indeed, in his home city, was . . . Well, it really didn't get any better than that.

Cavendish finished the 2012 Tour having added three more stage wins to his tally to make a total of twenty-three career wins at the event by that point. The sight of Wiggins in the yellow jersey leading him out for the stage victory on the Champs-Elysées on the final stage was quite something, confirming the sheer madness of British cycling's success.

No one could fault the commitment of the British national team when it came to getting behind Cavendish for races like the world championships or the Olympic road race. But after just one season with Sky, and having been on a Tour team that had been built around Wiggins, Cavendish decided to move to the Belgian Omega Pharma-Quick Step squad in 2013, where he could enjoy full support as undisputed team leader at the races he was targeting.

Following the 2012 Tour, Cavendish's focus switched quickly to the Olympic road race. While at the 2011 world championships he had enjoyed the luxury of seven other riders to help him win the title, at London 2012 he was part of only a five-man team, and it told. Wiggins, Froome, Ian Stannard and David Millar tried to control the race for him, but it wasn't to be, and an Olympic medal continues to elude him. There were rumours, however, that Cavendish could be tempted back to the track in Rio in 2016.

Four days after the Olympic road race, Wiggins won gold in the time trial, with Froome taking bronze, more than a minute down. Germany's Tony Martin took silver. London 2012 was, from a cycling point of view, just as successful as Beijing in 2008, but with the added lustre that being on home turf brought.

It was Victoria Pendleton's last hurrah before retirement. 'The golden girl of British cycling', as the newspapers always referred to her, had to settle for silver in the sprint, beaten by arch-rival Anna Meares, but struck gold in the Keirin, and could retire happy as the reigning sprint world champion.

Her replacement was needed, and she duly arrived: a new star was born in Laura Trott, who won gold in London in both the omnium and the team pursuit. The fact that Trott's an endurance rider and Pendleton was a sprinter matters little; it's inspiring figures that the sport and public requires, and Trott has whatever-it-is-that-she-has in spades.

It was a hugely successful Olympics for British cycling again, then, but there could only ever be one winner of the BBC Sports Personality of the Year Award. Step forward, Sir Wiggo.

'The most iconic trophy in British sport', Wiggins once called it, and you got the impression that he was as pleased to be recognized for his achievements as he was to actually win the Tour or his Olympic medals.

The award somehow manages to straddle the 'divide' between the Olympics loving public and the non-Olympic 'everyday' achievements of the athlete: a just reward for 365 days a year of training and commitment, rather than just the visible results. Very few athletes seem to have won the BBC Sports Personality of the Year Award on the strength of a single performance; the public requires a certain longevity from their sporting heroes.

Wiggins was the perfect winner: he could boast a career full of Olympic and international achievements, and then a single year when everything went right. People need a bit of time to get to know their athletes; perhaps it really is about 'personality' rather than solely achievement, after all.

But in the aftermath of Wiggins's 'Great British summer', he felt the pressure. Suddenly, he was one of the most famous faces in Britain; or, at least, his sideburns were. Froome had been too close for comfort at the Tour, and then in the off-season Lance Armstrong admitted to Oprah Winfrey that he had doped. More questions were, inevitably, asked of Wiggins, which he found difficult, despite maintaining his innocence. He later revealed that he'd had to move his children to a new school as a result of bullying; if Armstrong had cheated to win the Tour, the other kids had deduced, then their dad must have done, too.

In 2013, Wiggins chose to ride the Giro, which suggested that he might concentrate on that rather than the Tour, but he never looked in Giro-winning shape. He withdrew from the race after stage 12, suffering from both a chest infection and a knee injury, having crashed on stage seven.

In late May, the team announced that his knee was going to prevent him from starting the Tour. This meant that the hotly anticipated showdown between Wiggins and Froome – if there ever was going to be one – never materialized.

The 2013 season was, in short, all but a write-off for Wiggins, although he did come good again late in the season to win the Tour of Britain in September, and to take the silver medal – behind Tony Martin – at the time-trial world championships in Florence.

Some had called Wiggins's 2012 Tour win boring, such had been Sky's dominance. But British fans who had been waiting for a win since the Tour's inception in 1903 certainly didn't find it boring; neither did Sky. If you have the opportunity to win the greatest bike race in the world, and you find a tactical process that can gain you the title, then it stands to reason that you'll use it, and Sky went about winning the 2013 Tour in a similar manner.

Froome, lieutenant to Wiggins the year before, was now in the Wiggins role, while Richie Porte, instrumental in 2012, stepped up another level to become Froome's right-hand man. Would Porte then climb one more step to become Sky's next Grand Tour superstar in turn? The potential was there for some kind of perpetual Russian-doll production line (right-hand man becomes the following year's leader, and so on) and indeed Porte was initially being offered his own opportunity at the 2014 Tour of Italy, but was then pulled out of the Giro squad just a month before the start to ensure that he arrived at the Tour in July in the best possible condition to help the team.

Froome, almost unopposed, stormed to victory at that 2013 Tour, giving Team Sky their second win at the event in as many years. While Wiggins appears happy to have won the Tour 'just' once, Froome, five years Wiggins's junior, could perhaps win it four, five or six times.

It wasn't until December 2013 that it was announced that the two Sky teammates had put their past differences behind them, apparently having talked at the team's first get-together in Mallorca ahead of the 2014 season. 'To be honest, we should have done it a very long time ago, just to clear the air, but we are on good terms now,' Froome told the *Daily Mail*.

'The incident in 2012 was at the root of it all,' he continued. 'I'm not sure it was that big a problem, but it was all played out so much in the media, it was allowed to escalate.'

'I think there's a lot of internal rivalry . . . But in a healthy way,' Wiggins then told the *Guardian* at the start of the 2014 season. 'We all push each other, and everyone's vying for places in the Tour de France and other races, and there are a lot of good youngsters coming up.'

Having missed out on seeing Froome and Wiggins riding together at the 2013 Tour, a press corps that had been licking their lips at the prospect of the two men being at each other's throats come the 2014 race were left looking as though they were going to go hungry. Especially when it was announced that Wiggins hadn't been selected for the Tour squad. A nation wondered: did Sky not trust Wiggins to work for Froome after all?

Armstrong's confession in January 2013 to having doped to win his seven Tour titles, and the hangover from that, led to questions and doubts among fans and the media about Froome's dominating display, upsetting him and his team manager. Brailsford felt obliged to assert the riders' innocence during the 2013 race, just as Wiggins had had to do in 2012. Armstrong – and others like him – have caused a shadow of suspicion to be cast over dominating displays of bike racing, and it could take some time for the sport to be in a position to shake that off.

In September 2013, it was hoped that the election of new UCI president Brian Cookson – moving from his post as president of British Cycling – would herald a new dawn, with new leadership perhaps shaking up a sport that clearly still contains rotten elements, despite the efforts by many to clean it up. The change in the presidency, with the election held in Florence during the UCI road world championships, was preceded by what proved to be almost a war cry from Cookson who, when the preliminaries had gone on for far too long, decided to cut to the chase: 'Enough – let's vote!'

Five days earlier, in the same city, on the start ramp ahead of the team time trial world championship, another Briton – Katie Colclough – was similarly decisive as she put everything into what would be her penultimate race as a professional rider, determined as she was to go out with a bang.

'I didn't want to finish thinking I could have gone that bit harder or given that bit more,' says Colclough, 'and I knew that if I could tell people I was a world champion, it could make a big difference to the next stage of my life, so I was really committed to it.'

Colclough won, riding with her Specialized-Lululemon team-mates, the only world championship event in which riders represent their trade teams rather than their national squads. It was a huge achievement.

So her decision to quit cycling, aged twenty-three and at the top of her game having become world champion, surprised many.

She seemed to leave the sport without much explanation, which was her prerogative, of course. But when I caught up with her during her lunch hour at her new job in London I found she was more than happy to talk about it, and happy, too, to be working in the 'real world' now.

'I've never actually had any kind of job before!' she laughs.

Colclough should have been a poster girl for British Cycling, rising up through its Olympic programmes to become world champion, starting with the Talent Team, having been spotted, aged fifteen, at a local cyclo-cross (racing her mountain bike), before joining the Development programme and then the Academy, combining road and track.

Colclough became junior national points race champion in 1998, and was three times European team-pursuit champion. She then turned professional with HTC-Highroad in 2011, which became Specialized-Lululemon in 2012 – the year in which she also became under-23 national road-race champion.

'The chance to join HTC was too good an opportunity to turn down,' Colclough says. 'It was one of the best experiences I've ever had, and it was good to step out of the British Cycling bubble for a bit, so I wouldn't have changed anything. But at the start of 2013, I decided that I couldn't really see my future in the sport. I could imagine stopping at the age of thirty-six or thirty-seven and still being in the same position as I was, instead of having had another career or another lifestyle.

'There's also very little job security, you're always on the go, you never have a base, you never have a home, and I'd had a lot of bad crashes, too, to be honest: I'd hit my head again at the national championships, which smashed my helmet in two, so I think that was a big factor.'

Colclough nevertheless persevered, and contacted British Cycling coaches Paul Manning and Chris Newton to ask if she could be tested for racing on the track again, having concentrated on the road the previous season.

'I'm quite a goal-oriented person, so I thought going back to the track to ride pursuits and things might suit me better. But when it came to the night before the first training camp I was due to be at, in July, I just didn't want to go,' Colclough says, 'and I'd never felt that way about the sport before.'

She made a list of the pros and cons of remaining a pro cyclist, and the cons won out. Despite the lack of security, the money side of things never came into it; Colclough says she was getting by OK. 'There were so many factors, and it got to the point where I just had to ask myself whether this was what I actually wanted: whether I actually wanted to be a professional athlete any more.

'In the end it was a lifestyle change,' she explains. 'I'm enjoying living like a normal person now!'

Where does she see the future of women's cycling? In Britain, women's racing appears to be stronger than ever, especially since the introduction of the Women's Tour of Britain.

'From a British perspective, it perhaps looks like it, but in France you could turn up to a random race and it would have been cancelled, or there wouldn't have been any prize money, or none of the junctions would have been blocked off by the police. And nothing had changed in the five years I'd been doing it.'

Directly after retirement, Colclough became an athlete ambassador at the charity Right To Play, before plunging into the world of full-time employment, working for a sports-specific job agency. In May 2014, she announced that she'd joined sports-nutrition brand Science in Sport as their sponsorship and events manager.

On the same day, Colclough's former national-squad teammate Emma Trott announced her retirement from professional cycling.

Trott – older sister of double Olympic gold-medallist Laura – was racing at the inaugural Women's Tour, and chose the penultimate stage, which started in her home town of Cheshunt, in Hertfordshire, to reveal her decision to retire at the end of the race. The 24-year-old, who raced for the same Boels-Dolmans team as Olympic road-race silver medallist Lizzie Armitstead, told the press at the end of the fourth stage that she wanted 'a normal life'.

'I have not said anything until now, but I started thinking about retiring at the end of last year,' Trott explained. 'I lost two dear friends in the past year and that changed my perspective.'

Both Trott and Colclough had also been part of a horrific road accident in Belgium in 2010. The pair were with three other members of the national team when they were hit by a car, and were lucky to be alive. Trott broke her collarbone, while Colclough suffered severe concussion. The three other riders in the group were also injured: Lucy Martin suffered a cracked vertebra, Sarah Reynolds hurt her hand and Hannah Mayho broke her arm and leg.

Professional cycling – for men or women – is still a long way from being a normal career choice, and retirement from the sport will now give Trott and Colclough the 'normal life' that both cited as their motivation for leaving women's pro cycling behind them.

It's a huge shame for the sport to lose riders of such high calibre, but the public and media reaction to the Women's Tour suggests that women's cycling is nevertheless on the up.

Leaning on the bonnet of his team car, Sean Yates could be at one of any number of bike races across the world. The fact that he's in the BMW showroom on Park Lane in London doesn't matter; this is the launch of the new 2014 NFTO UCI Continental-level team, and Yates, having left Team Sky in 2012, is one of its *directeurs sportifs*.

'Cycling is on a massive high in this country at the moment,' he says. 'It just seems to be getting bigger and bigger, so it'd be great if, as a team, we could get even more investment and make the step up to Pro Continental, and get out and about racing in Europe.

'People – big-money people – now want to be involved with cycling, and now, with Team Sky, there's someone to follow, something to aspire to,' Yates says. 'The riders are buzzing: it's the opportunity of a lifetime, and they've got to grab it with both hands, and go with it.'

At the other side of the showroom, one of those riders, Russell Downing, resplendent in his red-and-blue-banded white circuit-race national champion's jersey, holds court.

Downing's seen it all in his sixteen years as a pro rider.

'Some years have been better than others,' he says. 'Some years it has been a struggle to pay the bills, but I'm still here at thirty-five, so I must have done something right. I'm still enjoying the sport – I'm as keen now as I've ever been – but I just wish I was twenty years old again. But then, don't we all?' he grins.

He means in order to take even more advantage of the status cycling enjoys in Britain today, but he's been a huge part of its history, and indeed of making it as popular as it is.

'My two years with Sky were great,' he says. 'To win that stage of the Critérium International with them, and then to ride the Giro d'Italia, was just fantastic. I'd always wanted to do a Grand Tour, and the Giro was the one I wanted.

'Today, I'm still mentally strong; I don't think I'll ever have enough of this sport,' Downing says. 'If I wasn't a pro bike rider, I'd still be riding my bike, so it's great to still be earning a living from it.'

A month later – Wednesday 12 March 2014 – would have felt incredibly special for Rod Ellingworth. On the same day, two of his former charges from British Cycling's Olympic Academy – Geraint Thomas, riding for Sky, and Mark Cavendish, now with Omega Pharma-Quick Step, but a Team Sky alumnus – took the race lead in two of Europe's oldest and most iconic bike races, which run concurrently each spring: Paris–Nice and Tirreno–Adriatico.

Thomas lost his lead in Paris–Nice two days later, and then crashed out on the penultimate stage, but he'd ridden well enough for people to start talking about him as a potential Grand Tour winner one day.

Cavendish, like Thomas, had to hand over his race leader's jersey at Tirreno after just two days, but the win on the opening stage to give him the lead hadn't come from a trademark sprint. Instead, it was the result of leading home his Omega Pharma squad in the team time trial – a discipline Cavendish loves even more than sprinting, as it means that the whole team gets to share the joy on the podium, rather than just in the team bus or back at the hotel with a glass of champagne, as they do when they've helped him win in a sprint.

Thomas looks set to concentrate on his road career rather than try to take a third Olympic gold medal in the team pursuit, while Cavendish, with such a successful road career already under his belt, might consider trying to win his first Olympic medal by returning to the track in Rio in 2016.

Other British riders outside of the Team Sky set-up are also finding success: riders of the calibre of Steve Cummings at BMC – a long-time member of the British track and road national squads, and winner of a stage of the Tour of Spain in 2012, and overall Tour of the Mediterranean title in 2014 – and time-trial specialist Alex Dowsett, who rides for the Spanish Movistar outfit, and in 2013 won the time trial on stage eight of the Giro d'Italia.

More evidence of British cycling's strength in depth are 22-year-old twins Adam and Simon Yates (no relation to Sean) who ride for the Australian Orica-GreenEdge team. Adam opened his account with a well-taken stage win and the overall at the Tour of Turkey in May 2014, while Simon was picked for the team's 2014 Tour de France squad. Their future is bright; British cycling – and British Cycling with a big 'C' – is churning out future champions by the dozen.

Modern bike racing in Britain is in rude health.

In the past, events have come and gone as a result of the stress of organization, the cost and cooperation of policing and the fickle nature of sponsorship. But, almost in their place, sportives have sprung up across the nation – not races, as such, but tough, high-intensity rides that often inspire faster riders to give full competition a try.

At the top level, British Cycling's nine-event Elite Road Series replaced the Premier Calendar in 2014, and is split into the three-event Spring Cup (including the iconic Lincoln Grand Prix, which will incorporate the national championship road race in 2015) and the six-event Grand Prix Series that runs through summer.

There's also the 10-round Women's Road Series, and a six-round circuit series, with burgeoning junior and youth series, too.

Add to that the Tour Series, the Tour of Britain and the new Women's Tour, plus the resurrected Milk Race, with a men's and women's edition.

Biggest of all, in 2014, was the hugely popular start of the Giro d'Italia in Belfast, and the Tour de France *Grand Départ* in Yorkshire, with a three-day stage race in Yorkshire set to run in 2015 as a legacy of the latter. There's the new London Velodrome in full swing, and the old London velodrome – Herne Hill – enjoying a renaissance. The new Derby Velodrome was set to open in late 2014.

Things have never looked better.

Extraordinarily – in contrast to how things used to be – we've now entered an era in which both fans and the media simply expect sprint wins from Cavendish, expect Lizzie Armitstead to be in the mix on the women's circuit against the very best in the world, and expect stage-race wins from Wiggins and Froome. On the track, expectation is huge in every discipline: for sprint events and endurance events, for both the men's and women's squads.

Getting to such a level has been hard; it's been a work in progress since James Moore set the bar so high by winning that first bike race in 1868 and winning the first-ever road race the year after. But with British cycling having reached such dizzy heights again, it's now the target for other nations ready and willing to adopt similar coaching, training and race tactics to take that crown for themselves.

Getting to the top is one thing, but staying there is quite another, as they say.

Stiff upper lip, chaps.

APPENDIX I

Winners (and nationalities) of Britain's major stage races, including the Tour of Britain and the Milk Race

Southern Grand Prix
1944: Les Plume (GBR)

Victory Cycling Marathon
1945: Robert Batot (FRA)

Brighton–Glasgow
1946: Mike Peers (GBR)
1947: George Kessock (GBR)
1948: Tom Saunders (GBR)
1949: Geoff Clark (GBR)
1950: George Lander (GBR)
1951: Ian Greenfield (GBR)
1952: Bill Bellamy (GBR)

Butlins Holiday Camps 7-Day
1951: Stan Blair (GBR)

Tour of Britain
1951: Ian Steel (GBR)
1952: Ken Russell (GBR)
1953: Gordon 'Tiny' Thomas (GBR)

1954: Eugène Tambourlini (FRA)
1955: Tony Hewson (GBR)

Brighton–Newcastle
1953: Frank Edwards (GBR)

Circuit of Britain
1954: Viv Bailes (GBR)
1955: Des Robinson (GBR)
1956: Dick McNeil (GBR)

Milk Race
1958: Richard Durlacher (AUT)
1959: Bill Bradley (GBR)
1960: Bill Bradley (GBR)
1961: Billy Holmes (GBR)
1962: Eugen Pokorny (POL)
1963: Peter Chisman (GBR)
1964: Arthur Metcalfe (GBR)
1965: Les West (GBR)
1966: Józef Gawliczek (POL)
1967: Les West (GBR)

Milk Race (*cont.*)
1968: Gösta Pettersson (SWE)
1969: Fedor Den Hertog (NED)
1970: Jiri Manus (CZE)
1971: Fedor Den Hertog (NED)
1972: Hennie Kuiper (NED)
1973: Piet Van Katwijk (NED)
1974: Roy Schuiten (NED)
1975: Bernt Johansson (SWE)
1976: Bill Nickson (GBR)
1977: Said Gusseinov (USSR)
1978: Jan Brzeźny (POL)
1979: Yuri Kashirin (USSR)
1980: Ivan Mitchenko (USSR)
1981: Sergei Krivosheev (USSR)
1982: Yuri Kashirin (USSR)
1983: Matt Eaton (USA)
1984: Oleg Czougeda (USSR)
1985: Eric Van Lancker (BEL)
1986: Joey McLoughlin (GBR)
1987: Malcolm Elliott (GBR)
1988: Vasily Zhdanov (USSR)
1989: Brian Walton (CAN)
1990: Shane Sutton (AUS)
1991: Chris Walker (GBR)
1992: Conor Henry (IRE)
1993: Chris Lillywhite (GBR)

Kellogg's Tour of Britain
1987: Joey McLoughlin (GBR)
1988: Malcolm Elliott (GBR)
1989: Robert Millar (GBR)
1990: Michel Dernies (BEL)
1991: Phil Anderson (AUS)
1992: Max Sciandri (ITA) *
1993: Phil Anderson (AUS)
1994: Maurizio Fondriest (ITA)

PruTour
1998: Stuart O'Grady (AUS)
1999: Marc Wauters (BEL)

Tour of Britain
2004: Mauricio Ardila (COL)
2005: Nick Nuyens (BEL)
2006: Martin Pedersen (DEN)
2007: Romain Feillu (FRA)
2008: Geoffroy Lequatre (FRA)
2009: Edvald Boasson Hagen (NOR)
2010: Michael Albasini (SUI)
2011: Lars Boom (NED)
2012: Jonathan Tiernan-Locke (GBR)
2013: Bradley Wiggins (GBR)

Women's Tour
2014: Marianne Vos (NED)

* GBR from 1995

APPENDIX II

The British Cycling Hall of Fame – 2010 inductees

In December 2009, British Cycling revealed the names of fifty cycling heroes who had been selected for induction into its new Hall of Fame as part of the organization's 50th-anniversary celebrations.

Pat Adams: Organizer of many of the leading enduro mountain bike events in the UK, including Mountain Mayhem and Sleepless in the Saddle.

Caroline Alexander: Fine all-round rider in MTB, cyclo-cross and road and the only British woman to have won an XC World Cup MTB race.

Brian Annable: President of the City of Edinburgh Club, long-serving track race organizer and one of the key figures behind the Scottish track scene which has produced riders like Chris Hoy.

David Baker: World Cup race winner and world championship medallist in MTB XC and one of a great first generation of British XC riders.

Sid Barras: A prolific winner in the UK pro road scene, he ended up with 197 professional wins. His sprinting skill made him a formidable opponent.

Stuart Benstead: Over fifty years a race organizer with the Archer GP and the hugely successful Hillingdon circuit events his crowning glories.

Chris Boardman MBE: Won the individual pursuit at the 1992 Barcelona Olympics and followed it up with a fine pro road career with forty-one wins, including several Tour de France prologues.

Bill Bradley: Winner of back-to-back Milk Races in 1958 and 1959 and twice national champion and an Olympian at the 1960 Rome Games.

Beryl Burton OBE: Five world pursuit and two world road titles topped off a career which included over 120 national titles – considered by many the best-ever woman rider.

Keith Butler: A national road champion and Milk Race stage winner, Keith has since become a driving force behind the highly successful Surrey League.

Arthur Campbell MBE: Long-standing and versatile official who was head of the SCU (now Scottish Cycling), an international commissaire and UCI committee member.

Brian Cossavella: A committed and enthusiastic event organizer, most recently of world and European masters track championships, but also of the 1990 junior road Worlds and 1996 track Worlds.

Doug Dailey MBE: Twice national amateur road champion; national coach from 1986 to 1996, since when he's played a central role in the GB team's management, including managing Olympic and Commonwealth teams.

Tony Doyle MBE: A very fine road and track rider, who won two world pursuit titles and was one of the most successful Six-Day riders of all time.

Malcolm Elliott: A leading road sprinter of the eighties, when he won numerous international races, including stages of the Tour of Spain, he is still racing and winning at national level [now retired].

Ian Emmerson OBE: British Cycling president from 1985-1995 and UCI vice-president, Ian is also a prominent race organizer, with the long-running Lincoln GP his best-known promotion.

Benny Foster OBE: Famed for his team management and race organization skills, Benny is perhaps best known as the director of the 1970 world championships held at Leicester.

Tim Gould: Winner of two World Cup XC MTB races in the first season of the competition, Tim was also a six-time winner of the Three-Peaks cyclo-cross race.

Eileen Gray CBE: A top rider, Eileen went on to found the Women's Cycle Racing Association and become BCF president. She was key to women's racing becoming part of the Olympics from 1984.

Dave Hemsley: Arguably the best British cycle speedway rider ever, he won three individual world titles and five national titles in his career.

Barry Hoban: A top road pro, he won eight stages of the Tour de France (a British record until Mark Cavendish came along) and his one-day wins included Ghent-Wevelgem.

Dale Holmes: One of the greatest BMX pros, twice winner of the elite men's world title. A multi national champion and also an international force in 4-Cross in his thirties.

Mandy Jones: Will always be remembered above all else for one remarkable result, winning the world road title when the championships came to Britain's Goodwood venue in 1982.

Peter Keen OBE: The first cycling Performance Director, Peter's sports science background helped him to convert lottery funding into a new culture of coaching excellence and racing success within the GB Team.

Peter King CBE: Peter's twelve years as British Cycling Chief Executive saw the organization become a world beater in competition and administration.

Stan Kite: A crucial figure for professional cyclists in the sixties and seventies, with the British Professional CRA, later the Professional Cycling Association.

Phil Liggett MBE: The voice of the Tour de France on TV, Phil has covered every Tour since 1973 and he has inspired several generations of cyclists with his commentaries.

Craig MacLean: A world champion and Olympic silver medallist in the team sprint and a silver medal winner in the sprint at the world championships.

John and Doreen Mallinson: A great example of the volunteering which underpins the sport in the UK, John and Doreen are mainstays of the NW cycling scene.

Paul Manning MBE: World and Olympic champion and world record holder in the team pursuit and an ever-present in the team's line up from the Sydney Olympics in 2000 through to Beijing in 2008.

Gerry McDaid: An outstanding international commissaire who has officiated at every level up to the Tour de France and who embodies the calm assurance this role requires.

Yvonne McGregor MBE: World champion and Olympic bronze medallist in the individual pursuit in 2000. Also a fine Time Trial and Road rider and world hour record holder.

Jason McRoy: Pioneering downhiller, tragically killed in a motorcycle accident in 1995 with the downhilling world at his feet. An icon of early mountain biking.

Chas Messenger: A fine rider who became an outstanding official, organizing events such as the Milk Race and managing the GB road team.

Robert Millar: A genuinely great road rider with outstanding climbing abilities – fourth place in the 1984 Tour de France and second in the Giro d'Italia were just two highlights.

George Miller: President of the SCU (Scottish Cycling), he was the organiser of the long-running Girvan stage race for over twenty years, as well as a ground-breaking pro critérium series.

Graeme Obree: World individual pursuit champion and hour record holder, Graeme was an innovator with his position on the bike and in bike design.

Hugh Porter MBE: A four-time world pursuit champion, Hugh was an outstanding road and track rider. He is now the BBC's voice of cycling.

Jason Queally MBE: A ground-breaking gold medal in the kilo at the 2000 Sydney Olympics heralded the beginning of a fine team performance by GB at the Games and a decade of success by GB's cyclists.

John Rawnsley: A very fine cyclo-cross rider who has organized the Three-Peaks race since he first launched it in 1961. He also won the first edition and rode the event forty-five times.

Brian Robinson: In many ways a pioneer of British road success on the Continent, Brian was the first British rider to win a Tour de France stage.

Alan Rushton: Prolific organizer of high profile events, usually with TV coverage – including the PruTour, world track championships and Kellogg's circuit series.

Tom Simpson: Britain's only pro road world champion [until Mark Cavendish in 2011], his tragic death in the 1967 Tour de France ended the dreams of a generation. He was BBC Sports Personality of the Year in 1965, reflecting his status in sport.

Eddie Soens: A Liverpool-based coach who has been credited with inspiring and informing several generations of young cyclists in the area – including Bill Bradley and Chris Boardman.

Colin Sturgess: The 1989 world pursuit champion, and one of a long line of outstanding British riders in this discipline.

Dot Tilbury MBE: The complete all-round volunteer, organizing, officiating, guiding, helping and even race reporting in the Isle of Man's thriving youth racing scene.

Graham Webb: World amateur road champion in 1967, Webb's pro career was dogged with ill-fortune – he returned to win a national Madison title in 1988, in Belgium, his home for the last forty years.

Les West: A double winner of the Milk Race, Les was second in the 1966 amateur world road championships and fourth in the pro race four years later.

Sean Yates: Tour de France time-trial stage winner and yellow jersey wearer, Yates was an outstanding pro and highly valued team rider.

Tony Yorke OBE: A well-respected coach, Tony made a huge contribution to the development of para-cycling as it moved towards UCI governance.

2014 British Cycling Hall of Fame additions

Nicole Cooke, Brian Cookson, Roger Hammond, Rob Hayles,
 Sir Chris Hoy, Victoria Pendleton, Norman Sheil.

Hall of Fame courtesy of British Cycling

FURTHER READING

So it turns out that there's rather a lot of British bike-racing history; this book really could quite easily have stretched to five or six volumes. Covering such a long period of time in just one book mcant that this could only cvcr bc an ovcrvicw – a jaunt through Britain's bike-racing history, if you like – which means that many of the events mentioned have been covered in a lot more detail by various autobiographies, biographies and specialist titles.

Although it was always my intention not to just regurgitate what was out there already – hence the proliferation of original inter-views – there was nevertheless plenty of research involved, and besides those books already cited in the text, I also found the fol-lowing useful, all of which I highly recommend for the student of British cycling.

Born to Ride by Stephen Roche (Yellow Jersey Press)
Brian Robinson: Pioneer by Graeme Fife (Mousehold Press/Sport & Publicity)
Days of Gold and Glory by Mike Price
Heroes, Villains & Velodromes by Richard Moore (HarperSport)
It's All About the Bike by Sean Yates (Bantam Press)
Roule Britannia: A History of Britons in the Tour de France by William
    Fotheringham (Yellow Jersey Press)
*The Little Black Bottle: Choppy Warburton, the question of doping, and the
    deaths of his bicycle racers* by Gerry Moore (Van der Plas Publications)

ACKNOWLEDGEMENTS

I have a number of people to thank, so apologies in advance to anyone I may have forgotten along the way. I'll make up for it in volume two . . .

Firstly, thank you very much to all those who agreed to be interviewed, either in person or over the phone. Twenty minutes often turned into half an hour, and then an hour or more, but luckily my apologies were always met with words to the effect of, 'I'm really enjoying talking about it after so long.'

So thanks to Chris Boardman, Michael Hutchinson, Jeremy Whittle and Pete Goding, to Colin Lewis and Simon Aske, to Brian Smith, Mick Bennett and Alan Rushton. Thank you Paul Watson, Tony Doyle and Gretel Yorke, Katie Colclough, Jamie Staff, Sean Yates and Russell Downing, John Herety, Matt Stephens and Kenny Van Vlaminck.

Special thanks to John Moore and Tony Hoar – both in their early eighties, I hope they won't mind my saying – whom it was a privilege to speak with at length, and who were additionally so generous with their time when it came to follow-up emails.

My extra special thanks to Brian Cookson and James Carr at UCI, and to Keith Bingham, who was invaluable in helping me to make sense of the timescale of things. Keith should really be doing his own book about his forty years with *Cycling Weekly*. I'd be the first in line to buy it.

As well as Keith, thank you to my other colleagues past, present and no doubt future, including, but not limited to, Robert Garbutt and Simon Richardson at *Cycle Sport* and *Cycling Weekly*, former *Cycle Sport* deputy editor Edward Pickering, author Richard Moore, and the old team on *Procycling* magazine – Peter Cossins, the already-mentioned Jeremy Whittle, Paul Godfrey, Pete Goding (again) and Daniel Friebe.

And thank you in particular to my co-editor on *The Cycling Anthology* range of books, Lionel Birnie, for his encouragement and support.

I'm thankful, too, to Abby Burton at British Cycling, and for the amazing resources that are the British Library and Ely Museum, and their staff.

Please also support the Dave Rayner Fund and the Braveheart Fund, who are an essential help to young British bike racers.

Huge thanks to my agent, David Luxton, for his expert guidance – and patience. The same to my publisher, Giles Elliott at Transworld, whose idea this book was in the first place. Thank you both for your faith in me.

And finally to my wonderful wife Lucy for putting up with me while I again went through the process – and it really is a process rather than a straightforward '9-to-5' job – of writing another book.

PICTURE
ACKNOWLEDGEMENTS

All pictures © Press Association Images, with thanks. Further copyright details as follows:

First section

Page 1: Early race and tricycle both © EMPICS/EMPICS Sport; Penny farthings © Press Association Images.

Page 2: Crowd © Topham Picturepoint/Press Association Images; Bartlett and Jones both © Barratts/S&G and Barratts/EMPICS Sport.

Page 3: NCU meeting © Between the Wars/Topham Picturepoint/ Press Association Images; Fields © Press Association Images; Brooklands © Barratts/S&G and Barratts/EMPICS Sport.

Page 4: All © Sport and General/S&G and Barratts/EMPICS Sport.

Page 5: New Raleighs © Barratts/S&G and Barratts/EMPICS Sport; Burton © Sport and General/S&G and Barratts/EMPICS Sport.

Page 6: Robinson both © Topham Picturepoint/Press Association Images; Burgess and Simpson © Press Association Images.

Page 7: Simpson and Robinson © Topham Picturepoint/Press Association Images; World championships © Barratts/S&G and Barratts/EMPICS Sport; Sports personality © Press Association Images.

Page 8: Rainbow jersey © Don Morley/EMPICS Sport; Mont Ventoux © Topham Picturepoint/Press Association Images; Funeral © Press Association Images.

Second section

Page 1: First Milk Race © Sport and General/S&G and Barratts/ EMPICS Sport; Bradley and Cowley/Burton both © Press Association Images.

Page 2: All © Press Association Images.

Page 3: Elliott © Jim James/Press Association Images; Millar © David Worthy/EMPICS Sport; Wiggins © Tim Ireland/PA Wire.

Page 4: Hoban © Press Association Images; Millar © Lionel Cironneau/ Press Association Images; Yates © David Worthy/EMPICS Sport.

Page 5: Cavendish © Peter De Jong/AP/Press Association Images; Wiggins © Laurent Cipriani/AP/Press Association Images; Froome © Tim Ireland/PA Wire.

Page 6: 1974 Tour both © Sport and General/S&G and Barratts/ EMPICS Sport; 1994 Tour © Peter De Jong/AP/Press Association Images.

Page 7: Prudhomme © John Giles/PA Wire; Wiggins © Gareth Fuller/ PA Wire.

Page 8: Women's Tour © Andrew Matthews/PA Wire; Yorkshire © Pete Goding/Goding Images/ Press Association Images.

INDEX

Bennett, Mick (*cont.*)
  training 100
  Women's Tour 118–19
  work with Rushton 102, 108, 109–10
  World Championships (1988) 126–7
Bentley, Pete 189
'Berlin-Warsaw-Prague Peace Race'
  (1952) 39–40
Beryl 72
Beyaert, José 37
Bic team 51
The Bicycle 52, 60
Bicycle Union 18, 19
Bidlake, Frederick Thomas 22, 33
Bidlake Memorial Plaque 22
The Big Breakfast 180–1
Bilsland, Billy 239, 247
Bingham, Keith 114, 137–8
Bishop Otter College, Chichester 125
Blue Peter 149
Blythe, Adam 237
BMX 21, 62, 103, 258
BMX Action Bike 103
Boardman, Chris 29, 168, 204–5, 221
  achievements 181
  bikes 75, 92, 93, 94, 188, 195–6
  helmets 196–200
  Hour record attempts 181–2, 196–7,
    215
  Olympic Games (1992) 3, 167, 180,
    187, 226
  Olympic Games (1996) 92, 93, 95
  road-race world championships (1997)
    165
  Secret Squirrel Club 183–6, 188–94,
    196, 197, 199–203
  skinsuits 199
  Tour de France (1994) 110, 111, 112–13
  using bikes for transport 195
Boardman Bikes 194, 195–6
Boonen, Tom 141
Bordeaux-Paris 25–6, 103, 141
Bortolami, Gianluca 113
Borysewicz, Eddie 168
Bottrill, Matt 215
Boulting, Ned, *On the Road Bike* 100
Boyer, Eric 146
Brailsford, Dave 177–8, 247

at British Cycling 1, 182, 186–8, 201,
  251–2, 260–1
Olympics Games (2004) 187–8
steps down from British Cycling 102
at Team Sky 200–1, 254, 266–7, 268
Team Sky accused of doping 283
Braveheart Cycling Fund 179, 239–45,
  247–8
Brighton-Glasgow 38
British Best All Rounder (BBAR) 32–3,
  41, 46
British Cycling (magazine) 70, 71
British Cycling Federation (BCF) 41–2,
  261, 289
  Dave Brailsford at 186–8, 201, 251–2,
    260–1
  David Millar 233
  Eileen Gray as president 70–1, 99
  funding 160–1, 179
  Hall of Fame 71, 120, 127, 130, 132
  John Herety at 176–8
  Olympic Academy 230, 288
  Olympic 'Class of 2008' 182
  and para-cycling 133
  racing licences 211, 220
  'Secret Squirrel Club' 182–6, 188–94,
    196, 197, 199–203
  Shane Sutton 102
  time trial national championships 220
  Tony Doyle as president 136–9
  track bikes 93
  Watson interview 156
  World Class Performance Plan 160–1
British Empire and Commonwealth
  Games (1954) 49–50
British Hercules team 51, 52–9, 60
British League of Racing Cyclists
  (BLRC) 35
  'Berlin-Warsaw-Prague Peace Race'
    (1952) 39–40
  BLRC-NCU feud 34–6, 40–1, 42, 60,
    120, 121
  merger with NCU 41, 120
  Southern Grand Prix (1944) 38
  Tour of Britain (1945) 38
  Tour of Britain (1951) 39
British National Cycling championships
  19

306

ABOUT THE AUTHOR

Ellis Bacon has been writing about bike racing for a living since joining *Procycling* magazine as deputy editor in 2003. He has since written for a number of other cycling publications and websites, including *Cycle Sport*, *Cyclist*, cyclingnews.com and *Cycling Weekly*, as well as for *The Times* and the *Observer*.

A keen linguist, he translated Bjarne Riis's autobiography, *Riis: Stages of Light and Dark*, from Danish into English, and he is also the co-editor, along with Lionel Birnie, of *The Cycling Anthology* series of books, published twice a year. *Great British Cycling* is his third book, following *World's Ultimate Cycle Races* and *Mapping Le Tour*.

Having lived in France, Denmark and the USA, Ellis now lives in Hertfordshire with his wife Lucy and their dog Sooty.